Strategy is not a physical shape;
instead, it is a pathway of thinking and action
through the unknown.

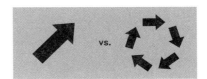

linear vs. cyclical

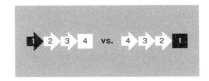

forward vs. backward

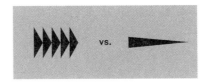

fast vs. slow

The Toolbox

The Toolbox: Strategies for Crafting Social Impact

Jacob Harold

WILEY

For general information on our other products and services or for technical support, please contact our Customer Care Department within the United States at (800) 762-2974, outside the United States at (317) 572-3993 or fax (317) 572-4002.

Wiley also publishes its books in a variety of electronic formats. Some content that appears in print may not be available in electronic formats. For more information about Wiley products, visit our web site at www.wiley.com.

Library of Congress Cataloging-in-Publication Data is Available:

ISBN 9781119863335 (Hardback)

ISBN 9781119863359 (ePub)

ISBN 9781119863366 (ePDF)

Cover and book design: Open (notclosed.com)

SKY10036290_100622

To my father, David Harold,
for giving me tools
of the heart, hand, and mind.

To my mother, Madeline Harold,
for teaching me
to ask if the ground was okay.

7   Contents

לִמְדוּ הֵיטֵב
Learn to do good.

Isaiah 1:17

Χαλεπά τα καλά
Good things are difficult.

Plato

万事开头难
All things are difficult before they are easy.

Chinese proverb

My beloved, let's get down to business.

Chuck D

Ieshia Evans protesting the murder of
Alton Sterling on July 9, 2016, in Baton Rouge, LA.
Photo by Jonathan Bachman

"Let's check to see if the ground is okay."

Kids tumble, knees scrape. As a toddler, when I'd trip and fall, my mother would scoop me up. She'd give me a kiss and a hug. Then she would turn our shared attention to the spot where I fell. My mother would kneel, place her hand upon the earth, and ask us to show compassion to a scrap of land: "Let's check to see if the ground is okay."

In part, this was a young parent's practical trick to distract a crying child from passing pain. But it was more.

My mother's strategy manifested a deeper belief: kindness is infinite. We have enough kindness for a world that has held us up, even enough for a world that has hurt us.

That kindness powers the greatest of human impulses: to serve, to build, to love, to witness.

It drives us to seek a better world — to multiply justice and joy.

But change is hard. The world does not easily yield to our visions of perfection.

How do we make change?

There are no easy answers.

Instead, there are tools.

"You imagine a circle of compassion,
and you imagine no one standing outside of it."

Father Gregory Boyle[1]

The work of social good is spread throughout society. Its burden falls upon the shoulders of people with and without power. Its challenges fall to those with formal training and to those who simply dream of something better.

It starts within the radius of community. One neighbor picks up trash along the sidewalk; another takes food to the homebound. The circle grows as people patch up the gaps in society from within the walls of a clinic or a school. Others build something fundamentally new, creating new products, new inventions, new art, and new institutions. Still others seek to change the systems that already exist — as executives on the inside or as activists on the outside.

Sometimes the change is part of a conscious vision; other times circumstances simply make it necessary. In a community hit by a natural disaster, people open their houses to neighbors who lost theirs. In a pandemic, fire chiefs transform fire stations into testing centers. In the midst of poverty, school administrators figure out how to feed a neighborhood so that they can educate it. A CEO looks out from a corner office window on a sea of demonstrators and realizes the time has come to confront the company's carbon footprint.

The path to something better is rocky, steep, and difficult. We quickly learn the limits of our understanding. There is no one single answer; there is no one technique; there is no silver bullet.

Let's all say it together: if all you have is a hammer, the whole world looks like a nail. **Narrow strategies invariably stumble against the complexity of the world.**

Alas, the work of social change is full of people with hammers. I have been as guilty as any. In my days as a grassroots organizer, I thought that bottom-up activism was the only way to make authentic change. In business school, I looked to markets for the possibility of scale. Working in philanthropy, I viewed decision-making through the lens of behavioral economics. When leading a technology platform, I used the frame of complex systems science to formulate our strategy.

How might we judge my strategic promiscuity? We might say I was always naïve, distracted by the latest shining object. Or we may say I was — unknowingly, perhaps — partially right each time. In fact, each tool offered a unique

"We need a multitude of pictures
about the world…
a gentle jeremiad against theoretical monism."

Kwame Anthony Appiah[2]

perspective for understanding — and acting in — the world. The complexity of the world forced me to assemble a toolbox that worked for me.

I wrote this book because **agents of change need a toolbox strategy**. By "tools" I mean frameworks for thinking and acting. By "toolbox" I mean an individual's collection of tools. And by "toolbox strategy" I mean an approach that brings multiple tools to complex problems.

In this book, we will — in a structured way — explore a set of nine tools that can help us build the better world we seek.

These tools have driven world-shaking social movements and billion-dollar businesses. But they are just as relevant for a neighborhood association or a farmers' market.

The nine tools do not represent every possible perspective on strategy impact strategy. But, together, they offer a mosaic view, a toolbox strategy for change.

Storytelling is the human impulse to understand the world through narrative.

Mathematical modeling is the essential practice of putting numbers to our assumptions.

Behavioral economics offers insights into human behavior as it is, not as we wish it to be.

Design thinking puts the user at the center of any process or challenge.

Community organizing is the art of building people power.

Game theory is a rigorous way to align our decisions with those of other people.

Markets represent the primary mechanism of resource allocation in our world.

Complex systems teaches how the whole can be greater than the sum of its parts.

Institutions form the essential infrastructure of our society.

Signs of wear are signs of use
Signs of use are signs of necessity
Necessity and use are
Signs of love

Rūta Marija Kuzmickas

The structure of this book

The Black feminist scholar Audre Lorde famously said, "The master's tools will never dismantle the master's house."[3] She argued that attitudes and systems of oppression cannot simply be turned against the oppressor. We must apply new approaches to solve old problems, otherwise, "only the most narrow parameters of change are possible." This is a warning that should echo in our minds.

Luckily, the tools in this book do not belong to the master. **These tools are the common heritage of humanity.** The question is, how do we choose to wield them? What purpose and what moral frameworks do we bring so that we may rebuild a house for everyone?

This book is meant to offer a hand to those on this fraught and thrilling journey. It is, admittedly, a hybrid: part textbook and part pep rally.

But mostly, it is meant to seed your intuition as you face the unknown ahead. Throughout, I've included stories, poems, quotes, diagrams, photos, and equations that represent a range of possibilities for social change. Some will resonate with you, others may not. That is the point.

You can think of the first three chapters as the "box" and the next nine chapters as the "tools." In Chapter One, we'll explore our early-21st-century context and why a toolbox strategy is necessary. Chapter Two provides a basic language for thinking about strategy. Chapter Three explores a set of moral and ethical dynamics that complicate and enrich the work of social change.

Then, the nine tools. Each of the tool chapters will explore a tool in depth, laying out its basic presumptions, concepts, and vocabulary. In each case we will explore times when this tool is appropriate and when it is not. And, for those ready to go deeper, I'll suggest more resources.

There is no chapter with architectural drawings for the perfect society. The tools in this book are just that: tools. They do not provide boldness, vision, or moral clarity. These tools must be brought to life by the force of human action. When the book closes, the rest is up to you.

"For the vanguards of the present dreaming up new ways to fight global warming or Black Lives Matter activists seeking alternatives to policing as we know it, this is an essential point: that the shape and extent of the change they seek depends as much on what tools they use as it does on their own will and hunger."

Gal Beckerman[4]

Commonalities and mindsets

The nine tools are not isolated or distinct; they overlap and intertwine. Throughout this book, you'll find common themes like listening, risk, power, information, and interconnection. (To highlight some of these commonalities, you'll find color-coded "hyperlinks" that show connections across chapters.)

A social change agent doesn't have to pick one single tool to solve one problem. Instead, the essence of toolbox strategy is multiplicity: there are many ways to understand and many ways to act. Our complex world asks us to go beyond our single hammer, and it is possible to do so.

Let me suggest four foundational mindsets to help you navigate the range of ways of thinking about social impact strategy.

The first is to **open yourself to a "both/and" mentality**. Toolbox strategy does not choose between qualitative or quantitative; it uses both the quantitative and the qualitative. Toolbox strategy is not limited to gradual change or to revolution; instead, it sees power in both the incremental and the disruptive. Toolbox strategy is not limited to radical outsiders or ambitious insiders; it recognizes the possibility of change both inside the system and outside the system.

Second, **recognize the power of clarity**. Clarity short-circuits confusion and enables collective action and learning. A clear hypothesis is more useful; direct communication is more effective. Clarity does not mean arrogance. Humility is itself a type of clarity. Sometimes the best way to equip ourselves for reality is to be honest about our own ignorance.

Third, **experiment with understanding**. We can explore which ways of thinking are most useful for a given problem. You can "try on" a given mindset or framework and see where it leads you. Then try another. Draw lessons according to how useful they are.

Finally, and most importantly, **the right thing to do is the strategic thing to do**. Even as you experiment with understanding, hold fast to your values. Human virtue offers a stable foundation for strategic creativity. And it works. Honest, compassionate behavior ultimately builds trust. Trust builds connection. Connection builds power. The most important piece of news in this book is this: kindness can be strategic, and strategy can be kind.

Language

The vocabulary of social good can be unsatisfying. We are stuck using words like "nonprofit" or "non-governmental" that are defined by a negative. Simple ideas end up conveyed through a complex stew of acronyms. (In the **Markets** chapter, we'll go through ESG vs CSR vs PRI vs SRI.)

This linguistic reality reflects a changing society. People are trying to sort out a new, cross-sector vocabulary for social good. This aspiration gives me hope, but it undoubtedly makes communication harder.

In this book, I've tried to use the words we have instead of making up new ones. Where appropriate, I'll highlight important linguistic nuance. (For example, I will later discuss what I see as the difference between "social change" and "social impact.") Other times, my word choice reflects an expansive view: "changemakers" or "social change agents" are just people working for a better world.

This generality is on purpose. Millions of people are positioned to do good in the world — and to do so in different sectors and at different scales. We cannot confine these lessons to nonprofit staff, social entrepreneurs, and philanthropists. Our world needs strategic action from nurses and pharmaceutical executives, accountants and tax officials, prime ministers and community gardeners.

I acknowledge the awkwardness of the social good lexicon. But let's try to see this linguistic confusion as a reminder that millions of humans are in the middle of something important: they're trying to figure out how to do good, together.

The power and limitations of perspective

Before I close this introductory chapter, I should say a few words about myself — and the strengths and weaknesses of my own perspective.

First, the weaknesses. Most fundamentally: I am only one person. My life has offered one perch from which to understand our shared complexity. Further, on almost every dimension of my identity — race (white), gender (male), sexual orientation (straight), citizenship (U.S. citizen) — I find myself in a privileged caste. This privilege has given me access and opportunity that I have tried to use for a greater good. And it has surely blinded me to realities that are obvious to others.

While I've had deep engagement with business and government, most of my work has been in the nonprofit sector. I've

The man pulling radishes
pointed the way
with a radish.

Kobayashi Issa

worked in many countries but have lived most of my life in the United States. I try to be conscious of these limitations, and readers should, too.

Now, the strengths. I've been blessed to spend two decades working for a better world. I've felt the sting of tear gas and the cut of handcuffs. I've sat in seats of power: in elite boardrooms and on the stages of august conferences. I count myself lucky that I've been able to work within some of the most influential, innovative, and impactful organizations in social change, from Greenpeace to Bridgespan to the Hewlett Foundation. Over the past decade, I've had the privilege of serving as CEO of GuideStar and to lead its 2019 merger with Foundation Center to create Candid, which *Fast Company* called "the definitive nonprofit transparency organization."[6]

These roles have been a blessing, not least because they have given me access to the lessons of a *field*. Ultimately, what is most important are not the organizations I've worked for but those I have worked with. My one perspective has allowed me to bear witness to the perspectives of so many others. **Their tools — our tools — offer hope in an age of flux.**

"The dogmas of the quiet past are inadequate to the stormy present.

The occasion is piled high with difficulty, and we must rise — with the occasion.

As our case is new, so we must think anew, and act anew."

Abraham Lincoln
December 1, 1862
Annual Message to Congress

An Age of Flux

In 2012, the Atlantic Ocean
swallowed the roller coaster at Casino Pier
in Seaside Heights, NJ.
Photo by Julie Dermansky

"The real problem of humanity
is the following:
we have paleolithic emotions,
medieval institutions,
and god-like technology."

E. O. Wilson[7]

"We are relying on
nineteenth century institutions
using twentieth century tools
to address twenty-first century problems."

Ann Mei Chang[8]

Life in a
plastic hour

**In 1862, a Dutch ophthalmologist
accidentally burdened the year 2020
with significance.** Herman Snellen's scale
set "20/20" as "normal" sight. Over time,
those four digits leaked into other realms
of life. "2020" came to evoke a sense of
visual — even strategic or moral — clarity.
Countless executives sought to capitalize
on that association by writing strategy
documents with names like "Vision 2020."
(I was as guilty as any.)

In retrospect, 2020 now feels like
a pivot moment away from clarity. The
COVID-19 pandemic shook an already
unstable world. Slowly building crises of
climate, democracy, and inequality all
seemed to explode at once.

Later in this chapter I will argue that
we are in a "plastic hour" (perhaps even
a plastic century), a time when change is
more possible. But to change the world,
you must first see it as it is. So, let us
set our toolbox down on the ground of
reality. Below is a whirlwind tour of our
early-21st-century moment, through the
good, the bad, and the fast.

Say it plain: that many have died for this day
Sing the names of the dead who brought us here.

Elizabeth Alexander

The Good

Billions have escaped extreme poverty.
Infant mortality has plummeted, and
lifespans and literacy have risen. Deaths
from violence — still too high — have
dropped since the bloodbaths of past
eras. And, inconsistently, in bursts and
with setbacks, the full range of humanity
is getting a chance to love whom they
would love, to be who they are, and to
recognize the immense diversity of the
human experience. We, in fact, have much
to celebrate.[9]

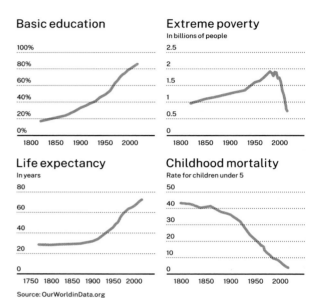

Basic education

Extreme poverty
In billions of people

Life expectancy
In years

Childhood mortality
Rate for children under 5

Source: OurWorldinData.org

These are but some of the things we overcome
But let us come to be more than their sum.

Amanda Gorman[10]

The Bad

And yet, we must confront the reality of raw injustice faced by billions and a struggling planet. 400 million people lack access to essential health services.[11] 2.4 billion people do not have access to toilets.[12] 860 million people are under-nourished.[13] 10 million tons of plastic are dumped into oceans annually.[14] 3 million tons of toxic chemicals are released into the environment each year.[15] 2 million people — disproportionately Black and Brown — are incarcerated in the United States.[16] The list of injustice goes on and on and on.

  As change agents, we face a paradox. The world has seen real progress. If we deny that progress, we insult those who fought for it. But if we ignore the challenges of the world, we betray ourselves and future generations.

Global average temperature change
Difference from 1951–1980 average, in degrees Celsius

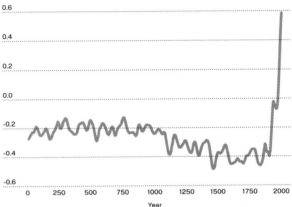

Source: Visualization by Femke Nijsse based on data from PAGES2k consortium published in "Consistent multidecadal variability in global temperature reconstructions and simulations over the Common Era," *Nature Geosciences*, volume 12, pages 643–649 (2019)

Wealth distribution

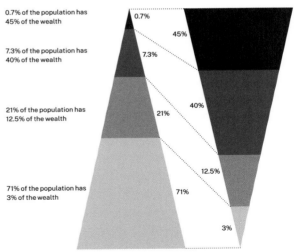

0.7% of the population has 45% of the wealth

7.3% of the population has 40% of the wealth

21% of the population has 12.5% of the wealth

71% of the population has 3% of the wealth

Source: Credit Suisse Global Wealth Databook

An Age of Flux

"Change is the one unavoidable,
irresistible, ongoing reality of the universe."

Octavia Butler[17]

The Fast

The metronome of history clicks faster.
We find ourselves in the middle of what
has been called "the great acceleration,"
where we witness a change in the very
pace of change. That is, we face not
only the velocity (speed) of ideas and
events but also the acceleration (increase
in speed). Information pours into our
minds; culture is a blur; politics moves to
a next phase before we understand the
previous one.

    Pope Francis called this phenomenon
"rapidification" and highlighted that it
is not just an external phenomenon but
a psychological one. He saw humanity
as being caught in a temporal vice:
"Although change is part of the working of
complex systems, the speed with which
human activity has developed contrasts
with the naturally slow pace of biological
evolution."[18] We are outpaced by the
change we have wrought.

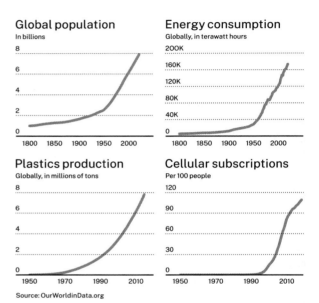

Global population
In billions

Energy consumption
Globally, in terawatt hours

Plastics production
Globally, in millions of tons

Cellular subscriptions
Per 100 people

Source: OurWorldinData.org

But, I think, the future is also another thing:
a verb tense in motion, in action, in combat,
a searching movement toward life,
keel of the ship that strikes the water
and struggles to open between the waves
the exact breach the rudder commands.

Ángel González

This acceleration has immediate implications for decision makers of all kinds. In 2017, Gen. Joe Dunford, then chairman of the U.S. Joint Chiefs of Staff, considered the effect on military affairs. He explained, "Decision space has collapsed" and the acceleration of time "makes the global security environment even more unpredictable, dangerous and unforgiving…Today, the ability to recover from early missteps is greatly reduced."[19] The compressed space for reaction is particularly acute in war, but just as relevant for social change.

There are many causes for the collapse of decision space. One core driver is "Moore's Law," Intel founder Gordon Moore's observation that the power and cost-efficiency of microchips tends to double every 18–24 months. We have all witnessed the extraordinary acceleration of computing power that has followed. It is so fast that it is most appropriate to show the graph logarithmically (that is, 10, 100, 1000, etc.).

Innovation theorist Bhaskar Chakravorti has countered that societal change happens only half that fast — what he has jokingly called "demi-Moore's law."[20] Technical innovation does not

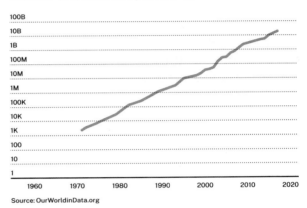

Number of transistors per microprocessor

Source: OurWorldinData.org

happen in a social vacuum. In an interconnected world populated by intertwined organizations, change requires the social and political wherewithal to align disparate efforts across multiple actors and organizations. This complexity is the brake pedal that balances the force of the accelerator.

Taken together, these two laws — Moore's Law and demi-Moore's Law — illustrate our predicament: constant, accelerating innovation constrained by increasing interconnection and complexity. Let's briefly examine four dimensions of this predicament: technology, culture, ecology, and politics.

"…as if time were not a river
but an earthquake happening nearby."

Roberto Bolaño[21]

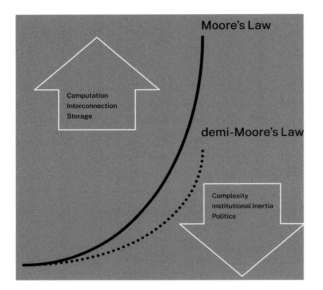

Technology: The Fourth Industrial Revolution

We are entering the Fourth Industrial Revolution. The first three technological earthquakes could each be summed up in a single word: steam, electricity, and computing. Each changed the structure of society. The upheavals of the Third Industrial Revolution — mobile, cloud computing, social media — are by no means over; they will echo for decades to come.

The Fourth Industrial Revolution has a different character. It cannot be distilled into a single technology; instead, it is a cluster of technologies emerging on the frontiers of change. I'll suggest the shorthand QARBIN (pronounced "carbon") to capture the key technologies that make up the Fourth Industrial Revolution: quantum computing, artificial intelligence, alternative energy, robotics, biotechnology, blockchain, new interfaces, the Internet of things, and nanotechnology.

QARBIN:

Q   **Quantum computing**
Molecular modeling,
quantum cryptography

A   **Artificial intelligence**
Machine learning,
neural networks, general AI

    Alternative energy
Solar, wind, batteries,
geothermal, fusion

R   **Robotics**
Drones, autonomous vehicles,
3D printing

B   **Biotechnology**
CRISPR, mRNA vaccines,
biocomputers

    Blockchain
Cryptocurrencies, non-fungible
tokens, distributed autonomous
organizations

I   **Interfaces**
Virtual/augmented reality,
metaverse, voice recognition,
brain-computer interface

    Internet of things
Distributed sensors, smart grid,
home automation

N   **Nanotechnology**

    Nanomaterials, smart dust,
molecular self-assembly

"Only the historian of the future will be able to assess the net effect of the machine age on human character and on man's joy in being and his will to live."

Helen and Scott Nearing[22]

Each technology could revolutionize our world. We cannot know which will be the most transformative. What we can know: this cluster of technologies is likely to cause dislocations equal to those of the first three industrial revolutions. The dreams — and nightmares — of science fiction are coming true: customized children, universal surveillance, fully autonomous warfare, self-replicating intelligence, and the metaverse.

Culture: The humanity of change

Technology has fundamentally re-structured human communications, bringing promise and peril to our work as changemakers.

For millions of years, communication was limited by the speed of human legs or the volume of the human voice. The print-ing press and postal services enabled ideas to move faster. The telegraph and the telephone connected vast distances in real time. Radio and television wove together a fabric of human stories. Through all of this, humanity has had to adjust, to evolve, and to react to the implications of these technologies.

In the second half of the 20th century, for better or worse, it seemed we might be heading to one global monoculture, where every corner would have a Starbucks and every teenager would listen to the same music. Many shared a sense that technology was driving cultural convergence.

The early part of the 21st century, however, has shattered a once-emerging monoculture into seven billion pieces. The Internet — and, in particular, social media — has thrown that once-confident understanding of the near future into question. The friction once inherent in communication seems to have played a crucial role in cultivating a type of cultural stability; conspiracy theories previously had to pass through intermediaries or at least find deep adherents before they could spread. Now, with a few quick "reshares," a once-unthinkable idea can permeate the discourse.

The past two decades would suggest that on some deep cognitive level we humans are ill-suited for the social media age: our attention is fragmented, our body images are distorted, and our sense of community — even reality — is filtered through screens.[24]

These challenges do not just test civic culture and human decency. There are deep practical implications for the work of social good. It is hard to solve problems with others without shared truth or shared trust.

For those trying to make a better world, we can take solace that our recent fragmentation reflects the diversity of the human experience. We can celebrate that we did not end up in a global monoculture. But we should also acknowledge that, in some ways, change has become harder as each of us lives in a self-reinforcing bubble. Our challenge is to reach through the membrane of our political world without breaking our connections with those closest to us.

Ecology: Mother Nature bats last

On Sunday, June 27, 2021, the Canadian village of Lytton, British Columbia, set a temperature record of 116 F (47 C). On Monday, it hit 118 F (48 C). On Tuesday, it set a national record of 121 F (49 C). Then, on Wednesday evening, a fire broke out that burned 90% of the town to the ground. Lytton's week from hell was a stark reminder of what we have in store amidst a changing climate.

Solving the climate puzzle is perhaps the greatest collective challenge ever faced by humanity. Technological growth

"By the middle of this century, mankind had acquired the power to extinguish life on Earth. By the middle of the next century, he will be able to create it. Of the two, it is hard to say which places the larger burden of responsibility on our shoulders."

Christopher Langton, 1987[25]

over the first three industrial revolutions has brought immense wealth, immense destruction, and a world-historical crisis. It is as if an impetuous demon is testing humanity: "I'm going to put all this useful stuff in the ground. But I'm not going to leave enough room for it in the atmosphere. Let's see what happens."

Climate change gets — and deserves — top billing. Like no other issue, the changing climate highlights our interconnections, our injustices, and our insufficient action. But let us not forget other ecological issues: the pollution of water, air, and life itself; the degradation of soil, habitats, and ecosystems.

Historians and anthropologists have repeatedly shown that environmental change often preceded societal collapse.[26] Sometimes this environmental change was beyond the control of the soon-to-collapse human community. They fell to volcanos, earthquakes, or storms. But in many cases, it was the choices of that community that led to their own downfall, whether by overfishing, deforestation, or polluting their water supply.

Technology and population growth have supercharged our ability to degrade the ecosystems upon which we depend.

Change comes faster, and we have less time to adapt to the new ecological context we ourselves have created. What's more, environmental issues have become truly global. Greenhouse gases do not have a nationality, and decisions made in Detroit or in Beijing affect the entire planet. The usage of fertilizers has transformed global agriculture, fed the world, and created global nitrogen and phosphorus crises. And, in a crisis that may soon become acute, the overuse of antibiotics is rapidly contributing to the microbes resistant to all the medicines we can throw at them.

If only the impacts of environmental degradation were distributed evenly. But environmental destruction weighs more heavily upon certain groups. In the United States, we see this clearly through the dimension of race. The evidence is clear: communities of color face a far greater burden of air pollution, poor water quality, and household toxins.[27] In the United States, Black and Brown neighborhoods simply have fewer trees. Around the world, the poorest countries — those least responsible for the problem — tend to face the worst impacts of climate change.

In all of this, we can despair at the injustice. And we should. But let this also be a clarion call for facing the ecological challenges that tie us together.

Politics: Power spread and clustered

The once unstoppable march of capitalism and democracy has shown itself to be decidedly stoppable. China's unique political and economic system has proven to be not only an engine of global growth, but resilient to global pressure — indeed, expectations — that it would shift towards the model of Western capitalist democracy. Across the globe, we have seen the rise of new forms of authoritarian government, often powered by populist and ethno-nationalist narratives.

Even as some countries have gained power, we have seen a relative weakening of the nation-state as the organizing principle of global society. Since the Treaty of Westphalia in 1648, the world has been a collection of countries. And the country remains the substrate of global politics. But now we've also seen an explosion of **non-state actors**. Transnational corporations operate at the scale of national governments, alternately facilitating destruction at a global scale and serving as beacons of responsibility.

Terrorist networks like Al Qaeda have shifted the contours of history. Organized crime networks like the Sinaloa cartel in Mexico or the 'Ndrangheta in Calabria alter politics and economies.

And through all of this, **civil society** organizations have emerged as a force. Whether a giant global network like Oxfam or Greenpeace, or a small village cooperative in Peru, these organizations have institutionalized the work of social change. Spanning the political spectrum, a range of different strategies, and a full set of social issues, these organizations have made the work of doing good part of the very structure of society.

More broadly, our assumptions about the roles of different institutions in our society are in flux. For-profit corporations face pro-social demands from customers, employees, and investors. Companies can no longer speak only of shareholder value. The very allocation of financial capital has been reset by the emergence of the multi-trillion-dollar socially responsible investing market.

"There are in history what you could call 'plastic hours.' Namely, crucial moments when it is possible to act. If you move then, something happens."

Gershom Scholem [31]

Military strategists speak of a VUCA world, one that is volatile, uncertain, complex, and ambiguous. Our challenge as agents of change is this: acknowledge the challenges of a VUCA world and succeed anyway.

V	Volatile
U	Uncertain
C	Complex
A	Ambiguous

Nonprofit organizations have built business models that are often the envy of the business community, with trillions of dollars of annual economic activity in the U.S. alone.[29] Society faces a promising but profound question: where does business end and social change begin?

Government roles have shifted as well. Sovereign wealth funds are some of the world's biggest investors. State-owned enterprises dominate entire sectors.[30] In many countries social services are outsourced to either for-profit or nonprofit organizations. The countless campaigns run to alter corporate behavior can be seen as a type of outsourced regulation.

All of this adds up to a social contract in flux. Once-stable assumptions about the roles of different institutions shift and crack. For the social change agent, this presents both a challenge and an opportunity.

It is undoubtedly a challenge to plan how to make a better world in the midst of such shifting sands. But it also creates an opportunity for growth, innovation, and nonlinear change; openings emerge in times of flux.

Acting in a plastic hour

Let us summarize this early-21st-century moment. Earth's ecosystems are on the brink of radical change or even collapse. Multiple technologies are transforming our very understanding of life. Human culture is fragmented, yielding ineffectual politics unable to come to grips with the challenges before us.

The systems of the world are shaken; components are loose, floating, and disconnected. But just like when a Lego set is broken into pieces, it is possible to build something new from the fragments. Instability offers opportunity. Perhaps the structures of society are ripe for change.[32]

(In the **Complex Systems** chapter, we will develop a language — equilibrium, feedback loops, and tipping points — to help us think through how to act strategically in a system out of balance.)

The author Arundhati Roy described the COVID-19 pandemic as a "portal." She challenged us to decide what we brought with us as we passed through: "We can choose to walk through it, dragging the carcasses of our prejudice and hatred, our avarice, our data banks and dead ideas, our dead rivers and smoky skies behind us. Or we can walk through lightly, with little luggage, ready to imagine another world. And ready to fight for it."[33]

Our window of opportunity remains open: perhaps this plastic hour is a plastic century. As long as our world continues to change, it will be susceptible to the will of those of us who would act. One thing is certain: this is a consequential moment in the human story — an era where our choices will matter for generations to come.[34]

Two words for "time" in ancient Greek:

1. **Chronos (Χρόνος)**
   clock time;
   the sequential structure of reality

2. **Kairos (καιρός)**
   an opportune moment;
   a season for harvest

"There is always a well-known solution to every human problem — neat, plausible, and wrong."

H.L. Mencken[36]

Seeing the moment clearly

We face a situation too complex for any of us to fully understand. If we organize our work through any single lens, we are almost certain to stumble upon the complexity around us. A given perspective might be morally neutral, but it is not strategically neutral. Each lens focuses our attention on some things and blinds us to others. Consider how different forms of media promote different ways of thinking: the political repercussions of social media are different from those of radio. Similarly, each strategic framework tends to tilt us towards a given way of thinking and thus way of acting.

We do not have to look far to see the limitations of narrow ways of thinking about the world. The siloed institutionalization of the U.S. intelligence community rendered it incapable of recognizing the danger presented by Al Qaeda in 2001. The 2008 Financial Crisis was an inevitable consequence of applying a market lens to every aspect of life. Compelling business narratives like WeWork[37] fell under the crushing weight of arithmetic. Countless nonprofits have brought a narrow solution to a complex problem — and failed.

Each of these failures was a consequence of the narrow application of one perspective on a complex world. As social change agents, we have an opportunity — and an obligation — to step back, take a breath, and do better.

In the next two chapters, I'll offer frameworks for social change strategy and ethics. Then we'll dive into the nine tools themselves.

I recognize this may seem like a lot to keep in your mind. But this multiplicity is the point. The human mind is a pattern recognition machine. **When we seed our minds with patterns, we prepare ourselves for an unpredictable future.** The age of flux demands a range of tools.

When you go to the eye doctor, they often sit down in front of a big metal machine called a phoropter. The optometrist cycles through a range of possible lenses — two at a time — and asks you, "Which is better: one or two?" That process helps find the right prescription for you.

Similarly, this book is meant to offer you a range of options to "try" in our complex world. It is up to you to choose which offers you the greatest clarity for thinking and acting in this plastic hour.

The 2020 California wildfires were a collision of intersecting crises.
Photo by Noah Berger

Clock of the sky,
you measure
the celestial eternity,
one white
hour,
one century
sliding
on your snow,
meanwhile the earth,
entangled,
is humid,
warm:
the hammers
hit
the tall ovens
burn,
the petroleum
shakes in its plate,
man searches, hungry,
for matter,
he corrects
his banner,
siblings gather,
walk,
hear,
cities
emerge,
bells
sing
in the heights
cloths are woven,
transparency
jumps
onto the crystals.

Pablo Neruda

Age of Flux Takeaways

1. If we deny the real progress the
    world has made, we insult those
    who fought for it; if we ignore the
    challenges of the world, we betray
    ourselves and future generations.
    History is contingent; it flows
    from our actions and from the
    forces that surround us.

2. As we try to change the world,
    our predicament is constant,
    accelerating innovation constrained
    by increasing interconnection
    and complexity.

3. A time of change is the perfect time
    to make change. Flux creates
    space for growth, innovation, and
    nonlinear change. In instability
    there is opportunity.

An Age of Flux

The Shape
of Strategy

Ray Charles — blind since childhood — loved chess. He watched the board with his fingers and played in his mind. Photo by Bill Ray

Finding
a pathway

How do we find a pathway to impact?
On such a journey, you need a language.
So we will begin with a definition.
**Strategy is the logic we use to
allocate our resources to achieve a goal.**

If you have a goal, but no logic, you
have only desire. If you have resources,
but no logic, you have only potential. If
you have logic, but no goal, you are only
a machine.

The challenge is this: each one these
three elements can *change*. You might
find yourself with more resources or a
new means of allocation. The context
around you may change, forcing you to
shift your logic. Or, as you learn more over
time, you might reframe your goal.

This, then, is the fundamental
paradox of strategy. At the beginning we
choose a goal and imagine a pathway to
that goal. But as we go through time, we
will learn. Things will change. Our path
will curve and split and end in ways we
cannot predict.

We need the *prospective* clarity of
an imagined pathway. But we also
need the flexibility to embrace a new
route to something better as we *retro-
spectively* learn.

The visual metaphor of a pathway is no accident. Social change is a journey. And one helpful way to map our journey is to talk about the *shape* of strategy. Over the course of this chapter, we will discuss several dimensions of this geometry of social change.

But, first, a story that is both an inspiration and a cautionary tale.

An invitation.

Bring a tent

The launch poster for Occupy Wall Street was a design masterpiece: a ballerina balanced atop the Wall Street bull, her grace somehow reining in — and reigning over — the strength of the bull.[39]

At the bottom are clear instructions: *bring a tent*. In that simple call, the logistics of the event were obvious. The events of the next several weeks cast a new kind of light upon the global financial system. For that time, "Occupy" protesters focused attention upon inequality in a new way. It injected the term "We are the 99%" into the public discourse to describe the U.S. concentration of wealth. Occupy Wall Street was a seminal moment in how American society thinks about finance, wealth, and power.

And, yet, it faded. Why? Perhaps there is a clue at the top of the poster. A question, there in red: "What is our one demand?" We might read this as a response to an oft-stated critique of Occupy Wall Street: it did not have a clear set of demands, or "asks." Or, more generally, critics argued that OWS did not offer a well-articulated plan for a better financial system. In the words on the top of the protest, the designers essentially admitted the absence of a definitive strategic logic for the protest. There was no exit strategy for themselves or their ambiguous opponents.

To many strategists, this is a searing indictment, an indication that OWS had a fundamentally unserious approach to making change. But perhaps it is more complicated than that. Two organizers, Astra Taylor and Jonathan Smucker, wrote that the lack of traditional policy proved to be a powerful kind of flexibility: "As it turned out, the lack of demands became one of Occupy's greatest assets, enabling a wide range of people to see themselves in the same struggle. Popularizing a broad critique of inequality was far more important, politically, than writing out detailed policy prescriptions."[40]

So perhaps we may choose to be more generous. Instead of locking itself in a single answer or a single logic, maybe we can think of Occupy Wall Street as having a different kind of purpose. Can we think of this question — "What is our one demand?" — as a strategy to imagine a different kind of society? Perhaps it is a window to a desire that cannot fit on a single placard but instead involves conversations and actions across thousands of people. Taylor and Smucker continue, "The whole point of the phrase 'We are the 99 percent!' was its capaciousness. It functioned as an invitation. The curious didn't have to pass a political litmus test; they could show up and ask questions. If they stayed long enough, they'd see how their hardships aligned with the hardships of others."

There is no simple lesson here. Occupy Wall Street might have been more consequential with a strategy based on clear logic and a clear ask. I admit that I believe that. But we also should acknowledge a different kind of consequence. Occupy did not change practice or policy, but the changes it made to the social and political conversation have survived long after the tents left Zuccotti Park. It turned out that a few hundred people with tents nudged the curve of history.

The next year, 2012, saw the launch of the new movement for economic justice, Fight for 15, which pushed for a $15 minimum wage. Consider the contrast between the names of the two movements: Occupy Wall Street was named after its tactic; Fight for 15 was named after its goal. But that contrast ultimately proved strategically powerful.

OWS created political and cultural space for the concrete asks of Fight for 15. Importantly, it also offered personal inspiration during the Fight for 15 battles. Many workers said that OWS gave them confidence that their dream of a just wage was not just fair, but possible.[41]

And it worked. Over the subsequent decade, Fight for 15 campaigns secured a $15 minimum wage (twice the federal minimum wage) in dozens of cities, states, and companies across the country. One analysis suggests that, in aggregate, these victories have led to 22 million workers receiving wage increases totaling $68 billion.[42]

We cannot draw a straight line from the tents of Zuccotti Park to increased wages at a particular fast-food restaurant in Illinois. But we can see the connections across history — and the ultimate importance of both capaciousness and clarity.

"Hope is definitely not the same thing as optimism. It is not the conviction that something will turn out well, but the certainty that something makes sense, regardless of how it turns out."

Vaclav Havel[43]

The shape of history

History is the history of successful change. Over and over again, people have sought to change the world. Great cities were built from the Andes to the Himalayas. Systematic efforts to gather human knowledge took place from Timbuktu to Beijing. Humanity has etched the crust of the Earth from Panama to Suez with canals that linked the world in overlapping circles. Entire continents fought for and gained their freedom.

From the sweep of history to the sweep of a neighbor's stoop is a continuum of change. You sit on that continuum. Your choices help carve the contours of history. This chapter explores how we translate our ambitions — however modest or grand — into action.

But first, a book about effective social change needs an effective definition of social change — of those efforts to bend the shape of history. Here is my definition: **social change is work to make the world better.**

Let's break this down. We can start with the word **work**. Social change is action, on purpose. There is no such thing as passive social change. It takes people waking up and acting. Change is, as historian Lawrence Goodwyn said, "in no sense spontaneous, it is the work of human hands."[44]

Then, consider the word **make** — social change is, ultimately, about consequences. It is instrumental. And it should be judged relative to the *counterfactual* — that is, whatever would have happened without our action. But accident is not social change; it is the background static of the universe. We are trying to bend the course of the future *versus* what might have been. *Social impact* is the result of our work; social change is the work itself.

We can make change at multiple scales of the **world**. We can think globally, think locally, act globally, and act locally. All are valid. What matters is this: social change is an act outside of our own self-interest; it is a gift to the other. And, as we will discuss throughout this book, transformation of the world often involves transformation of ourselves.

And what about **better**? Importantly, it can be either adding a good or subtracting a bad. Painting a magnificent mural on the wall of the community library counts. As does preventing the clearcutting of an old-growth forest. Social change includes both capturing opportunities and addressing challenges.

The shape of strategy

The mathematician Jordan Ellenberg remarked that "geometry is a form of honesty."[45] And, indeed, thinking about the "shape" of strategy is one way to honestly confront the challenges of social change. Of course, strategy is not a physical shape; instead, it is a pathway of thinking and action through the unknown. The good news is that it's possible to articulate the characteristics of that pathway.

Imagine we are on a hike. Our path depends both on our mental approach and on the physical terrain. We might choose to follow the existing trail or to bushwhack a new one; we might seek adventure or simple relaxation.

Whatever our mindset, the world will present us with practical questions. Do we cross the river? Do we dare enter the cavern? Do we rest on that rock? Are we strong enough for the steep slope?

So, as we think about the shapes of social change strategy, we need to think about both the shape of your mindset (how do you approach the problem?) and the shape of your situation (what is the context of your work?).

This chapter is meant to define the general contours of social change strategy. In the notes you'll find a set of tactical tools for tackling specific parts of the strategy process — from creating a theory of change to building a social enterprise business model.[46] ■

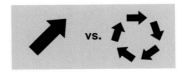

linear vs. cyclical

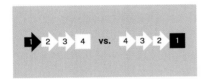

linear vs. cyclical

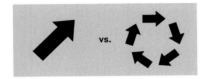

forward vs. backward

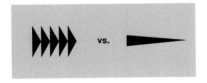

fast vs. slow

Linear mindset

We will start by considering the two basic mindsets for strategic action and why both are essential. The first is the *linear* mindset and the second is the *cyclical* mindset.

The linear mindset shows up across sectors. In the nonprofit sector, it often manifests as a "logic model," in international development as a "logframe" (from "logical framework"), and in the business world as a "value chain." All are related to the same basic idea: the articulation of a series of steps from action to achievement of a goal.

Let's talk through an example: a logic model for a job training program.

Think of the path as calligraphy —
narrow where it borders
the farm house and horse pens.

Think, how beyond the open gate,
the stroke fattens, traveling
upward into the dark.

Cynthia White

Recruit training program participants	*number of sign-ups*
↓	
Execute training program	*available seats in program per year*
↓	
Ensure program quality	*number of participants who graduate from program*
↓	
Match participants to jobs	*number of graduates matched to a job*
↓	
Participants find stable careers	*number of graduates who stay in job more than three years*

The linear mindset is powerful because it encourages clarity. It allows — even forces — you to articulate assumptions and steps along the way. Also, describing your strategy "out loud" in this way also creates the possibility of a future feedback loop. As the poet Amanda Gorman says: "To be accountable we must render an account."

The clarity of the linear mindset lends itself to measurability. We can identify metrics along the way to track our progress. Those metrics explicitly help us identify where our logic might break down. What if the numbers show us that people do complete our program, but they don't get a job? We've learned something about the assumptions that underly our strategy.

The linear mindset brings three challenges. **First**, as you move down the chain of logic, measurement tends to become more difficult. **Second**, each step leads us away from our control over our own actions. To the right, we place our fate in the hands of others and the world. **Third**, linear models tend to lose out to nonlinear reality. For as we all learn, the world is curvy.

Cyclical mindset

The cyclical mindset takes the position that iteration is a better approach to progress than prediction. Since we cannot know what will happen, we constantly cycle through a series of steps. Like a blind person testing the ground with a cane, we create a pathway out of the information we gather as we move through the world.

Cyclical thinking is now firmly embedded in the global economy. It has been applied to manufacturing (Kaizen[47]), computer programing (Agile[48]), new business development (Lean Startup[49]), and even aerial warfare (OODA loop[50]).

The specifics depend on the context. But the essential idea is to rotate through a cycle of learning. We plan, act, learn... and then choose our next step according to what the world has told us. We do not lock ourselves into a particular path if that path is no longer feasible.

This kind of iteration is especially powerful in a rapidly changing world. It enables what the activist and strategist adrienne maree brown described as "emergent strategy." In many ways, this mindset is a fundamentally humble approach that relies on constant learning.

The cyclical mindset tends to run on the fuel of feedback. You are constantly asking the outside world how you are doing — whether by watching their actions (are people downloading your tool?) or listening to their words (what do people say about what you're doing?).

The cyclical approach is, thus, a good ethical match for social change. It does not put the social change agent above those they serve. And, importantly, in a complex and rapidly changing world, the cyclical approach can simply be more effective because it can be more responsive to change.

With that said, we should keep in mind two challenges in the iterative mindset as applied to social change.

The first limit is that, ironically, the linear mindset can be important for achieving nonlinear change. If you are trying to fundamentally shift the behavior of an entire system, your logic may rely on reaching a "tipping point" where a situation suddenly changes. (We'll discuss this kind of nonlinear change more in the **Complex Systems** chapter.)

Aiming for a tipping point can require patience. If — in the spirit of the cyclical mindset — you rely on quick-response

A system can suddenly shift from one equilibrium to another.

data, it may appear that your approach isn't working. So you give up too soon.

The second limit of cylcical thinking is that big change often relies on imagining a wholly different world. This is as true in business (imagine Steve Jobs describing the iPhone) as it is in social change. But cyclical strategy tends to rely on feedback from constituents. If your constituents cannot yet imagine a different world, their feedback will constantly — if unconsciously — pull towards the status quo.

It is the ineffable power of human vision to imagine something differ- ent — something that requires patience and faith. The challenge is to evolve that vision as it meets up with reality.

Two clever acronyms

A goal should
be "SMART"

Specific
Measurable
Achievable
Relevant
Time-bound

People will often rally
around a "BHAG"

Big,
Hairy,
Audacious
Goal

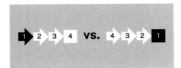

forward vs. backward

Thinking, forward and backward

The philosopher Soren Kierkegaard said, "Life must be lived forward but it can only be understood backwards." In determining strategy for social change, our challenge is to have the courage to imagine what the future could be but have the humility to recognize that our well-articulated goals may not manifest just as we imagine them.

First, we can start by drawing lessons from the past to apply to work going forward. The past may be behind us on a timeline, but it is still relevant as a source of learning. (To quote another thinker, Snoop Dogg, "You've got to always go back in time if you want to move forward."[51])

For many of humanity's greatest achievements, a different future was articulated by an architect, political leader, or social visionary. That vision creates an opportunity for a second technique: we can think "teleologically" — that is, backwards from a goal. In this, we mentally place ourselves in a future moment where we have succeeded. And then we precisely articulate the pathway that got us from the present moment to that possible future success.

The danger is that we have so much faith in our ability to navigate uncertainty that we do the math wrong. To guard against this, we can use a third approach: assume a "learning stance" where we constantly check the data and let it guide us as we move forward. (We'll discuss this more in the Design Thinking chapter.)

Fourth, we can do a "pre-mortem" exercise where we imagine a future state where our efforts failed — and think through what might have gone wrong to lead to that possible failure. (In the **Ethics** chapter, we'll explore this act of shifting temporal perspective.)

Swedish activist Greta Thunberg has called for "cathedral thinking" as humanity faces the threat of climate change. Such long-term, teleological vision is both necessary and possible — if it tempered by steady humility and constant learning.

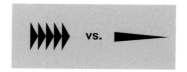

fast vs. slow

The Way It Is

There's a thread you follow. It goes among
things that change. But it doesn't change.
People wonder about what you are pursuing.
You have to explain about the thread.
But it is hard for others to see.
While you hold it you can't get lost.
Tragedies happen; people get hurt
or die; and you suffer and get old.
Nothing you do can stop time's unfolding.
You don't ever let go of the thread.

William Stafford

Urgency and patience

History happens on the stage of time. As social change agents we have to decide how fast we want to move and how patient we're willing to be. In social change, we often confront the inertia of changing long-standing rules, practices, and beliefs. That inertia can demand patience — but patience should be a strategy, not an excuse.

The writing of Martin Luther King Jr. illustrates the tension between urgency and patience. He famously spoke of the "fierce urgency of now" in his *Letter from Birmingham Jail*. In the Letter, King spoke directly to a set of moderate pastors who had urged more patience, saying, "I guess it is easy for those who have never felt the stinging darts of segregation to say 'wait.'"

To King that desire for patience was itself a form of structural racism, an imposition of the timelines and pacing of the dominant group upon the needs of an oppressed people. Even as he sat in his cell in the Birmingham city jail, where the passing of time lost its connection to the outside world, each word of this letter conveyed his sense of urgency.

our past doesn't contradict our future;
they're swatches of the same fabric
stretching across our minds,
one image sewn into another

A. Van Jordan

But King also recognized the need for patience in his statement, stating, "The arc of the moral universe is long, but it bends towards justice." King is often misquoted, "the arc of history bends towards justice." In that misquotation, we can find two essential lessons as we struggle with the dimension of time and social change.

First, King did not suggest history was a linear march through a series of dates. He instead spoke of the curves of the moral universe, powers beyond our understanding that shape the consequences of our actions. In this, King was speaking against inevitability, against a belief that we need not act because things would get better on their own. But he was also speaking for hope, offering a sense that change was in fact possible. And not only was change possible, but the universe was on the side of good.

The second misquotation of King is that "long" disappears. The exclusion of the word "long" is itself a denial of what King was saying. He knew the perverse strength of the systems of oppression even as he had hope that the moral universe was on his side. He did not expect immediate change, even if he knew it was justified.

This tension between urgency and patience can be both a strategic and an emotional challenge for changemakers. The clearer you are about your situation and your strategy, the easier it will be to understand what timeline might be realistic. Then you can match your communications and your expectations with that timeline — even as you always remember that change might come faster or slower than you expect.

The spiral mindset

The tensions among these strategic approaches will always be with us. Strategy requires both vision and iteration; it requires both urgency and patience.

Ultimately, we can aspire to what I call the "spiral mindset," a combination of the linear and cyclical approaches that spirals like a corkscrew. When you open a bottle of wine, the corkscrew points the way, but you have to turn it to dig through the cork and get to your goal.

When you develop a social change strategy, you orient towards a better future and prepare yourself to turn and dig and turn some more. You create a pathway as you walk, watching the ground ahead of you even as you take step after step towards your goal.[52]

Linear
*e.g. rural
vaccination
campaign*

S-curve
*e.g. new
product
introduction*

**Discrete
endpoint**
*e.g. ballot
initiative*

Cyclical
*e.g.
seasonal
fundraising*

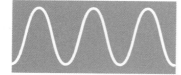

Preservation
*e.g. protecting
a disappearing
language*

The shape of situations

The world is the way it is because of the way it was. The past, for all its flaws, is a good predictor of the future. Or, put another way, the circumstances of the near-past tend to be like the circumstances of the near-future.

There are moments of discontinuity — consider the COVID-19 pandemic — but even in an era of rapid change, there is an underlying continuity to most of history.

That fact is what makes the work of social change so difficult. Forces — social, economic, cultural, technological — have conspired to create the situation we are in. If you want to solve a problem that exists now, you will confront the mechanisms that created the present moment.

Understanding your current situation is essential to your future success. If we ran back the tape, chances are we would end up in a similar situation. After a drought-ending rain, the streams will flow down the same valleys; water will gather in the same basins.

The work of social change is, thus, the work of tilting, not against windmills, but tilting the contours of the present so that the future might curve in a different way.

I dwell in Possibility —
A fairer House than Prose —
More numerous of Windows —
Superior — for Doors —

Emily Dickinson

"The senses lag, but Self runs ahead."

The Upanishads[53]

We've discussed the "shape" of our mindsets and argued for a spiral approach to thinking about strategy. Now let us ask what is the shape of your strategic situation?

Each social change situation is unique, but they do tend to cluster in patterns that reflect the way you might progress over time. In the charts on the previous page, I suggest five such patterns. All are oversimplifications, but I believe useful ones. The x-axis represents time — as you move from left to right you move from past to future. And the y-axis represents the status or progress of your work.

Direct service provision tends to be **linear**. You feed one person, provide one vaccination, or offer one training at a time. You may get more efficient or effective, but your service provision will always be bound to the limits of people.

Some successful campaigns follow an **S-curve** that starts slow, accelerates, and levels off. You might see this when introducing a new product to market or a new idea in a discourse. (S-curves are discussed in more detail in the **Mathematical Modeling** chapter.)

For some social change strategies, like a voter referendum, there is a **discrete end point**. After election day, it is a waste to try to get more votes — but you might, for example, shift your attention to ensuring enforcement of a new law.

Other strategic contexts are fundamentally **cyclical**. Philanthropic giving tends to be concentrated at the end of the calendar year — for reasons of both tax strategy and holiday generosity. Accordingly, many nonprofits find that their contributed revenue follows a cyclical pattern with a spike in the fourth quarter.

Other change strategies are not about driving change, but about preventing it — about **preservation**. If you are trying to defend an old-growth forest or protect a disappearing language, your "situation" will stay flat for as long as you succeed.[54]

Most social change strategies will map to one of these patterns — or a combination of them. These patterns will not answer your strategic questions, but they can help provide a language or framework for discussion. Which model best reflects what you are trying to accomplish? And then you should attempt to locate yourself on the chart. In finding your place on these lines and curves, you don't ask "where am I?" but, instead, "*when* am I?"

"Nothing can remain immense
if it can be measured."

Hannah Arendt[55]

The reality of any change process is, of course, more complicated than any simple line. Reality is a tangled mix — with unexpected setbacks, stasis, and surges. But a sense of the basic shape of your situation will help you organize your thinking and your action.

Measurement and learning

What can be known, and when? As social change agents, we gather information about the world around us and, importantly, about how much (if any) effect our work is having on the issues we care about. That is, we monitor, evaluate, and learn. **Monitoring** is collecting signals about your work while it is happening. **Evaluation** is analyzing your progress against your goals so far. **Learning** is extracting lessons from monitoring and evaluation.

Monitoring can be known as a "formative" process that takes place as you are acting, whereas evaluation is a "summative" process that tries to make judgments about what has happened so far.

On a road trip you might **monitor** speed, gas level, and the hunger of your passengers. At the end you can **evaluate** whether you actually got to your destination. And you **learn** to avoid the food at the gas station and instead check out that great barbeque joint on Route 52.

There are many techniques and approaches to monitoring, evaluation, and learning. (For additional resources, please see the notes.[56]) These techniques encompass both qualitative and quantitative methods.

Qualitative methods range radically, from a single conversation to a multi-year ethnography. Qualitative information could be as simple as a single anecdote from a volunteer that changes the way an organization understands a problem. Or it might be a systematic effort to collect life stories from every resident at a homeless shelter. Qualitative data — and it is *data* — offers humanity and insight.

What qualitative data doesn't offer is scale and proportion. For that, we look towards quantitative methods. Numbers do not necessarily create a higher form of truth. But quantitative data does lend itself to strategic insight, resource allocation, and accountability.

At their most basic, quantitative methods are simply counting. That counting enables the sense of proportion that is so important to understanding your influence relative to context. Counting, however, does not guarantee causality — that is, did the result happen because of your action? Demonstrating causality is difficult but sometimes possible.

Many argue for a "gold standard" of a randomized controlled trial (RCT) where participants are chosen at random and there is a comparison between two groups that. RCTs do include mechanisms that help us have more confidence in causality. They have immense analytical power. They can help you draw on others' experience. Sometimes the best strategy is to simply do what someone else has already shown to be effective (see the notes[57] for resources). In the **Mathematical Modeling** chapter, we'll go into more detail about the power and limitations of RCTs.

In the end, my advice is simple to say and hard to do: be as rigorous as possible while acknowledging the messiness of reality.

Articulate the logic you believe will work to allocate resources to achieve your goal. Then, step by step, seek to describe a way — imperfect as it might be — to judge your progress, learn, and move forward.

> "It is not skepticism about the very idea of truth that guides us; it is realism about how hard the truth is to find."
>
> Kwame Anthony Appiah[58]

Proportion and power

In some circumstances you can identify the concrete outcomes of your work: a kid graduates or a fragile ecosystem is permanently protected.

Other times you want to change the way the system works, to understand why kids aren't graduating in the first place, or know why people aren't eating healthy snacks. You shift your mindset from symptoms to causes. This argues for "root cause analysis" that traces a problem back to its roots.

When we search for root causes, we often reveal one or both of the following dynamics: (1) the structure of the **system** tends towards a certain result or (2) there is a **power** imbalance. Both will be explored in more detail later in the book — especially in the **Complex Systems** and **Community Organizing** chapters.

When looking at systems and power, we quickly come to understand that proportion matters. A dozen people protesting in front of the Parliament of India will probably be ignored. A dozen people showing up at a village meeting might shift the fundamental trajectory of that community.

Some interventions require saturation: the 911 emergency number works because it is the same number everywhere; cigarette taxes would not reduce smoking if they were charged at some stores and not others.

Other interventions simply require meeting a threshold: mobile payments began to work as a system of finance for the unbanked once they were accepted in enough places.

Each situation is unique. There's no one single proportion that will work in all contexts. Part of the work of strategy is determining what proportion might be necessary to reach to shift the balance of power in a situation. It might be smaller than you think. Researchers Erica Chenoweth and Maria Stephan systematically looked at nonviolent social movements across the globe and found that deep engagement from 2.5–5% of the population was often sufficient to spur major change.[59]

Power is a deeply human phenomenon. We rarely confront questions of power alone; there will be others — allies, opponents, bystanders — who act in ways that matter for our goals. This field of power is politics. As Jenny Odell explains, "politics necessarily exist between even

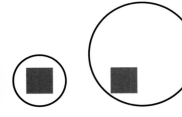

How big is your pond? The same scale can dominate a small context but be lost in a large context.

two individuals with free will; any attempt to reduce politics to design...is also an attempt to reduce people to machines."[60] We can be clear and rigorous about our goals, strategies, resources, and analysis. But — thank God! — we can never remove the human element from social change.

The battlefields of social change

As social change agents, we'd be wise to understand how proportion and power play out in change, especially in those cases where we are "outgunned" — whether by an opponent or by a situation. For millennia, military strategists have wrestled with related power dynamics. Those of us working for a more peaceful world may wish to move beyond the language of war, but we would be foolish to ignore its lessons. So, let's take a moment to focus on the strengths and weaknesses of war as a metaphor for social change.

In social change we always face a situation, a status quo we wish to change. That situation is often a pattern of behavior in a society, a community, or an institution. Unlike in war, your opponent is not necessarily a conscious, well-defined enemy. But if we bring the moral frame of war — an intention to destroy or subjugate — we preclude the possibility of redemption or transformation. We lock ourselves into zero-sum thinking; we guarantee there will not be a mutually beneficial resolution. Military history offers profound analytical lessons; our challenge is to learn from them without adopting the moral frameworks of war.

I'll briefly mention three lessons from military strategy, apply them to social change, and then speak more generally about ways to address imbalances of power.

The first lesson is this: the defense has an advantage — primarily because they can pick their positions and have easier access to supplies. In the pre-mechanical era, this advantage was estimated at 3:1; that is, an offensive (invading) force needed to be at least three times the size of the defensive force to have an even chance. Modern technology has changed the quantitative balance, but the basic lesson remains.[61] The advantage presented by the defense is partly balanced by the key advantage held by offensive forces: they can pick the timing and means of their attack.

Second: willpower matters. Napoleon famously said, "In war, three-quarters

Mapping strategy

It is often valuable to draw strategy. Throughout this book, we'll consider different "maps" that can help us as we work towards social impact.

In Storytelling, we'll consider the "story map" of the Hero's Journey.

In **Community Organizing** we'll talk about how we might diagram influence with a "power map."

In **Complex Systems**, we'll think about how to understand the components and interactions that make up a "systems map." ■

turns on personal character and relations; the balance of manpower and materials counts only for the remaining quarter."[62] Troop morale is an essential ingredient in battlefield success. Further, a cause seen as "just" has more moral force behind it; emotional motivation has kinetic implications.

Third, in the middle of war, the decision-making environment can be confusing and ambiguous. Soldiers operate within what Carl von Clausewitz called "the fog of war." Communication is essential for alignment — yet inherently difficult amid conflict.

All three of these dynamics were visible in the first months of Russia's 2022 invasion of Ukraine. Ukraine's early success resisting a larger force reflected both the advantages of defense and the importance of willpower. This conflict has also demonstrated a modern version of "the fog of war." In the Internet era, the "fog" is composed not of ignorance but of surplus — the overwhelming amount of information, misinformation, and disinformation that clogs the decision-making environment.

Each of these lessons are immediately relevant to the work of social change.

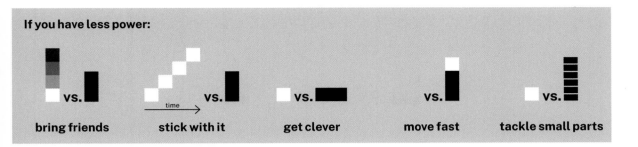

If you have less power:

bring friends vs. stick with it vs. get clever vs. move fast vs. tackle small parts

In short, impact is hard because you (the offense) are trying to change an entrenched situation (the defense). Willpower — passion and energy — is relevant both strategically and morally. And social change actors are constantly acting in contexts of imperfect information — whether too little or too much.

With those signposts, let's step beyond the language of violent conflict and think about power imbalance in general. I'll suggest five ways to think about situations where you have less power than the entity or situation you wish to influence.

You can **bring friends**. In social change, this is the work of recruitment and coalition-building. (We'll discuss this more in the Game Theory chapter.) You can **stick with it**, which is to say, change the discourse and the story simply with your lasting presence ("every Monday at City Hall"). You can **get clever** by reframing an issue or taking a disadvantage and turning into an advantage (civil disobedience does this). Or one might simply **move fast** enough that you reset the situation. This can happen in a farcical way (the riot at the United States Capitol in 2021) or a majestic one (the occupation of Cairo's

Tahrir Square in 2011). Or you can **tackle small parts** one at a time, as in door-to-door canvassing.

These images and ideas are, of course, overly simple. They are not solutions, but categories of approaches you might consider for your specific situation. Moreover, scale, proportion, and change are not always easily measurable. As we saw in the story about the Occupy movement, some changes are inherently qualitative — they shape society's conversation or the metaphors we use to understand our world.

Even in a foggy world, we can lean ourselves towards our work with integrity: soberly seek to understand root causes, assess our relative power in the situation, and think about how to wield that power.

	gathering	understanding	navigating
individuals	Storytelling	Behavioral Economics	Design Thinking
organizations	Community Organizing	Mathematical Modeling	Game Theory
context	Institutions	Complex Systems	Markets

Strategy and the nine tools

In this chapter, I've offered many "shapes" for strategy. Before we move on to the next chapter, I want to leave you with one more shape: a matrix to help you think about the nine tools.

This mapping is one of many ways to think about these (and other) tools. It suggests some possible signposts as you think about when each tool might be relevant to your needs.

In the matrix, the first row is made of tools that operate primarily at the level of the individual person. The tools in the second row are especially relevant for thinking about groups, organizations, and interactions. The third row includes tools helpful when placing your work in a broader context.

We can — loosely — think of the columns as representing different challenges. The first column ("gathering") includes tools especially helpful for bringing people and power together. The second column ("understanding") is a set of ways to make sense of people, progress, and interaction. The third column ("navigating") includes tools especially useful for figuring out how to act amidst complexity.

This matrix represents just one way to understand these tools as a group. I'd encourage you to come up with your own categorization. And, as importantly, I'd invite you to add your own tools to your toolbox.

"Roots. Creativity. Strategy. Fire. That's the magical combination."

Ayana Elizabeth Johnson[63]

Suggested reading

Ann Mei Chang
Lean Impact

Paul Brest and Hal Harvey
Money Well Spent: A Strategic Plan for Smart Philanthropy

John Doerr
Measure What Matters

Lawrence Freedman
Strategy

Strategy with integrity

Ultimately, strategy requires both intellectual and ethical integrity. It needs to be rooted in the clearest possible line connecting the present with a better future — a logical pathway connecting action to results.

Strategy with integrity also includes the humility to recognize that we do not have all the answers and we are part of something much larger. Integrity takes seriously the possibility of change. The world is the product of our choices and our efforts.

Recognizing our own power and agency — constrained as it may be by forces around us — is itself an act of courage. This brings us to the challenge of the next chapter: acting with effectiveness *and* ethics.

Ethics and Social Change

"Senseless Kindness," a performance with
dancers Alison McWhinney, Isaac Hernandez,
Francesco Gabriele Frola, and Emma Hawes
of the English National Ballet
Photo by Dylan Martinez

> "How should we live?" someone asked me in a letter
> I had meant to ask him
> the same question.
>
> Again, and as ever,
> as may be seen above,
> the most pressing questions
> are naive ones.
>
> Wisława Szymborska

Do the right thing

Social change is a tangle of ethical puzzles. As we work to build a better world, we find ourselves confronted with human complexity: different people have different beliefs about what is right; different perspectives offer different understanding; different choices lead to different outcomes.

While this book is oriented towards people who want to build a better world, the tools themselves are ethically neutral. They do not include a hidden check on intentions — or on outcomes. Smart strategy can reduce poverty, or it can concentrate wealth. Insights into human behavior can be used to build agency or manipulate minds. Storytelling can set the stage for justice or for genocide.

Our task is to put these tools to good work. Social change requires strategic flexibility, as described in the previous chapter, and ethical constancy, as explored in this one. As the activist Shira Hassan says, social change can be "a mutable process with only its values set in stone."[64]

"This is the divine law of life:
that only virtue stands firm.
All the rest is nothing."

Pythagoras[65]

**Eight ethical dilemmas
in social change**

Beliefs:
Know what is true to you

Consequences:
Acknowledge winners and losers

Time:
You are both ancestor and descendant

Money:
Resources are power

Truth:
Describe reality with humility

Identity:
Acknowledge who you are

Relationships:
Act with others, not upon them

Organizations:
You are not your organization

Below, I will suggest eight ethical dilemmas common in social change. In each case, I'll explain the contours of an ethical challenge and offer suggestions for how social change agents can navigate it.

Importantly, each dilemma offers an opportunity for strategic insight. We can turn these puzzles to our advantage, use them to reveal the essentially human in our work. And, throughout, you will see traces of my own belief: *in the long term, the right thing is always the strategic thing.*

I dreamed of classifying
Good and Evil, like wise men
Classify butterflies:
I dreamed of pinning down Good and Evil
In the dark velvet
Of a glass box…

Dulce María Loynáz

"Neutrality is dead and it has a place."

Alix Guerrier[67]

Beliefs:
Know what is true to you

Every human being has beliefs about what is right. Those beliefs sculpt the way we understand the world, and they drive our actions.

Social change is the work of turning beliefs into verbs. We would be wise to recognize, however, that one dimension of human diversity is diversity of beliefs. Changemakers who acknowledge diversity of beliefs are simply more likely to succeed. Why? Because they will better understand their strategic context.

One of the most complex ethical puzzles facing the social change agent is how to reconcile our beliefs with those of others. Not everyone can or should believe the same thing. We fail to honor that diversity when we do not acknowledge that the person standing in front of us thinks differently than we do.[66] In a time of stark political polarization, this challenge has become more acute and more urgent.

I'll offer a lesson from my own experience. When I was CEO of GuideStar, many of our users told us they worried about nonprofits that were promoting an agenda of hate. GuideStar was the most widely used source of data about nonprofits, so we felt an obligation to act. And, in addition to the millions of users on guidestar.org, we provided data to giving platforms that facilitated billions of dollars in donations each year.

We were confident that the proportion of nonprofits pushing a hateful agenda was small. But where could we find a list of "hate groups"? We turned to the Southern Poverty Law Center (SPLC), which had spent decades researching hate groups across the United States. GuideStar staff cross-referenced the SPLC's hate group list with our own and posted the data on our site.

Then, I got a call from the Associated Press. The reporter revealed to me our blind spot. The very definition of "hate group" had become a flashpoint in the culture wars that plagued our country. The SPLC's definition of hate group — those that discriminated against others for their immutable characteristics — was coherent but, as we discovered, contested. The definition made sense to us, and indeed it still makes sense to me. But the truth is that others had a different view. For example, the SPLC's list included groups that sought to restrict immigration. To the SPLC these groups were engaged in a racist campaign. But the organizations themselves insisted their work had economic or environmental motivations. Even by the SPLC's definition, we had to impute motives to make a judgment.

As we navigated this experience — which later involved lawsuits, threats, and eventually removing the data — we got a stark lesson in the diversity of belief. We can and should fight for what we believe in; but we only succeed when we acknowledge that others may feel differently. Ultimately, our choice to flag a handful of nonprofits only seemed to enflame existing tensions and harden a cultural standoff.

Our experience trying to identify hate groups forced me to confront how I relate my own political beliefs to the rest of the world. I proudly consider myself a political progressive. I believe society can and must systematically tackle inequality and ecological destruction. I believe that bias and bigotry are embedded in the structures of our society. But I will not succeed in building what I see as a better world if I speak and act as if everyone feels the same way.

Consequences: Acknowledge winners and losers

Choices yield winners and losers. There are those who benefit from a choice and those who do not. In the Game Theory chapter, we explore how to maximize the number of cases where everyone wins.

But, if we are to approach social change ethically, we ought to be honest about trade-offs. It does us no good to pretend that choices only have the consequences we favor.

At the beginning of their careers, physicians pledge the Hippocratic Oath. There is a reason that the Oath's famous first line is *do no harm*: even those tasked with healing can do the opposite. People building a better world should begin with the same aspiration. Unintended consequences are a real danger, even from the most innocent-seeming act. We should all pause to ponder this haunting question from novelist and historian Ada Palmer: "how could the inventors of glitter know that they would poison the manatees?"[69]

The challenge is not to allow uncertainty to freeze our will. Instead, we can see uncertainty as an inspiration to clarify our purpose, think through the range of possible consequences, and hold ourselves accountable. Even as the road to Hell is paved with good intentions, so is the road to Heaven.

There is also a strategic dimension to this ethical stance. When we are honest about the consequences of our choices, it is much easier to understand why different constituencies have different beliefs. Then we can use this information to anticipate objections, neutralize opponents, and recruit allies.

Consequences bring communications challenges. As we'll explore in the Storytelling chapter, we need to articulate a narrative as we draw support for our mission. Sometimes we'll have an option. Do we want to highlight — or minimize — an "us-versus-them" dynamic? In a battle to shut down a coal mine, it would be strategically unwise and morally problematic to frame it as a conflict between environmentalists and mineworkers. Instead, a climate campaigner could frame it as a contest between a victimized community and a profit-obsessed coal company. We cannot stop there. We still must confront the fact that mineworkers will lose their jobs and, therefore, there is an obligation to invest in how to support them once the mine has shut down.

The more we honestly acknowledge winners and losers, the better we can frame a story that aligns with our moral framing and our strategic context.

Time:
You are both ancestor and descendant

In African American communities there's a common phrase, "I am my ancestors' wildest dreams." Pause to imagine the dreams of a great-great-great-great-grandmother, enslaved in the moment but persevering out of hope for generations ahead. And a great-great-great-great granddaughter, thriving despite it all. Across the generations we witness mutuality, tragedy, and hope.

Our responsibility as ancestors is intertwined with our responsibility as descendants. Perhaps the knottiest trade-offs that change agents face are those between the present and the future. We regularly have to decide whether to push a challenge off until later, to tap a resource, and to invest or to save.

There's a powerful technique to bridge these different time perspectives: imagine that you are already living in the future. Sigal Samuel tells a story:[71]

In 2015, 20 residents of Yahaba, a small town in northeast Japan, went to their town hall to take part in a unique experiment.

Their goal was to design policies that would shape Yahaba's future. They'd debate questions typically reserved for politicians: Would it be better to invest in infrastructure or child care? Should we promote renewable energy or industrial farming?

But there was a twist. While half the citizens were invited to be themselves and express their own opinions, the other half were asked to put on special ceremonial robes and pretend they were people from the future. Specifically, they were told to imagine they were from the year 2060 — so that when deliberating with the group, they'd be representing the interests of a future generation.

The results were striking. The citizens who were just being themselves advocated for policies that would boost their lifestyle in the short term. But the people in robes advocated for much more radical policies — from massive health care investments to climate change action — that would be better for the town in the long term.

And they managed to convince their fellow citizens that taking the long view would benefit their grandkids. In the end, the entire group reached a consensus that they should, in some ways, act against their own immediate self-interest in order to help the future.

We see these trade-offs throughout society. The entire purpose of the discipline of finance, as we discuss in the Markets chapter, is to mediate across time and across risk. Investment is, by definition, a bet on the future at the expense of the present.

These questions become ethically complex especially as we stretch to longer time horizons.[72] Many social issues — notably climate change — are issues of generational trade-offs. We also see this dynamic in pension reform, infrastructure investment, and education.

The ethics of time also have immense practical implications for social change institutions. For example, in philanthropy, we've seen a roaring debate over the question of foundation "perpetuity." Should foundations manage their endowments so as to forever maintain the real value of their assets? Or should they "spend down" their assets by giving away more money, faster? Related questions come up in the management of social enterprises or nonprofits that have to decide whether to save for a rainy day or spend on mission now.

There is no single answer for how we should make trade-offs from one generation to the next. In the **Mathematical Modeling** chapter, we will discuss ways — such as the social discount rate — to think explicitly about these questions. These models can then help us honestly articulate trade-offs *over time*.

Perhaps, though, the most powerful step is to regularly pause and remind yourself: I am both ancestor and descendant.

Money:
Resources are power

If you articulate the ethical dimensions of your decisions involving money, you will use it better — whether earning it, spending it, raising it, or giving it away.

This ethical clarity is essential for two reasons. First, it is the right thing to do. If money is power, we need to acknowledge the way it influences us in our actions. Second, understanding the ethical dimensions of money helps us navigate the inevitable pushback, challenges, or conflicted sense of identity that comes with organizing capital for good.

Quite simply, many people working for social change are uncomfortable with money. It can be an almost physical reaction. I know one nonprofit leader who insisted he was prone to getting sick after fundraisers where he handled a lot of cash. For most, though, it is a moral quandary. They recognize the inequalities of our society — and that the systems of money helped to create those inequalities. But they also know that money enables them to pursue their organization's mission.

Actual engagement with money quickly raises those tensions. That engagement could be fundraising — whether collecting donations for a nonprofit, investments for a business, or taxes for a government. Invariably, questions of power come up when money is used for social good. In the relationships section below, we'll explore how money hierarchies can be twisted into power hierarchies.

Our ethical anxieties around money can quickly get personal. Many of us feel the weight of an essential question: how much is enough? The philosopher Peter

"Peacemakers truly 'make' peace...
we need to be artisans of peace,
for building peace is a craft that demands serenity,
creativity, sensitivity, and skill."

Pope Francis[74]

Singer presents a simple thought experiment. Imagine you saw a drowning child. You could save her, but only by jumping into the river and ruining your suit. Most people say they'd save the child.

But there are many nonprofits that have evidence-based interventions to save a child's life for less than the cost of your suit. If all lives are equally valuable, are we not then similarly obligated to donate?[73] I do not claim to have a definitive answer. But I am sure that it is a question worth pondering.

In the Strategy chapter, we defined strategy as a logic for allocating resources to achieve a goal. Inherent in that definition is an assumption of scarcity. You don't need logic if you have infinite resources. That scarcity is often present, not just in money but in time, attention, or voice.

But when it comes to money, it is worth pausing to consider its abundance. There are trillions of dollars sloshing around the global economy. Every year in the United States alone people donate — simply give away! — almost a half a trillion dollars.[75]

There is not an infinite amount of money. But there is a lot. And there are many people who would be happy to see their money put to a different kind of use, who would celebrate the use of their money for public purpose. So, while the objective scarcity of money demands rigor, the subjective reality can be one of abundance.

These challenges extend to people's professional identity. Millions of people around the world are paid to make the world better. That is a sign of a healthy society. But it also raises ethical dilemmas. Should people expect less — or more — compensation if they are doing good for the world? How much should a nonprofit pay its executives? Is it okay for an investor to get rich off renewable energy? Should public health officials get a bonus if they drive down infection rates?

Social change agents get the benefit of others' perceptions of their own altruism. But that brings with it a higher standard, a new set of expectations, about how the work of social good does or does not benefit those involved.

To navigate these ethical puzzles, our best hope is honest acknowledgment. Acknowledge the inherent power dynamics between those asking for money and those providing it. Acknowledge the necessity of money to accomplish

> "It does not require many words to speak the truth."
>
> Hinmatóowyalahtqit
> (aka Chief Joseph of the Nez Perce)[76]

> "The only path to justice runs through truth."
>
> Darren Walker[77]

our important work for social change. Acknowledge our personal need for some, but not too much.

Truth:
Describe reality with humility

It is not easy to talk about truth. We grasp for the right words; we talk past each other. So let me start with some definitions. Like all definitions these are imperfect, but they at least can help us frame the conversation.

1. **Truth** is the actual state of reality. It has an objective existence. But the limitations of human perception (and, indeed, quantum physics) make it impossible to perfectly describe or access that reality.
2. **Truthfulness** is a state of doing your best to tell the truth, of sincerely attempting to be accurate.
3. **Truthiness** is communication that disregards actual truth; to speak without any commitment to accuracy, precision, or sincerity. As the philosopher and TV talk show host Stephen Colbert explained, "truthiness" is "the belief in what you feel to be true rather than what the facts will support."[78]

The philosopher Richard Reeves argues that the only solution to our current crisis of truth is an ethical one. He says, "Trust is built on truthfulness rather than truth…the most important thing is to strive to present their work in a way that's as objective as possible (accuracy), and to present a range of reasonable results wherever possible, giving the fullest possible picture (sincerity)." Reeves continues, "Certainly, being truthful is a hard task. But without it, free societies cannot function. And nobody said freedom was easy."[79]

Truthiness cannot last forever. Eventually, reality wins. And despite our era of waning trust, trust still matters. It has immense practical implications in business. I recall a conversation with the leader of a radical environmental group who had worked in the business world before. He remarked at how struck he was that there was less trust among environmental nonprofits than he had seen among businesses.

The lesson here is that trust is not simply a moral act. Trust is a practical prerequisite for many activities. It lubricates relationships and removes barriers. And by its very nature, trust compounds over time, growing as one party's bet on another pays

Ethical glossary

Utilitarianism: greatest good for the greatest number

Categorical imperative: act as if you would make your action universal

Golden Rule: do unto others as you would have them do unto you

Platinum Rule: do unto others as they would have done unto themselves

Morality: what you believe to be right

Ethics: collective norms of behavior

Causistry: an ethics of causes and circumstances

off. In the Game Theory chapter, we will explore some of the consequences of this trust. And we will fully acknowledge that there are times when trust is not justified.

Truthfulness yields trust among others. And, importantly, seeking truth also makes it more likely we do not lie to ourselves and, instead, listen to what the facts are telling us.

Identity:
Acknowledge who you are

Societies are arrangements of individuals. The caste system in India assumed that each individual was chained to a spot in an immutable social hierarchy. The history of race relations in the United States is a history of structural inequality, and, indeed, may be thought of as its own kind of caste system.[80]

Not all social structures or sources of identity are so nefarious. Many are sites of human flourishing: families, communities, congregations, and sports teams.

Good or bad, it is essential that we recognize that these structures are real. That recognition is at the heart of many efforts to build a better world, as organizations work to erode the immoral structures and build better ones.

But our recognition of identity must go deeper than abstract external analysis. It should include an understanding of where we, as individuals, fit in a structure. That placement may or may not be fair. We may be privileged or disadvantaged through no fault of our own.

This simple acknowledgment forces a reassessment; once we know how we got here, we can be honest about how to move forward. (See further discussion in the **Behavioral Economics** chapter.)

Our identities are a combination of dimensions: race, ethnicity, birth sex, gender identity, sexual orientation, religion, class, ability, political beliefs, and more. All are a part of how we show up in the world. And these identities have consequences. Many other books have explored in depth the power of these dimensions. But it so important to social change strategy that I would like to pause to note the key elements.

1. Each dimension of identity matters on a personal level: it helps define — consciously and unconsciously — our sense of self, our understanding of who we are in the world.
2. The dimensions do not operate independently; they intersect. Being a Black woman is more than just being a woman and being Black.
3. Identity changes how people perceive and relate to each other, again both consciously and unconsciously.
4. These changes compound over time and end up embedded in language, practices, and institutions.
5. This "structural" effect creates an unequal distribution of power and resources in our society. As a general rule, that is unfair. But it is real.

Consciousness of our identity need not mean we accept the structural effects. But it does mean that we admit they exist. A wealthy white man can do compassionate and effective work in an under-resourced Hmong community. But he cannot paper over his race or economic privilege. Ignoring it does not make it go away.

Ultimately, acknowledgment of difference creates space to find commonality.

Relationships:
Act with others, not upon them

We are not alone. We act as individuals in constant interaction with others; we act

> "If you have some power,
> then your job
> is to empower somebody else."
>
> Toni Morrison[81]

in *relationship*. A thousand libraries have been written on human relationships. Here, let me suggest we organize our brief exploration around the "direction" of the relationship: up, down, and sideways.

"Up" relationships are with those in power. To influence them, we would be wise to acknowledge two things. First, we can admit they have power. It may not be fair that these individuals have influence over others: they might not be smart, good, or representative. But they have power. Our job as social change agents is to influence their actions. Second, when looking up at one who has power over us, we can remember that we have power, too. Those in power always need those with less power. They are defined by it: bosses are not bosses without employees; teachers are not teachers without students; wardens are not wardens without incarcerated people.

"Down" relationships are those with less power than we have. In most situations we're in, there will be people who are structurally subordinate to us. They could be employees, volunteers, children, grantees, or students. The first step is to acknowledge this power dynamic.

Acknowledgment can protect against two perversions of power dynamics: abuse and guilt freeze. Abuse is self-explanatory; history is rife with examples of the exploitation of power. Guilt freeze is when those with power are ashamed of their power and so fail to act at all. It is useful to recognize those moments when you have power that you did nothing to deserve. But we also can remember that the call of social change is to act with justice, not to wallow in guilt.

"Sideways" relationships are the heart of social change. We walk with others. Those who seek transformative change alone always fail. Our colleagues and others who share our path are not just our companions; they are our only chance to succeed. So much of the success in social change is recruiting — through stories — companions in making a better world. I'll discuss this process more in the **Community Organizing** chapter.

It is worth pausing on two types of relationships in social change that should be sideways but often are up-and-down. First is the relationship between agent and beneficiary. The social entrepreneur employing people just out of prison may aspire to a sideways relationship with their employees. If they find themselves in an "up-down" relationship, they might alienate the people they're supposed to help and miss valuable first-hand insights that would bolster their business.

Similarly, money often equates to power. And in social change, those with capital (whether providers of grants, debt, or equity) often find themselves with power. The challenge is this: the funder and the funded are on the same team. They are fellow travelers towards a better world. The funder and the funded should be in a sideways relationship, but too often the funders are up and the recipients down. These power dynamics can work at cross-purposes with truth, leading to what Nanjira Sambuli called "narrative ventriloquism…a creative nonfiction for anyone who's ever had to fundraise."[83] Money can distort relationships, which distorts trust.

In each of these three directional relationships, the best relationships are defined by dignity. When in doubt, we can use dignity as the criterion by which we judge our choices. We can all aspire to a story with shared dignity. One of the greatest fuels for dignity is listening, a core focus of the Design Thinking chapter.

In the end, the most powerful transformation contains elements of both altruism and authentic self-interest. As the Australian Aboriginal leader Lilia Watson memorably said, "If you have come here to help me, you are wasting your time; but if you have come because your liberation is bound up with mine, then let us work together." In an act of beautiful consistency, Watson herself emphasized that she does not alone deserve the credit for this quote; it was created as part of a collective effort.

Organizations:
You are not your organization

Many social change agents spend so much time encased in the identity of an organization, they forget they are separate from it. This attitude is especially true for founders and executives who are externally perceived to represent an organization (whether for-profit, non-profit, or government). It also can be true for front-line workers who are seen as the voice of an organization.

This sense of shared identity is understandable, but we are wise to remember we are distinct: we can believe something different from our organization's official talking points. We contribute to and bear responsibility for the successes and failures of our organizations, but they are not wholly ours. I'll mention two concrete places where this concept comes into play. Across sectors, there is the challenge of "founder's syndrome," where the person who started an organization sticks around for so long that the organization gets stuck. After many years, disentangling the relationships and the ethos of an organization from its founder can become difficult. This problem is solvable with intention and a plan for transition.

Versions of organizational identity crises can emerge for executives, especially chief executives. I felt it myself during my time as CEO of GuideStar. Indeed, I had to give up a part of my identity (being a chief executive) to enable the merger of GuideStar and Foundation Center to form Candid. It was a strategic sacrifice to advance the mission. But it was still painful; it is easier to change a business card than an identity.

The conflation of self and organization is not always a figment of an arrogant leader's imagination. It can be reinforced — or even imposed — externally. The receptionist at the health clinic bears the emotional burden of beneficiaries' experience at that clinic.

Related to the confusion between self and organization is the confusion between self and job. At times this confusion leads to arrogance or intransigence. But, in work for social impact, the bigger problem is exhaustion and burnout.[85] This is acute in healing professions like nursing, therapy, and social work and extends across many types of work for a better world.

As social change agents, we walk a fine line, because our emotional and ethical investment in our work builds power and effectiveness. That investment creates vulnerability, which then engenders trust. By definition, vulnerability creates the possibility of harm. Social change agents would be wise to remember the advice of flight attendants everywhere: put on your own oxygen mask before helping others.

The final chapter of this book — **Institutions** — explores some of the ethical questions facing organizations — whether government agencies, businesses, or nonprofits. What are the rights and responsibilities of organizations to their stakeholders and society as a whole?

"I say more: the just man justices."

Gerard Manley Hopkins

Ambition, humility, and kindness

The best of modern social change is characterized by a contradiction: it is both ambitious and humble. Major societal change doesn't tend to happen accidentally. It is powered by intentionality. And intentionality for impact is — by definition — ambition.

But ambition without humility is arrogance; arrogance leads to delusion; delusion leads to failure.We don't have to look far to find reasons for humility: we exist in an immensely complex world that is calcified by institutional inertia and distorted by human biases. Reality itself asks us to be humble.

And yet we still must claim our own power. Our challenge is to do so in a way that honestly confronts the ethical dilemmas that arise when you try to do something that matters.

I'd like to close with an emphasis on the connection between kindness and effectiveness. In the Game Theory chapter, we will explore this connection more formally — not just formally in the sense that we will spend time on it, but formally in the sense that one can *mathematically* show the power of kindness.

We don't need an equation to know that kindness can work. Every day we have a chance to test this hypothesis with friends, family, colleagues, and strangers. Even in a harsh world, those who invest in others are ultimately rewarded.

And for change agents like us, our rewards are not just personal, but in the impact we see.

Ethics and Social Change Takeaways

The work of changing the world comes with unique ethical responsibilities. Ethics is not separate from strategy; ethical dilemmas also offer opportunities for strategic insight.

Eight essential dimensions of social change ethics and how to navigate them:

Beliefs:
Know what is true to you
Acknowledging and reconciling diversity of belief is central to your actions as a social changemaker. Today's stark political polarization makes this challenge more acute and more urgent.

Consequences:
Acknowledge winners and losers
Be honest about trade-offs; there's no upside to pretending that choices only have the consequences we favor. Exploring why others disagree helps us understand how we might change their minds.

Time:
You are both ancestor and descendant
Change agents face knotty trade-offs between past, present, and future. Take time to imagine the dreams of those who came before you and the needs of those who will come after you.

Money:
Understand both resources and power
Always be prepared to articulate the ethical dimensions of your decisions involving money — whether you are earning it, spending it, raising it, or giving it away. People see your work as altruistic, so it carries higher expectations about how it does and does not benefit everyone involved.

Truth:
Describe reality with humility
Follow the truth to where it leads you, not to where you want it to go. A stable, long-term foundation of trust cannot be built on lies and half-truths. Present a picture that is as accurate and as sincere as possible. Warts and all.

Identity:
Acknowledge who you are
Our identities have consequences. Ignoring identity does not make it go away. Acknowledging difference creates space to find commonality. Analyzing where we fit in the social structure (whether that structure is fair or not) casts light on our own path forward.

Relationships:
Act with others, not upon them
Those who seek transformative change alone always fail. Impact requires other people. We can pay attention to how power flows within those relationships. Whatever the arrangement, the best relationships are defined by dignity.

Organizations:
You are not your organization
That attitude can lead to arrogance, intransigence, exhaustion, and burnout. We can believe something different from the organization's talking points. Neither the successes nor failures of an organization are wholly ours.

In the end, the key lesson of social change ethics is this: kindness is effective.

Torah

Tao Te Ching

Dhammapada

Bhagavad Gita

Analects

The Bible

Quran

Storytelling

Turn Off the Plastic Tap," by Benjamin Von Wong. In February of 2022, the artist placed this mammoth installation outside of the headquarters of the United Nations Environment Program in Nairobi, Kenya. It served as an inspiration — and as a warning — for delegates working inside to negotiate a global plastics treaty.

All the world's a stage

Tell all the truth but tell it slant —
Success in Circuit lies
Too bright for our infirm Delight
The Truth's superb surprise
As Lightning to the Children eased
With explanation kind
The Truth must dazzle gradually
Or every man be blind —

Emily Dickinson

Those who set the narrative set the stage for the actions of others.

In this chapter, we'll explore two kinds of narrative that are essential for social change. The first form is deep in our bones: the **story**. A story usually traces the path of a protagonist who overcomes challenges. It is time-bound, with a beginning, a middle, and an end.

There is also a second kind of narrative that subconsciously explains a situation. It's how people filter information and make sense of the world around them. I will call this the **"invisible narrative."** An invisible narrative is not a single story, instead it is one way we collectively organize our understanding of the world.

Some invisible narratives are modest in scope — the assumptions a community makes about its park. Others are immense — the myths that create the substructure of entire societies.

The power of these two kinds of narratives is a consequence of the way the brain makes sense of the world. We perceive reality through a tangle of sense, emotion, and reason. Narratives are an efficient way to weave data together; a storyline is a mental thread that connects dots over time.

In social change, we are trying to define new pathways toward a better world. For this reason, storytelling is an essential tool for anyone with a dream of something better.

This chapter cannot hope to cover the vast universe of storytelling. What it can do is lay out a basic framework and offer a set of lessons for how narrative can be wielded for the social good.

"Storytelling is one of the primary building blocks of civilization. Everything that is important to us as a species has been contained in stories...
We can't have a just, equitable society unless we imagine one."

Levar Burton[87]

So, first, a story.

The Capitol Crawl

Once upon a time, an astonishingly short time ago, there was no such thing in the United States as rights for people with disabilities. And for many disabled people, that injustice was internalized. "People with disabilities... didn't think the issues we faced in our daily lives were the product of prejudice and discrimination," Kitty Cone, the late disability rights activist, wrote in 1997. "If I thought about why I couldn't attend a university that was inaccessible, I would have said it was because I couldn't walk — my own personal problem."

The consequences of such a framing were grave. Disabled individuals weren't just stigmatized; they were institutionalized, sterilized, and denied the most basic rights afforded other Americans.

Inspired in part by the passage of the Civil Rights Act of 1964, a group of young people with disabilities saw — and lived — a different story. Instead of focusing on what individuals "lacked," they talked about where society was coming up short. In other words, rather than seeing the limitations of disability as a personal problem, the activists recast it as a problem of an inaccessible society.

Over the course of many years, disability rights activists like Cone filed lawsuits, led sit-ins, and lobbied for equal access in employment, education, housing, and public transportation. In parallel, they worked to empower people with disabilities and called for independent living opportunities. Their struggles led to slow progress, but disabled people still faced barriers built into the architecture — physical and cultural — of society.

They engaged in a decades-long effort to reframe the story of disability. The Capitol Crawl, on March 12, 1990, was a thunderbolt to the narrative. The Americans with Disabilities Act (ADA) had stalled in Congress. Activists decided they needed to demonstrate the moral and political urgency of the disability crisis.

Sixty disabled protestors made their way to Washington, DC, discarded their wheelchairs, and crawled up the steps of the U.S. Capitol. One of them, Jennifer Keelan, was only eight years old. From their hands and knees, chanting "ADA Now!" and "Access Now!" participants scaled each and every stair of the country's foremost symbol of democracy as more than a thousand people cheered them on.

This was a story told visually as much as verbally, providing a powerful metaphor for the barriers Americans with disabilities faced in the United States. Inaccessibility laid bare part of an unjust invisible narrative. Participant Bob Kafka remembered, "We wanted to show that 'access is a civil right' is more than just words, that we were willing to take action. We wanted to make sure the statement we made was symbolic and visual."

The Capitol Crawl was an exclamation point after decades of work. Four months later, President George H.W. Bush signed the ADA into law stating, "Let the shameful wall of exclusion come tumbling down."

From that rubble, the disability community built a new — truer — story about what the "pursuit of happiness" could mean in American society.

Stories and invisible narrative

The Capitol Crawl shows how stories and invisible narrative come together. The status quo invisible narrative was rooted in the fundamental limitations of disability. It saw disability as something lacking, as a set of perhaps tragic circumstances that could not be remedied. It was a force so powerful and unchallenged that many people with disabilities like Kitty Cone had, at some point, even believed it about themselves.

But the dramatic images of the Capitol Crawl made clear the moral courage of the disabled activists. It was political will that was lacking. Members of Congress just needed to show a fraction of the courage of the activists and sign the ADA. In the end, the Capitol Crawlers didn't just change policy, they helped define a new invisible narrative.

Social change may even be described as the use of stories to reimagine the invisible narrative. But to do so we need to understand the basic shape of stories and how they may be used to shift the invisible narrative. If we change the invisible narrative, we shift the context in which decisions are made and how society is formed and reformed.

The human mind perceives reality through a mix of senses, emotion, reason, and memory.

Narrative is a **line** through that data.

It might be a **timeline** that connects events over hours or years.

It might be a **storyline** that scripts characters and events together.

Or it might be what Australian Aboriginal peoples call a **songline**, a path through a particular land (or sky) that links together events and characters in space.

A common story

Folklorists have identified thousands of motifs common across human stories. Some have endless variations in modern culture: "rags-to-riches," "mistaken identity," and "vengeance."[89] Other motifs surely remain hidden in our collective subconscious.

Any single archetype is an oversimplification of the library of human stories. But it is undoubtedly useful to have a framework to guide us as we seek to use stories for good. In this chapter, we'll focus on one archetype: the "Hero's Journey" as formally articulated by Joseph Campbell in 1949.[90]

In the Hero's Journey, a protagonist is called from their known life to go on a journey. In that journey they pass into the unknown, meet companions, find a mentor, pass through trials, confront darkness, and return transformed.

You do not have to look far to find examples of the Hero's Journey in popular culture.

Harry Potter was called from 4 Privet Drive on a journey to the unknown: Hogwarts. There he met Ron and Hermione and found wisdom from Dumbledore. He then confronted Voldemort and was, ultimately, transformed.

In *The Wizard of Oz*, Dorothy was swept up from Kansas and called to a quest to meet the Wizard. Along the way she found guidance from the Good Witch, met the Scarecrow, the Cowardly Lion, and Tin Man, and confronted the Wicked Witch. She then returned to that place like no other, home.

The Hero's Journey is sometimes called the "monomyth" — a single Ur-story that explains all others. That is, quite simply, wrong. Human experience is too diverse to be captured in a single framework. In fact, some critics have argued that the Hero's Journey reflects a particularly individualistic — not to mention white and male — way of understanding the world. I must emphasize this is only one of many ways of thinking about the structure of stories. With that said, the Hero's Journey is, by my judgment, particularly useful as a narrative framework for social change.

We are all protagonists in our own stories — and many want to be the hero of our stories.[91] But, first, we need a "call" to something greater, a call that brings us into an unknown world. Along the way, we

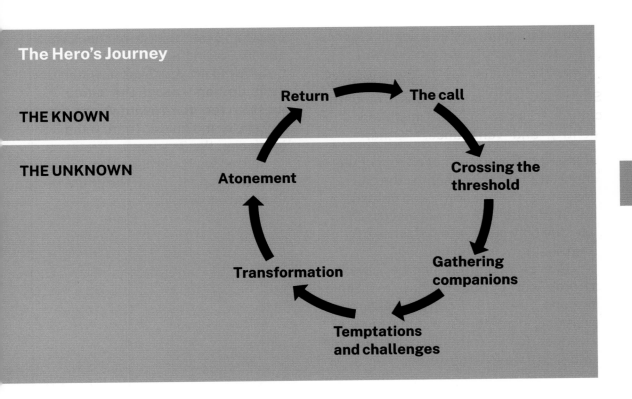

The Hero's Journey

THE KNOWN

THE UNKNOWN

Return → The call → Crossing the threshold → Gathering companions → Temptations and challenges → Transformation → Atonement → Return

Our brains chemically reward us for stories. A study of hospitalized children found that those who were told stories showed higher levels of oxytocin and lower levels of pain.[92] ■

need companions, and we need guidance. If we do anything ambitious, we will confront challenges. And challenges lead to transformation.

Each of these elements has a parallel in the work of social change.

Below, I will focus on three elements of the Hero's Journey that are particularly important for social change: the call, describing the unknown, and personal transformation. Then I will discuss the roles we play and the importance of tragedy, irony, and humor.

Before we continue, another caveat: a Hero's Journey does not have to be epic in scope. The pattern can emerge in the everyday: in a meeting, a conference, or a protest. To illustrate this point, imagine going for a walk in the woods.

One day you look out your window and see a beautiful sky. So you walk out the front door and head into a nearby forest. There you look up at a giant tree. Inspired by its stability and its grandeur, you find yourself emotionally rooted, calmed, and strengthened.

Then you discover that you are not alone — you see two squirrels chasing each other through the branches. You hear a dozen birdsongs around you. You pause and feel an urge to check your phone. But, instead, you take a deep breath and lift your eyes to watch the light filtering through the leaves.

For a few more minutes you continue to wander the forest. Then, you turn around and return home, refreshed.

In that walk, perhaps over 15 minutes, you have gone through the entire cycle of the Hero's Journey.

is a myth, not a mandate,
fable, not a logic by which people are moved."

win Edman[93]

"You are never strong enough
that you don't need help."

Cesar Chavez[94]

he call

/e cannot change the world alone; we
eed others to join us. Recruitment is
entral to social change and stories are
entral to recruitment. A social enterprise
ust recruit investors; a community
leanup needs volunteers; a protest
ithout participants is not a protest.

As social change agents, therefore,
e have to craft "the call" to invite others
o join us on our journey. Indeed, I would
uggest that the very definition of **leader-
hip is an invitation to a shared story**.

Social change leaders need to factor
he question of power into their invita-
ions. When making "the call," we need to
nderstand the voice we will use and how
e relate to the person with whom we are
peaking. Are we recruiting from a posi-
ion of perceived wisdom (as a "mentor"),
spiration (as a "petitioner"), or equality
as a "partner")?

Most of us gravitate towards the
partner" frame. We should; that equality
s firm ethical ground to craft a call. But
here are times when the person we are
peaking to will perceive us as having
isdom and look to us as the "mentor."
egardless of whether they are right, we
annot ignore that power dynamic.

Similarly, if our recruitment is in a
context where we have less power, it is
wise to acknowledge that we are the
"petitioner." Indeed, we may choose to
turn that frame to our advantage and craft
a story that places the one with power in
the role of hero. When they do what we
want (such as make a donation or pass a
law), they are victorious in the story.

In each case, we should be thoughtful
about how we situate our power relative to
the other characters in our story.

The call is not always intentional or
predicted. Sometimes the companions on
a social change journey emerge through
circumstances beyond our control. This
certainly matches many classic examples
of the Hero's Journey. Consider the stories
of J.R.R. Tolkien. In *The Hobbit*, Bilbo's
companions simply showed up at his door.
The "fellowship" in the *Fellowship of the
Ring* began as a collection of bickering
political representatives. It took crisis for
them to offer their sword, bow, and axe
towards a common cause.

Describing the unknown

A sought-after skill in literature is "world building," the ability of an author to craft a context that feels real and is internally consistent. This is a prominent part of speculative fiction; indeed, for some readers its core appeal is the immersion in a different world. But it is relevant for even the most realistic fiction. Yes, Octavia Butler, Cixin Liu, and Frank Herbert built worlds. So did Zora Neale Hurston, Leo Tolstoy, and Emily Brontë.

The revelation of the unknown is core to social change storytelling. In the Hero's Journey, a protagonist crosses a threshold and is introduced to a broader world. Something beyond "normal" is revealed. Social change agents can reveal something new to those around them.

In some circumstances, we may wish to paint a picture of something new and beautiful. If we hope to build a community garden, we need to weave a story for our community of what it will be like when it is complete. Similarly, if we want people to confront an injustice, we have to describe its roots, its reality, and its resolution.

It is possible to convey an invisible narrative directly through human stories. Yaa Gyasi's novel *Homegoing* is a notable modern example. It traces seven generations of a Ghanaian family. One branch navigates the transition from colonialism to democracy and another is enslaved in the United States. As you follow the lives of Gyasi's characters, you learn about the forces, policies, and institutions — sharecropping, convict leasing, Jim Crow, redlining, mass incarceration — that constrained their choices and set their pathways.

Such a narrative places the present moment in the middle of a chain, a chain linked to the past and perhaps to be broken in the future. It is situational analysis that builds a world in the reader's mind and helps make the present intelligible.

Some story-starting phrases from the world's languages

Arabic (Moroccan):
"I've told you what's coming..."

Armenian:
"There was, there was not..."

Bantu (Mozambique): "Once upon the time, there was a truly great friendship..."

Chinese (Classical): "Anciently..."

Czech: "Beyond seven mountain ranges, beyond seven rivers..."

English: "Once upon a time..."

German: "Back in the days when it was still of help to wish for a thing..."

Gujarati: "This is an old story."

Hindi: "In one era..."

Kazakh: "A long, long time ago, when goats had feathers..."

Korean:
"On an old day, in the old times..."

Persian: " Someday, sometime..."

Scottish Gaelic:
"A day that was here..."

Slovak:
"Where it was, there it was..."[96]

Personal transformation

Humans yearn for agency. We desire some degree of control over our path through life. Even in an unjust world, we still want to believe there is a connection between our actions and our outcomes. Rooted in our desire for agency is a yearning for personal transformation.

We tend to want to make ourselves better. The work of social change is, in this way, not only an opportunity for external impact, but also an opportunity for *personal transformation*.

Personal transformation can be a source of psychological empowerment and thus of agency. But, more, it can serve as a kind of parallel track to social transformation: we watch changes in ourselves as we see the external fruits of our labor. The internal process of personal transformation and the external process of social change can intertwine and reinforce each other over time.

Some of the greatest challenges of personal transformation are when we look in the mirror and see ourselves in a new way. In the Hero's Journey, the final confrontation involves a deep sense of self-reflection. Indeed, the ultimate antagonist is often a reflection of the dark side of the protagonist. (Spoiler alert: so, it turns out that in *Star Wars*, Darth Vader is Luke Skywalker's father.)

A version of this transformation dynamic can play out directly in social change. Personal transformation can be terrifying, even as it is essential. Sometimes, social change work requires that we confront our own shadows. A philanthropist can sit alone and guiltily brood about their own wealth or, through reflection, find insight into the sources of inequality that help them act with clarity and kindness.

Sometimes transformation comes not in spite of terrible circumstances but through them. Nelson Mandela transformed his 27 years in prison into an opportunity for profound growth. The early years of Mandela's work for freedom were driven by (justified) anger and at times descended into violence. But somehow, within the experience of his incarceration, he found the wisdom and power to help lead his country peacefully away from the ravages of apartheid.

Three cautions are worth noting. First, personal transformation can be twisted and fall into blame-shifting. That is,

we cannot simply "blame the victim" and demand transformation from those facing the currents of injustice. Heroism takes many forms; for some, survival is victory. Second, personal transformation driven solely by guilt or shame will not lead to social action; it needs agency and hope to succeed. Third, for those who have a history of trauma, personal transformation is psychologically fraught and especially benefits from having a wise guide. In each case, our growth ought to be sensitive to what my father, who spent his life working at the intersection of psychotherapy and social change, calls "our own woundedness."

With those caveats, some degree of personal transformation is always possible even in the bleakest of circumstances.

Gandhi's (likely apocryphal) dictum "be the change you wish to see in the world" is both a moral and a strategic statement. That is, goodness is good in and of itself. It also makes one a more effective advocate, immune to charges of hypocrisy. But internal change is not, by itself, enough for external change.

Transformation positions us to act; then act we must.

Tragedy, irony, and humor

It is easy to aspire to a clear story, one with obvious good guys and bad guys. But the truest and most effective stories are often characterized by a fog of ambiguity or contradiction. Truth complicates the simple story — and as we see in the **Ethics** chapter, truth builds trust.

The complexity of truth can show up in stories as tragedy, irony, and humor.

Let's start with tragedy. In the narrative framework of Greek tragedy, a hero is haunted by a tragic flaw. In some twist, that flaw leads to their downfall. Tragedy can be an important angle in social change narratives because it can be deeply self-reflective and compassionate. Aristotle argued that listeners connect to tragedy in two ways: they see themselves in the hero (*mimesis*, or imitation) and they weep for the suffering they see (*catharsis*, or cleansing).

These two elements are directly relevant to social change storytelling. First, we need to place ourselves — and those we recruit — as heroes in a story. And most of social change is an attempt to confront the suffering of the world.

Irony is a twist on this formula. The actions of a character have the opposite effect of what they intended. The theologian Reinhold Niebuhr wrote in *The Irony of American History* about the many times when U.S. foreign policy had exactly the opposite impact of what was intended. Why would a theologian write about foreign policy? Because in the negative outcomes of good intentions, we can find important lessons about human morality.

The activists of the Capitol Crawl used this technique to great effect by highlighting the irony that the United States Capitol — supposedly a symbol of accessible, democratic government — was inaccessible to many citizens. Law-makers inside the Capitol weren't taking action to represent those citizens. Social change narratives like this can highlight the elements of absurdity that pepper our life, highlighting the contradictions that make up our messy reality. In 1960, four Black college students in Greensboro, N.C., created a new narrative when they did the unthinkable: they sat at a lunch counter and asked to have lunch. The righteousness of the students highlighted the ironic absurdity of not serving lunch at a lunch counter.

Humor is the more joyous reflection of these contradictions. As with irony and tragedy, it flips expectations, offering an outcome or a contradiction that surprises the audience. It can reveal a tension or an insight. But, more, it can lighten the mood. So much of social change is Very Serious.

Political cartoons, costumes, and pranks can transcend the dreary seriousness of politics. During the 2000 U.S. presidential campaign, I was part of a team trying to inject discussion of global warming into the political conversation. My friend Matthew Anderson dressed up as Captain Climate — a superhero who had traveled back in time to warn politicians about climate change. And one night in New Hampshire, it worked. Senator John McCain — amused by the galivanting superhero at his rally — invited him up onto the stage for a conversation. Matthew stood there in tights, hands on hips in classic superhero pose, and got McCain to commit to holding hearings upon his return to the Senate. In part because of this stunt, McCain eventually became a much-needed Republican champion for climate action.

Oscar Wilde was exaggerating when he said, "If you want to tell people the truth, make them laugh, otherwise they'll kill you." But there are very practical reasons to use humor in social change narratives. It works. Funny stories are often the most memorable; laughter can carve an idea into our minds.

Some common narrative roles

Protagonists:
Hero
Friend
Mentor

Antagonists:
Tyrant
Henchman
Beast

Neutrals:
Rogue
Nature
Jester
Bystander

Finding our roles

We exercise power when we define roles in a story. At times, categories of good and evil will be useful; the hero and the villain are obvious. But often the choice is not so simple.

Imagine you are organizing a beach cleanup. There is no single villain. Countless individual actions and social forces have led to the trash on the beach. Right now, the garbage is there. It does not care where it came from. Blaming past actions does not solve present problems.

What if the true villain is our inertia or apathy? What if we who stand by are the ones who bear responsibility? Suddenly the story is flipped, and we are the bad guys. But there is a solution! You — yes, you! — have an opportunity to go from being a passive villain to being an active hero. Pick up a bag and gloves and let's get to work. Let us transform ourselves as we transform the beach.

The simple answer of framing can inspire action and reflection. If we cast ourselves as the good guys, we risk ignoring our own complicity. And if we cast our opponents as irredeemably evil, we foreclose the possibility of their redemption.

Now, evil does exist. Sometimes it must be called out and resisted. But storytelling also allows us to see our roles in a situation with more nuance and potential. It gives those we target space to change for the better. And, if we are wise, storytelling also creates a pathway for our own transformation.

Crafting a public narrative

Marshall Ganz spent sixteen years as an organizer with the United Farm Workers. Then he decided to take what he had learned in California's fields and apply it to broader questions of social change strategy. He got an appointment at Harvard's Kennedy School of Government and focused his attention on teaching and studying the use of story in social change. Ganz suggests a framework he calls **public narrative** — a technique for stacking stories to change invisible narrative.

Ganz argues that an effective social change communication tends to have three essential elements. First, it is rooted in personal experience with a "story of me" that explains how a person came to care about an issue. Second is "a story of us" about how that "me" is a part of something bigger, a component of an "us" with common purpose. Third is a "story of now" that connects the listener or reader back to the current moment and where to go from here.

Stacked together, these three stories can serve as a complete communications strategy. First, you capture attention ("story of me"), then you connect to the listener's experience ("story of us"), and then you offer a pathway for action ("story of now").

"The assumption that whatever we now believe is just common sense, or what we always knew, is a way to save face. It's also a way to forget the power of a story and a storyteller, the power in the margins, the potential for change."

Rebecca Solnit[98]

A story of us

One afternoon when I was a junior in high school, I went to watch a friend's soccer game. On the drive over, I stopped to get gas. And, well, I forgot to pay. (This was before the days of credit card readers at the pump.) About an hour later, at the game, I realized it. I immediately drove back to the gas station to admit my mistake and to pay. Inside, the cashier looked confused and said, "Oh, we called the police and told them two young Black men had driven off without paying." I stood in momentary shock, corrected them, paid for the gas, and left.

It was impossible to miss the racial dimension of the situation: I, a young white man, had committed a crime. And two young Black men were handed the blame. In that moment, I finally began to grasp the realities of structural racism. I saw how the stories of the innocent, the guilty, and the bystander were intertwined. My story of petty theft was part of a far larger story of injustice. In that linkage is opportunity, a way for us to build stories that drive us to a more just society.

In this way, we can weave our own stories into a far greater fabric. Let me

close with an epilogue from the Capitol Crawl. Over the recent decades, the Americans with Disabilities Act has yielded widespread practical benefits for people across society. We all profit from the "curb cut effect": sidewalk ramps originally put in place for wheelchairs make life easier for people with bicycles or strollers or wagons.[99] Each time I smoothly push my children in a stroller up a sidewalk ramp, I owe a thanks to those who crawled up the Capitol steps; their heroism made a better world for us all. Like the best narratives, it was not a "story of them"; it was a "story of us."

Storytelling Takeaways

1. **Different narratives set the stage for social action.** A story traces the path of a protagonist who overcomes challenges. It has a beginning, a middle, and an end. An invisible narrative is a way that people collectively organize their understanding of the world. A public narrative combines both by stacking stories to change the invisible narrative. It connects a story about "me" to a story about "us" and then a story of where we go from here.

2. **There are many storytelling archetypes to choose from.** They are simplifications, but they allow us to be intentional about how we use stories for social good.

3. **The Hero's Journey is a particularly useful frame for social change.** The protagonist passes into the unknown, meets companions, finds a mentor, passes through trials, confronts darkness, and returns transformed.

4. **Recruitment is central to social change,** and stories are central to "the call" that invites others to join us. Be aware of power dynamics. And make people feel victorious when they help us do good.

5. **Revelation of the unknown world is core to social change storytelling.** Craft a world that feels real and internally consistent.

6. **Power analysis attempts to understand how society really works.** It helps people understand how we got here and where we might go. Most driving forces are hidden in plain sight.

7. **Social change is an opportunity for personal transformation.** Even in an unjust world, people want to believe that there is a connection between their actions and outcomes.

8. **Social change calls on us to confront our shadows — how we have contributed to the problem.** Consciousness of our own behavior makes us more effective and guards against hypocrisy.

9. **True stories are complicated.** Tragedy, irony, and humor are tools for complex storytelling. In tragedy, a fatal flaw leads to a downfall. In irony, a character's actions have the opposite effect of what they intended. Humor flips expectations; the outcome surprises the audience.

10. **Frame stories beyond simple good and evil.** More nuanced stories give targets a chance to change for the better. Wise storytelling inspires action and reflection and creates a pathway for personal transformation.

Joseph Campbell
The Power of Myth

Ursula K. Le Guin
Steering the Craft

Patrick Reinsborough and Doyle Channing
Re: Imagining Change

Rebecca Solnit
Hope in the Dark

Tyson Yunkaporta
Sand Talk

Mathematical Modeling

**The Taj Mahal is a work of art
and a work of mathematics.**
Photo by Arpit Jawa

Counting
what counts

**For our chapter on mathematics,
let's begin with a poem.**

Write it down. Write it. With ordinary ink
on ordinary paper; they weren't given food,
they all died of hunger. All. How many?
It's a large meadow. How much grass
per head? Write down: I don't know.
History rounds off skeletons to zero.
A thousand and one is still only a thousand.
That one seems never to have existed

Wisława Szymborska

For years this poem has echoed in my
soul. *History rounds off skeletons to
zero*. Tens of thousands of Jews, Poles,
Ukrainians, Roma, and Russians died at
the Szebnie camp east of Jasło, Poland
between 1941 and 1944. Szymborska's
poem is a call for dignity for those lives
amidst the unimaginable. When we ask
historians, "How many people died in
Nazi death camps?" the answer rounds
off skeletons to six zeros: 11,000,000.
We can see the shape of the horror
that happened, but the vastness of the
tragedy blurs the details of the truth.
Human stories can get lost in zeroes.
　　Does that mean we give up on
numbers? No. This poem reminds us why:

"You don't see something
until you have the right metaphor
to let you perceive it."

Thomas Kuhn

there is a profound difference between "a thousand and one" and "a thousand." That difference: "one." What was their name, that one thousand-and-first soul? We do not know. But let us count them, nonetheless. Those who are counted, count.

Some see the use of mathematics in social change as dismal or disrespectful. It is the opposite: math is a way to honor the things that matter. Most of the work of social change is not as tragic as Szymborska's poem. Instead of murders, we count vaccinations delivered, lives transformed, or acres protected. And each act of counting confers its own kind of dignity — sometimes modest, sometimes profound. And that value is magnified because math helps us do our work well.

Mathematical modeling can help us plan for the future and learn from the past. The rigor of math, applied to social change, ensures clarity, keeps us honest, and helps us imagine what is possible.

Sometimes math is simple counting. That can be morally invaluable. It is also strategically essential. We can use mathematical equations as metaphors, stories to help us explore an uncertain future.

As the mathematician Mary Everest Boole said, "This method of solving problems by honest confession of one's ignorance is called Algebra."

This chapter will explore a set of basic mathematical tools for social change. First, we'll look at simple linear models that work with elementary arithmetic. Then we'll look at how reality, in fact, tends to be curvy, and how math can — imperfectly — address that challenge. Next, I'll suggest four ways to find meaning in numbers. And I'll close with cautions about how we use math to make a better world.

> "You better cut the pizza in four pieces because I'm not hungry enough to eat six."
>
> Yogi Berra

Linear models

Equations are stories, and variables are characters. The simple act of assigning variables to different parts of our strategy allows us to think more clearly about our work. To begin, let's think about some basic "linear" mathematical operations: addition and multiplication.

Addition

We can start by **adding up the parts** of our work. Imagine a job training program with three teachers: Juan, Eleanor, and Philippe. The total number of students served in this program is the sum of the number of students (S) served by each individual teacher.

$$S_{total} = S_{Juan} + S_{Eleanor} + S_{Philippe}$$

Multiplication

Impact is not simply a question of quantity; quality matters, too. Maybe Juan is the most successful teacher. His students get an average of five job offers (J_{Juan}). If Juan supports three students, he is responsible for fifteen job offers ($S_{Juan} \times J_{Juan}$). Accordingly, the total number of job offers across the entire program can be represented as follows:

$$J_{total} = (S_{Juan} \times J_{Juan}) + (S_{Eleanor} \times J_{Eleanor}) + (S_{Philippe} \times J_{Philippe})$$

With this combination of addition and multiplication, we begin to see how the varying performance of teachers plays out in the total impact of the training program.

Impact is, thus, often as simple as **how much times how many**. If we are seeking to maximize the number of job offers our students receive, this equation suggests two strategies. First would be an "addition" strategy of adding more teachers or more students. Second would be a "multiplication" strategy of deeper training and support of teachers to increase the quality of the teaching.

This basic addition/multiplication framework forms a powerful starting place for social change strategy. An — undoubtedly oversimplified — equation for social change is $I = Q_N \times Q_L$. That is, impact equals quantity times quality. Let's look at another example.

When I served as CEO of GuideStar, we relied on a set of a dozen different revenue streams. It was a blessing to have multiple sources of revenue. But it was, frankly, confusing. What did it all mean? Who were the people and what were the actions behind the numbers?

We could look at our financial statements and see a set of dollar signs representing total revenue for each product. But those aggregate amounts often obscured what was actually happening to bring in this revenue. How many foundations were using our products? How much were technology platforms paying?

To understand what was happening, we needed to build a simple linear model that combined addition and multiplication. We called it the "RENT Equation":

$$R = \sum_p N_p T_p$$

The variables are important; bear with me here. Revenue (R) is all the money we'd get in a year. Σ means "sum" across all our different products (p). N_p is the number of customers or donors for a particular product. T_p is total average revenue in a year from a given customer of that product. And that's how we paid the rent.

For an example of how you might use the RENT Equation, imagine a small opera house with four "products" — ticket sales, concessions, sponsorships, and donations. We can think about the number of people and the average revenue the opera house gets in a year from each.[100] In their accounting software or on their financial statement, the opera house will only see the column on the far right. The stories of actual people are obscured. By revealing the people and (average) prices beneath the revenue numbers, it becomes much easier to have strategic discussions about each line item. The numbers in the two middle columns — number of customers and average revenue — raise questions that might offer fruitful pathways. How does the number of tickets sold in a year compare to capacity? Could we drive up the donation line item by focusing on fewer big donors?

products	total "customers" in a year	average revenue per "customer"	total revenue by product
P	N_p	T_p	$N_p T_p$
tickets	5000	$200	$1,000,000
concessions	2000	$30	$60,000
sponsorships	50	$10,000	$500,000
donations	500	300	$150,000
total ("R")			$1,710,000

Mathematical Modeling

The math of simple risk

One challenge with many linear models is that they are retrospective: that is, they look backwards on a more certain past. But we also want to look forward (prospectively). We can't predict the future, but we can use math to make a structured guess.

The expected value (EV) model simply takes a potential result and multiplies it by the percentage chance that outcome will happen.[101] EV allows us to compare different alternatives. For example, consider two different strategies for investing $100,000 to reduce greenhouse gas emissions. In a first strategy, we take $100,000 and use it to plant trees in a deforested area. This is a low-risk strategy; it is almost certain to lead to a net reduction in greenhouse gas concentrations. As an alternative, we might invest that same amount of money in a lobbying campaign to introduce new local regulations to encourage installation of heat pumps. The second strategy might have a much higher potential impact but a much lower chance of success.[102]

The second strategy has an 80% chance of failure but a higher expected value. The act of mapping out expected value makes it much easier to make trade-offs according to risk tolerance. If we are cautious, Strategy One is a safe bet; if we are aggressive, Strategy Two offers greater upside.

These calculations are not always easy. Estimating the chance of success can be especially tricky. But the mere exercise of having people say out loud what they believe their chance of success to be can be helpful in revealing assumptions and refining strategy.

Served with a significant dose of humility, expected value calculations can be a valuable way to think about risk. At times, these calculations can help justify making a bet on a strategy with more risk and greater potential impact. But EV does not change the fact that we cannot predict the future.

It is worth pausing to emphasize the difference between "risk" and "uncertainty." Risk is a well-defined description of different possibilities: you know when flipping a coin that you have an equal chance of getting either side. Uncertainty, however, reflects a lack of knowledge about the possibilities in the future. Surprising events — the attacks

	annual CO_2 reduction if successful	multiplied by chance of success	equals expected value
strategy 1: direct reforestation	100 tons	x 90%	= 90 tons
strategy 2: lobbying for heat pump incentives	1000 tons	x 20%	= 200 tons

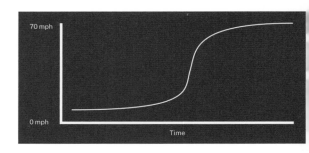

of September 11, 2001, for example — can emerge outside of expected categories. (More on these "black swan" events later in this chapter.)

The RENT Equation and EV are examples of "linear" models. They rely on elementary arithmetic — addition and multiplication. Accordingly, they represent a world defined by straight lines. The challenge, of course, is that the world tends to be curvy.

Nonlinearity

Mathematics offers many tools — exponents, calculus, trigonometry — that represent the curviness of the world. This is not the place to dive into the details of the mathematics of curves. But we can and should consider how "nonlinear" ideas from mathematics can be metaphors that help us understand our path through a curvy world. What is a curve but a story of change over time? We'll start with the story arc known as the S-curve.

In business, a successful product will follow an S-curve of growth as it goes from launch to early adopters to market maturity. In politics, public acceptance of new policy proposals may follow a similar path — years of advocacy with minimal progress, followed by a period of rapid success that evolves into more modest growth. (In the United States, consider gay marriage, Social Security, or national parks.)

S-curves show up throughout science, especially in biological systems: a population (whether ants or cancer cells) may grow slowly for a while, then fast, and then reach the limitations of its ecosystem.

Just as two and two is four
I know life is worth the pain
Though the bread is precious
And the freedom rare

Ferreira Gullar

Let's take a closer look at the parts of the S-curve. (You can find an explanation of the equation behind the S-curve in the notes.[103])

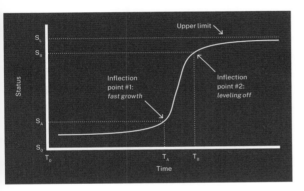

The above chart is a generalization of the S-curve to any situation. Think back to when you were learning how to read. You started out at time T_0 and you didn't know how to read (you were at S_0). You spent a long time learning basic sounds of letters. At first it didn't make a lot of difference. But then, you reached some moment where it started to come together (time T_A) and you hit the inflection point.

Then, you learned very quickly. Your past learning (letters, sounds, and words multiplied current learning. And, eventually, you reached a second inflection point (at T_B) where you pretty much knew how to read (S_B). You might still learn a few new words, or get faster, but you had mastered the tool and now could use it, for example, to learn about strategy. You will probably never learn every single word, and there is an upper limit beyond which you cannot pass (S_L). That upper limit represents the fundamental constraints of your context.

If you believe your work will face an S-curve relationship (such as product development, fundraising, or adoption of an idea), then you can use it as a planning tool.

Your first task: *locate yourself on the S-curve.* Where — when — do you think you are? If you have not yet hit the inflection point, ask when that might happen. (When is T_A?) What will your status be then? (What is S_B?)

It is not possible to predict exactly when you will hit an inflection point in a complex system (more on this in the **Complex Systems** chapter). Still, you can bring additional clarity to your thinking if you at least offer a hypothesis.

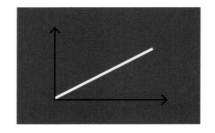

linear
e.g. rural
vaccination
campaign

The shape of situations

As we discussed in the **Strategy** chapter, the S-curve is one of several common situation "shapes" that we often see in social change strategy. The first and last are "linear" shapes and the middle three are "nonlinear" shapes.

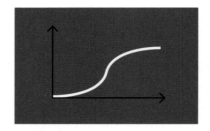

s-curve
e.g. new
product
introduction

These shapes are, first and foremost, useful to help orient you to "when" you are in your strategic situation. But for the brave among you, they also offer an opportunity for more rigorous analysis. For example, cyclical strategies can be modeled using the trigonometric functions sine and cosine. But we don't even need equations to find value. Simply defining the period (how long to go through a cycle) and amplitude (how much changes over the course of a cycle) can help transform a discussion.

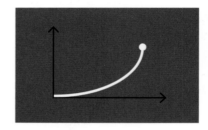

discrete
endpoint
e.g. ballot
initiative

You can use the clarity of a discrete end point to help allocate resources — for example, you might determine your weekly budget by dividing your assets by the number of weeks until your end point. In contrast, in a "preservation" situation it may be more essential to preserve resources for future use — arguing for a calculation fundamentally focused on what spending level you could sustain in perpetuity.

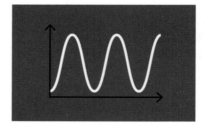

cyclical
e.g. seasonal
fundraising

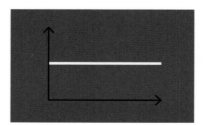

preservation
e.g. protect
a disappearing
language

Let's pause to "zoom in" on the linear model. It looks smooth from a distance. Is it? When we look closely at most "linear" changes, we see they look more like a staircase. In mathematical terms, they are a "step function." Consider the example cited above, a rural vaccination campaign. Each vaccination bumps up the line by one. What looks continuous and smooth from a distance is composed of discrete, human victories. Even linearity may have nonlinear characteristics.

Four ways to find meaning in numbers

Thus far we have focused on mathematical models that help us *plan*. These models give us a sense of proportion, help us isolate key variables, and offer metaphors to facilitate conversations among our stakeholders. Now, we will move on to mathematical models that help us learn. Below, we'll look at four methods for finding meaning in mathematics.

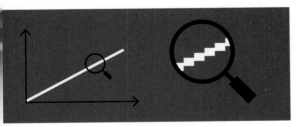

Basic statistics glossary

Sample size: the number of data points (sometimes called the "N").

Standard deviation: a measure of the amount of variability in a data set.

Statistical significance: confidence that a relationship is not coincidence.

Regression analysis: mathematical technique used to determine the relationships in a data set.

P-value: a measure of the likelihood that a relationship is a coincidence. Often, P-values under 0.05 (5%) are considered to be statistically significant.

R^2: a measure of how much of the difference is "explained" by a given regression analysis.

Normal distribution: a common distribution of results often known as a "bell curve." Normal distributions tend to result from the aggregation of many events that have the same likelihood.

The power and limitations of statistics

In the Strategy chapter, we discuss evaluation and the need for active feedback loops to enable constant improvement. We also look at standards of evidence and the importance of both qualitative and quantitative sources of information.

But how do we make sense of the data that comes in through your feedback system? When faced with large amounts of data, we often use statistics to extract meaning from the information.

Statistics begins with data. We often forget that the word "data" is plural. Data are a set of points of information. The art and the science of statistics is to make sense of data sets. Life is full of variation: trees of the same species are different heights; lakes are different shades of blue; human lung capacity varies. Sometimes there's a good reason: trees might draw nutrients from different types of soil; lakes might have different mixtures of algae; smokers might have gunked up their lungs.

Old Faithful Eruptions

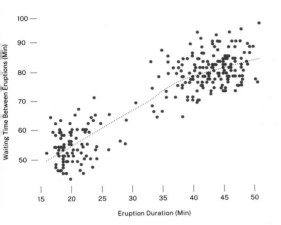

This graph of the eruptions of the famous geyser Old Faithful shows how data can visually tell a story. The graph is a scatter plot of eruptions, with the X axis showing how long it lasted and the Y axis showing the time between eruptions. A quick glance shows how there are two categories of eruptions: short ones with short breaks and long ones with longer breaks.

Statistics helps us draw out the meaning or "signal" from all this variance or "noise." In simple terms, if we believe that one factor accounts for much of the variance of another, we pair them up with a common type of analysis — linear regression — to see if our hunch about their relationship is true.

Since this kind of analysis is easy to do in a standard spreadsheet, it is a boon for amateur analysts. But such simplicity makes it a challenge for society, as we shall see.

The clean relationships found in a linear regression analysis offer a simple story. But it is worth noting that it is rare that a real-life data set shows such a simple relationship. More often, the relationship is less clear-cut and is more complicated.

Indeed, many basic assumptions of statistics have been challenged. Central to statistics is the concept of the "P-Value," which measures the likelihood that the relationship is a coincidence. A low P-value indicates greater confidence in your results. A common — and often unconscious — statistical sin is "P-hacking" — trying out a whole set of relationships until you find one with a low

P-value. (There are countless statistical tools available that can more rigorously test the validity of a relationship — for those, it is best to consult with an expert.)

To make things more complicated, data sets can have the same characteristics while telling very different stories. Consider the four scatter plots below, known as Anscombe's Quartet. Each of these four scatter plots has the same basic statistical characteristics (mean and standard deviation for both the X and Y sets, correlation, and linear regression line). But each one obviously tells a different story.

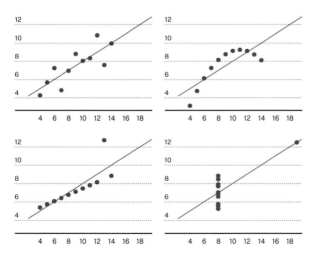

For all of these reasons, we use statistics to inform decisions, not to make decisions for us. Further, we must remember that statistics is based on the data in the world, and the data in the world reflects injustice. (This is not a mere accident; many of the tools of modern statistics were developed by early-20th-century eugenicists.[104])

These challenges have become more urgent with the increasing use of artificial intelligence. If, for example, you "train" a machine learning algorithm to identify potential criminals based on socio-economic data, you are almost certain to reproduce the impacts of structural racism. **Statistics is a powerful tool for helping us understand how the world has been, but it does not tell us how it could be.**

Common patterns: normal distributions and the power law

Certain patterns often show up in data sets. Two of them can be highly relevant for strategy. The first is the normal distribution — often known as the bell curve.

Normal distributions arise when you look at aggregate data across independent events that have the same statistical probability. For example, imagine flipping 100 pennies. If you did this 1,000 times and looked at the results, you would likely see some patterns. Chances are, most of the time the number would be around 50. There might be a lot of cases of 49 or 52 — and fewer of 35 or 61. Probably not very many — if any at all — of 7 or 92. Normal distributions are found throughout society: from voting patterns to stock prices and medical outcomes.[105] If a soup kitchen mapped the number of volunteers they get each day over the course of a year, those totals might reflect a normal distribution.

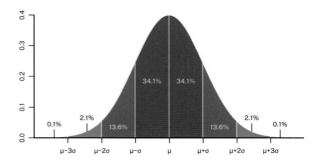

A normal distribution
Because of their "normality," normal distributions offer some convenient shortcuts: 68% of the observations will be within one standard deviation from the mean; 95% within two; 99.7% within three.

A key characteristic of normal distributions is that events far to the left or right are extremely unlikely. But reality often manifests in another way: the **power law distribution**.

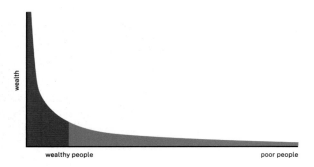

A power law distribution

In this example, the X axis makes up every person in society, ordered from richest to poorest. The Y axis is their wealth. As we see, a small proportion of individuals are responsible for a large portion of the total wealth.

Power law distributions have a specific mathematical formulation but are often simplified as the 80/20 rule. For example, 80% of your revenue might come from 20% of your customers, or 80% of your best ideas come from 20% of your employees.

The power law relationship shows up throughout science, especially in physics and ecology. In a simple example, there are millions of species of small animals, but a disproportionate part of the planet's total body mass is attributable to a few very large species, such as whales and elephants.[106]

Power law distributions are relevant for what Chris Anderson christened the "Long Tail" — when you add up all of the users with niche interests, you end up with a large part of the marketplace.[107] On the power law distribution chart in the box, these customers make up the market to the right in light blue, which has historically been very expensive to serve. Traditionally, businesses have focused on the market in dark blue, where they could get enough volume to find economies of scale. But the Internet and cheap transportation have allowed new business models to capitalize on this Long Tail.

Consider how eBay thrived by creating a platform for sales within niche markets.)

Social change agents can look for similar opportunities for impact: is the "long tail" being served, or are resources over-allocated to the obvious, prominent cases?

The power law distribution also shows up as a reflection of "probability distribution" of possible outcomes. If we always assume that events will have a symmetrical distribution (like we see with a normal distribution), we will discount events that seem unlikely.

Sometimes a distribution has a "fat tail" because those possibilities off to the side are more likely than in a normal distribution. Nassim Nicholas Taleb called these "black swan" events. (European thinkers believed all swans were white until they discovered the black swans of Australia.[108]) For example, if a nonprofit's government funding has for decades come within a narrow range, it is easy to discount the possibility of a windfall (given, for example, a government stimulus program in response to a pandemic) or an instant erasure of funds (given, for example, a radical shift in policy).

Data visualization

The world is overwhelmed with information. The marginal cost of data storage is approaching zero, allowing us to keep information that we might have discarded in the past (old emails or security tapes). The data are often contradictory, unstructured, or of mixed quality. In short, a mess.

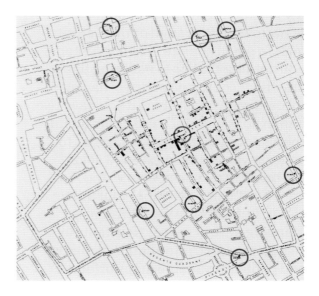

John Snow's map of the 1854 cholera outbreak allowed him to pinpoint which of the public water pumps (here highlighted in red) was the source of the outbreak.

An entire movement and industry have emerged to help us visually make sense of this immense amount of information. As one of the prophets of the industry, Edward Tufte, says, "We shouldn't abbreviate the truth but rather get a new method of presentation."[109]

I'll suggest a few principles for data visualization. First, use graphic displays to reveal truth, not conceal it. For example, avoid the common sin of narrowing the range of the Y axis to make a small change look big. Second, add nothing that does not bring understanding. There's no sense in having a three-dimensional chart if you have two dimensions of data. Third, think about the visual cues that make it easier for your viewer. For example, add color if it helps to reveal meaning. And, for goodness' sake, just label your axes.

A critical tool in visualization is mapping data in *space*. New tools like GIS (geographic information systems) and publicly available maps offer comprehensive coverage and the ability to cross-reference different data sets visually. Geospatial mash-ups take many data sets (whether tree cover, public art, or great burritos) and display them geographically.

More generally, data visualization tools offer ways to make use of the immense amount of information available to us — and to use that information to make better decisions, not just stand agape at the sheer quantity of it all.[110]

This has been true for centuries. The science of epidemiology was, in a sense, born out of a data visualization. In 1854, a major cholera outbreak hit London. Physician John Snow mapped the cases and public water pumps and was able to pinpoint the source of the outbreak as the public pump at the corner of Broad Street and Cambridge Street. This offered both a conceptual breakthrough and a practical solution: cholera was transmitted via public water infrastructure, so the authorities removed the handle to that particular pump.

nderstand correlation; seek causality

very time the rooster crows, the sun
ses. Those full-throated cock-a-doodle-
oos and sunrises are correlated: they
end to happen at the same time. That
henomenon does not, of course, mean
at roosters cause the sun to rise. But
is easy to see causation where there is
nly correlation.

Determining the direction of causality
often difficult. For example, wealthier
tudents do better on average on stan-
ardized tests than students from fami-
es with few resources. This relationship
oes not mean the wealthier students
re smarter; in this case, correlation
bscures other mechanisms of causation
.g., tutoring, nutrition, high-speed
nternet access).

There are certain experimental
esigns which offer more power for
dentifying causality. As we discussed in
he **Strategy** chapter, randomized con-
rolled trials (RCTs) randomly assign test
ubjects and a control group. RCTs are
xtremely powerful in certain cases — for
xample, in experiments around tactical
overty interventions by Nobel prize
inners Esther Duflo, Abijit Banerjee, and
ichael Kremer.[112]

But RCTs also face a number of
limitations. First, they rely on a control
group, but many social interventions do
not lend themselves to measure a "counterfactual" — we cannot, for example, do an
"experiment" in a parallel universe without
a Sierra Club to measure the effectiveness
of the Sierra Club in our universe.[113]
Second, RCTs can raise ethical concerns:
can you withhold mosquito netting from
a control group in a malaria zone to test
the efficacy of your program? Third, the
results are often context-specific in ways
that are hidden to the researcher, making
it difficult to apply results from one geographic area or constituency to another.

Causality is what we care about.
It is — by definition — core to our work.
But like so much in social change, it also
demands humility.

Finding meaning with humility

We use math to help us find imperfect
meaning in a complex world. Mathematical modeling is a form of storytelling
that tries — and sometimes succeeds —
to precisely link with reality. That is not
just an analytical act, it is an ethical one.
In the end, math is a tool to ensure that
in our work, everyone counts.

Mathematical Modeling Takeaways

1. **Math helps social change agents like us be more successful.** A mathematical mindset provides clarity, reveals insights, and keeps us honest.

2. **You don't have to do any math to benefit from mathematical modeling concepts.** For example, most social change strategies map to patterns. By thinking through a pattern's shape, you'll find a language or framework that can transform strategy discussions.

3. **Math helps us learn and plan.** It allows us to find meaning and to tell a story about our past, present, and future.

4. **The stories we derive from math are important communications tools.** Numbers need a narrative context, a good story, to effectively communicate with stakeholders. Metaphors bring the power of math to social change.

5. **Math provides a sense of proportion.** It helps us understand the scale of a problem relative to the resources we have to solve it.

6. **Math helps you think more clearly about your work.** It articulates underlying assumptions and reveals what's happening behind aggregate numbers. In complex situations where predictions are difficult, you can offer hypotheses that clarify your thinking.

Statistics extract meaning from information generated by your feedback system. They help you draw a "signal" from the "noise" of information overload. Basic statistical analysis is easily done on common computer spreadsheets.

8. **Use statistics to inform decisions, not make them.** Statistics begin with data. Data are a set of points of information. That means statistics tell us how the world has been, not how it could be.

9. **Color, scale, connection, distance, and proportion are all tools you can use to visualize data.** Use graphic displays to reveal truth, not conceal it. Everything you add should bring understanding. An entire movement and industry have emerged to make visual sense of information.

10. **Mathematics still requires caution.** Our challenge as social change agents is to root our work in data while recognizing it is difficult to find absolute meaning in that data.

- Real-life data sets rarely show a simple story. Data sets with the same basic statistical character-istics can tell different stories when plotted on a graph.
- Events that seem extremely unlikely mathematically can and do happen.
- Numbers can be misleading when they are viewed alone. They are most useful in the context of other numbers.
- Understand correlation; seek causality. Statistical analysis alone cannot guarantee causality
- Finding the right model can be difficult. The right data

Behavioral Economics

An elephant has a mind of its own.

Reaping
habits

As social change agents, we must deal with the human mind as it is, not as we wish it to be.

Let us begin with a metaphor. Imagine an elephant with a human rider. Together, they travel down a pathway. A skilled rider can indeed influence where the elephant goes. But basic physics suggests that the elephant has an immense advantage.

In this metaphor, the rider represents the conscious, rational mind. The elephant is the unconscious, emotional mind. The pathway is the context in which the mind acts.

This chapter will explore how social change agents can navigate the dynamics of the human mind.

We'll start with ten **biases** — think of them as the elephant's natural tendencies.

Building on these biases, we'll explore seven **illusions** — broader phenomena where conscious understanding often misses a deeper truth.

The next section offers five solutions, effective ways to respond to the reality of the mind as it is. We'll focus on interventions that change the context of human behavior: the path on which the elephant treads.

The elephant metaphor oversimplifies centuries of philosophy and cognitive science, but it serves our purpose: to understand the biases and illusions that shadow the rational mind. And to develop social change strategies accordingly.

The elephant/rider metaphor is imprecise, as is any description of the human mind. A more explicit framework has been suggested by the Nobel Prize–winning psychologist Daniel Kahneman. In his book *Thinking, Fast and Slow,* he describes an ongoing interchange between two "systems" in the human mind. The unconscious and emotional aspects of the brain make up "System 1." The deliberate and rational aspects of the mind are "System 2."

System 1 is fast, system 2 is slow. Both are essential parts of what makes us human. ■

Nudging toward efficiency

Pauline Lubens, a public health educator, was used to being the teacher. Then an email from her utility company taught her a big lesson.

Pacific Gas & Electric, Pauline's utility, sent her a "Home Energy Report" that compared her energy use to 95 homes within a mile of her own. "You used 49% more than efficient homes," it said. The report gave her a standard happy face. The top homes rated a huge grin.

"I wanted to be better than I am," Lubens said. "It appealed to my competitive instinct. I got the B. I want the A." So she started switching off the TV and the power strip and unplugging electrical cords when she wasn't using them. Within a week, she was getting estimates to install solar power for her home.

The Home Energy Report was an example of a "nudge," a conscious effort to tilt behavior, while still allowing people full agency over their decisions. By design, those smiley faces made Lubens less content with her energy use, so she made better choices.

Alex Laskey, one of the choice architects behind Home Energy Reports, says the idea began with a social science experiment in San Marcos, Calif. Graduate students hung different signs on homeowners' doors, asking them to turn off air conditioners and turn on fans.

Signs about cost savings, helping the environment, and good citizenship flopped. What worked? A sign that said 77% of their neighbors had already switched to fans.

The moral, Laskey says, is that social pressure "is powerful stuff. And harnessed correctly it can be a powerful force for good."

In 2007, Laskey co-founded Opower, now a division of Oracle. The company's tools, such as the Home Energy Report, have created enough energy savings to eliminate 15.2 million metric tons of carbon dioxide from the atmosphere.[115] That's what 3.3 million passenger vehicles would produce in a year.

Cognitive biases

The brain uses shortcuts to navigate our complex world. These shortcuts — sometimes called "heuristics" — are an essential way to sort through the immense amount of information our senses glean from the world around us. These heuristics create leanings of our mind that tilt our actions. They are neither good nor bad, but they are crucial for understanding human behavior. Below, I've listed ten common cognitive biases.

Social proof

People look to those around them to decide what behavior is acceptable.

Reciprocity

We are hardwired for exchange. If some-one gives us something, we are inclined to give them something back.

Sunk cost bias

We tend to make future choices in a way that validates our past choices. This is starkly irrational if a past choice is unchangeable.

Anchoring bias

Our perceptions are influenced by nearb information. In experiments, participant asked to guess a number were influence when presented with a random number.

Outcome bias

We tend to assign value depending on results, not the cause of those results. A wealthy person is perceived to be smart, even if their wealth was gained through luck.

Risk aversion

It hurts more to lose a certain amount than it is pleasurable to gain that amoun

Consistency

We will work to avoid contradictions across our actions and our words. We all aspire, even subconsciously, to consistency.

In-group bias

Consciously or not, we tend to have a bia for those in our group. We perceive those that are like us to be more valuable, and our decisions reflect this bias.

Competence bias

We tend to overrate our competence relative to others. Most people believe they are better-than-average drivers. It is impossible for us all to be correct.

Ambiguity effect

We crave clarity in decision-making and will tend to choose options with well-defined probabilities.

This list is not meant to be illustrative, not comprehensive. These and other biases operate differently in different people at different times. They are not always possible to see or understand, but they matter profoundly for how we live our lives.

You believed in your own story,
then climbed inside it —
a turquoise flower.
You gazed past ailing trees,
past crumbling walls and rusty railings.
Your least gesture beckoned a constellation
of wild vetch, grasshoppers, and starts
to sweep you into immaculate distances.

The heart may be tiny
but the world's enormous.

And the people in turn believe —
in pine trees after rain,
ten thousand tiny suns, a mulberry branch
bent over water like a fishing-rod
a cloud tangled in the tail of a kite.
Shaking off dust, in silver voices
ten thousand memories sing from your dream.

The world may be tiny
but the heart's enormous.

Shu Ting[116]

The sum of our biases: seven of life's illusions

The cognitive biases discussed above are leanings in the moment, a hand on the scale that nudges us towards certain behavior. They add up over time and create broader tendencies in the mind that I will refer to here as "illusions." These "illusions" are mental frames we use as we navigate a complex world. No matter how much they feel like trustworthy products of the rational mind, illusions always reflect an imperfect understanding. Social change agents can try to correct for these illusions or, at times, even use them to their advantage.

Below, I'll discuss seven of these illusions. This list of seven is not meant to be a formal taxonomy of human behavior. Instead, it's simply a framework to highlight some tendencies of the mind that are relevant to our work.

Rationality

We humans are gifted with consciousness. With that gift comes the perception that we are free to make choices. For millennia, poets, philosophers, and scientists have argued about whether that perception reflected reality. That is, they have argued about free will.

I believe in free will. Our choices matter. Our brain's capacity for reason is core to who we are — one of our greatest gifts and our greatest tools. But in social change, we need to recognize the limits of rationality. The fundamental insight of behavioral economics is that people are not in fact isolated, rational actors. Our biases frame our perceptions and tilt our decisions. There is an elephant beneath us.

I've been guilty of forgetting this. In my time at the Hewlett Foundation, I too often assumed that if donors simply had access to good data about nonprofit performance, they'd make better giving decisions. The reality was much more complex. It turns out that charitable giving is personal, emotional, and context dependent. We devised a number of ways to inject rational thinking into the giving process — but always with an eye to the

"It is only in relation to other bodies
and many somebodies
that anybody is somebody."

Jimmy Boggs[118]

omplexity of human behavior. (We'll
iscuss this case more in the **Complex
Systems** chapter.)

The illusion of rationality has broader
mplications. The dominant economic and
olitical frameworks of the 20th century
vere built upon an assumption: individu-
ls rationally act according to their own
elf-interest. This belief spanned the
olitical spectrum (it is central to both
ommunism and neoliberal economics).
's hard to overstate the consequences
f this often-hidden assumption. The
ery way we understand society has been
uilt — at least in part — upon an illusion.
Many economic and political structures
f our society have followed from that
nderstanding. (As John Maynard Keynes
oted in 1936, "Practical men who believe
hemselves to be quite exempt from any
ntellectual influence, are usually the
laves of some defunct economist."[117])

Throughout the work of social impact,
e find ourselves correcting for others'
alse assumptions about universal ratio-
ality. Along the way, we can be humble
bout the limitations and the power of our
wn reason — even as we try to wield it
or good.

Independence

It is easy to experience life as if we were
alone and in control. But we are not alone.
Human experience is fundamentally
mediated through other people, and our
choices are constrained by the systems
we live in.

And yet, the illusion of independence
is psychologically powerful and socially
consequential. It yields the belief that
all people "get what they deserve and
deserve what they get."

Social psychologists consider this
belief — a consequence of the illusion of
independence — so important that
they've labeled it "Fundamental
Attribution Error."

The illusion of independence is part of
why systemic social change is so difficult.
Consider, for instance, how the fundamental attribution error conveniently
assigns responsibility for poverty to
the very people who lack resources and
opportunities rather than to the powerful
system that apportions them.

It also provides a tidy excuse for
the failure of past policies. Instead of
sparking a search for root causes and new
answers, this illusion makes the blame
game feel like a rational choice for the

127   Behavioral Economics

people who are more comfortable with the status quo of the existing system.

Social change agents regularly find themselves countering the fundamental attribution error. They work to identify those forces that are actually responsible for the state of today's world. They highlight our interdependence and shared responsibility.

The illusion of independence has implications for social change beyond the way we describe a problem. It is central to strategy, as well. Strategy relies on situational analysis, and a thorough analysis requires recognition of interdependence.

In the **Community Organizing** chapter we will discuss power mapping, a process for visually representing the forces that influence a decision maker. Even the most distant-seeming autocrats or the most powerful investors are themselves interdependent. Because people in power often labor under the illusion of independence, they don't understand their own vulnerabilities to the beliefs, actions, and influence of others. This contradiction can create an opportunity for social change agents.

Identity

We build our identity upon shifting sands. Political, religious, or ideological identity can change in a day. Race does not exist as a coherent genetic category. Gender has different meanings in different cultures. Social class is an unstable amalgam of wealth, education, family heritage, and attitude.

But these dimensions of identity don't need to be stable to be important. They influence how others treat us and are reflected in the broader systems in which we operate. The illusion of identity has obvious ethical implications that we discuss in the Ethics chapter: people are granted differential treatment according to their identity.

The challenge for social change actor is to recognize the tenacious strength of these illusions. A campaign for transgender rights that doesn't acknowledge the strength of culturally determined beliefs about gender (even when those beliefs are themselves illusions) is less likely to be successful.

Many humans manage to override the illusion of independence when it comes to their own community. They can perceive their local interdependence,

The best lack all conviction, while the worst
Are full of passionate intensity.

William Butler Yeats

but they fail to extend that perception to the rest of the world. Consider the classic line from the radio show *A Prairie Home Companion*: "Where all the women are strong, the men are good-looking, and the children are above average." As with any good joke, it reflects a deeper reality: people regularly perceive that those they identify with are exceptional compared with the rest of the world (an illusion some call the "Lake Wobegon Effect" based on the fictional town from the show).

Statistically, U.S. citizens believe that Congress is dysfunctional but that their representative is great. They believe the educational system is a mess but their school is an exception. Social change agents have to bridge this contradiction when working on an issue like democracy reform or better schools.

More generally, we have to recognize that identity matters, even as it is in many ways a product of our own minds.

Narrative

Stories are a powerful mechanism we use to make sense of the world; they weave together characters, perceived causality, and time. And, as we discuss in the Storytelling chapter, narratives work.

The challenge is this: a given narrative may or may not be true; it may or may not be representative of a broader situation.

As powerful as stories can be, they can also be their own type of illusion — or even a distraction. Consider what Shankar Vedantam calls the "empathy telescope."[121] He tells a heartwarming story of how people raised $250,000 to rescue a dog named Hokget left on an abandoned oil tanker 800 miles south of Hawai'i. Then Vedantam asks why we don't see a similar response for individuals impacted by genocides and famines. His explanation: "The brain is simply not very good at grasping the implications of mass suffering…Hokget did not draw our sympathies because we care more about dogs than people; she drew our sympathies because she was a single dog lost on the biggest ocean in the world." It can be easier for the human mind to become invested in a single story with a single protagonist than a general, structural problem diffused across many people (or creatures).

Other times, the challenge is the nature of the narrative itself. Social change agents may have to dig out of the illusions that old stories have left behind.

The gay rights movement in the United States had to counter decades of false narratives about homosexuality with scientific research, individual stories, and new narrative frames like "love is love."

Indeed, many narratives have a political edge, making engagement all the more difficult as you tug in the opposite direction. As narrative hardens into a belief system — and becomes tangled up with identity — people tend to perceive new facts through the lens of that system.

This is not just a passive process; the mind will actively seek information that confirms current beliefs. You might think that intelligence would be a bulwark against that kind of twisted interpretation, but research suggests the opposite. People with more developed analytical skills have more available methods to bend new information to their current beliefs. One set of researchers explained that people will "use their quantitative-reasoning capacity selectively to conform their interpretation of the data to the result most consistent with their political outlooks."[122] Narrative frames are resilient. They defend themselves.

Expectations

To the ascetic, pleasure is a racket. To the psychologist, pleasure is a ratchet. Our expectations shift with new experiences and can "ratchet" up with time. Psychologists call this phenomenon the "hedonic treadmill." Once we've experienced something we perceive as better (such as subsidized gas prices or first-class travel), we can quickly come to assume it will continue.

The hedonic treadmill has significant implications for social change. It creates constituencies for the status quo — even among those who might benefit from broader change. In the United States, the mortgage interest deduction primarily subsidizes the upper classes and does little to achieve its original aims of broadening home ownership. But it is politically locked in place, difficult to remove because of support from middle-class voters who might stand to benefit more from alternate uses of public dollars. In India, water subsidies create a raft of problems with broad implications — from pollution to food security. But the entire agricultural economy has structured itself around these subsidies.

130   The Toolbox

"Humans are symbolizing, conceptualizing, meaning-seeking animals. The drive to make sense out of our experience, to give it form and order, is evidently as real and as pressing as the more familiar biological needs."

Clifford Geertz[123]

The illusion of expectations can play out in the psychology of social change agents, too. As wise women and men have warned for millennia, we set ourselves up for failure if we bet our happiness on a single victory.

Similarly, many practitioners of social change — myself included — are guilty of believing that once we implement a single solution (such as carbon pricing or campaign finance reform), we will have finished the work of building a better world. We believe our one solution will have so many positive side effects that it will automatically solve countless other problems. For our sanity — and for the sake of strategic clarity — we'd be wise to remember that change is a constant process. It does not end with victory; it begins again.

Language

Language is a bridge from one mind to another. Many philosophers and linguists argue that language creates the very framework humans use to understand the world.

In this sense, language is the ultimate illusion. The words we use guide our behavior and constrain our sense of the possible.

This has obvious implications for social change. Do we call a political position "pro-life" or "anti-choice"? Is it unpatriotic to oppose the Patriot Act? Language is a battleground, a place where political and moral questions are represented in letters and in sounds. Social change agents have little choice but to work to control the terrain of language. Politicians know this well; consider the title of an influential — and notorious — 1990 GOPAC memo to legislative candidates: "Language: A Key Mechanism of Control."[124]

This defining process can become complicated by aspects of language that relate to power. The use of derogatory terms is an expression of power, a way for one group to impose its will upon another. Marginalized groups also reclaim the power of certain words as an act of their own agency. Taking a once-derogatory word like "queer" and turning it into an expression of pride and power was a profound act of social change jujutsu.

In the 21st century, language has become further politicized — even weaponized — and reflects some of the deep divisions in our society. Consider the term "LatinX." It is an authentic reflection of a desire to empower those descending from the peoples of South and Central America and to do so in a non-gendered way. But advocates for the term face a significant challenge: most LatinX people do not describe themselves as LatinX. Opponents have successfully capitalized on this contradiction; instead of gently promoting an inclusive vision, "LatinX" has been turned into a tool of cultural warfare.

The contradictions of language can, though, be leveraged with great constructive power. In 1968, 1,300 striking Black sanitation workers in Memphis famously carried signs stating simply, "I AM A MAN." The signs referenced the famous first line of Ralph Ellison's Invisible Man, "I am an invisible man," which highlighted the narrator's experience of not being seen by the society around him. By removing of qualifying language ("invisible"), the workers clearly and directly asserted their dignity while also highlighting the fact that so many in society did not treat them as human.

Social change agents can and should try to change the contours of language — while also recognizing the stickiness of language and the history embedded in it.

Scarcity

It is all too easy to assume that something that benefits you will hurt me. Some institutions of modern society — i.e. the market economy — can support this illusion. Sometimes it is true: if I eat this Pop-Tart, you can't.

Luckily, it is often possible to transcend Pop-Tarts and bake a larger pie. The presence of refugees can enrich a community. A shift in the tax structure can grow the economy. An acknowledgment of another's freedom can enhance everyone's scope of possibility.[126]

The scarcity illusion mistakes the very real scarcity of some situations for scarcity across all situations. It can be tragically self-defeating. For decades, many U.S. public swimming pools were only available to white residents (that is, they were not actually "public"). The pools were crucial summer amenities in the days before most homes had air conditioning. During the era of desegregation, communities faced pressure — moral, legal, financial, and political — to allow Black residents access to the pools. Some communities found a hateful and self-destructive resolution; they filled the pools with concrete and shut them down.

Heather McGhee has called this "drained-pool politics."[127] This tragic example reminds us that the illusion of scarcity is not just a rational desire to get more for oneself; it can lead to an irrational desire to prevent others from getting anything. In the section on abundance in the Game Theory chapter, we explore how to transcend the traps of a scarcity mindset.

A note on neuroscience

The brain is a tangle of sub-regions; each sub-region is itself a tangle of neurons and synapses. Neuroscience has begun to make sense of the brain's patterns, but much work lies ahead to unravel the mysteries of consciousness.

We do know that the brain is a dynamic system that brings together the ancient, unconscious instinct of the limbic system with the more modern and rational frontal cortex. Mechanisms like the amygdala direct the traffic of thought, bypassing reason when instinct is necessary.

Through it all, flows of chemicals help to define our conscious experience. These flows connect us as individuals; when you give someone a compliment, you'll get oxytocin, and they'll get dopamine.

Researchers have recently discovered evidence that confirms millennia of religious speculation: the mechanisms of human cognition extend beyond the brain. The idea of a "gut reaction" is not mere metaphor: there is a network of 100 million neurons in the average human digestive system.[128] We do, in some ways, think with our bodies.

Scientists and social change agents have only begun to translate this neurological dance, but we can be sure that great potential (and great danger) lie ahead as we map the workings of the brain to the work of social impact. ∎

Solutions

These biases and illusions represent core patterns of human behavior. Below, we'll discuss a set of techniques for confronting them in the work of social change.

Discipline

Over the centuries countless people — nuns and sages, athletes and artisans — have worked to bring discipline to their minds. We social change agents also have an opportunity to invest in mental capacity. We can build abilities (such as focus and clarity) and cultivate virtues (such as wisdom and compassion).

For centuries, sages have highlighted the connections between discipline and virtue. Across the Himalayas, you'll see rocks carved with the Tibetan words *om mani padme hum*. This phrase is directly translated as, "hail to the jewel in the lotus." But it has a deeper meaning. The lotus flower lives in muddy water; its roots draw nutrients from the deep murk. Wisdom (the lotus) rises from our disciplined engagement with the messiness of the world. Compassion (the jewel) flowers from that wisdom. True discipline is not harsh self-denial; it is fuel for kindness.

We are more than just stimulus-response machines. There are many techniques to cultivate mental — and thus physical, strategic, and ethical — discipline. Prayer, exercise, and art can all be forms of meditation. When we build consciousness of our own mental activity, we create space for understanding and for control. As psychologist and author Tara Brach says, "There is a space between stimulus and response and in that space is freedom."[129]

Consciousness often — though not always — includes a momentary gap for at least some decisions. (I will leave it to you whether you describe that gap as "free will"!) As social change agents, we can watch for that gap as we try to live up to our own standards of ethical and strategic excellence.

Activist adrienne maree brown remarked that she was, "thrilled by how humans have continuously stood up against our own weaknesses."[130] That courage is a source of hope for humanity and a source of power for changemakers.

Systems design

I promised early in this chapter that I would take you back to explore interventions in the elephant's path. That path is the context for how the mind works. Sometimes we can provide cues and clues that lead to better outcomes. In this way, you can become what Richard Thaler and Cass Sunstein call a "choice architect."

It is sometimes possible to shift the context of a decision without constraining choice. To use the language of Sunstein and Thaler, we can "nudge" people to make better decisions. For example, evidence suggests that shifting sign-up for retirement investment programs from an "opt-in" (you have to act to sign-up) to an "opt-out" (you have to act to not participate) can significantly increase the amount of money people save for their future. Effective nudging is not always possible (or advisable). But it is often examining the context in which a choice is made.

The choice architect's first step is to map out a choice system. Or, put another way, we try to understand the elephant's path.[131] What are the set of processes over time that a target individual is passing through? Can we identify discrete steps and their order? Do they include signals that guide a given person one way or another? From that, we can sometimes intervene to make the pathway more conducive to good outcomes. Below, I'll suggest four techniques.

First, as noted above in the example about retirement investment programs, be intentional about default settings. In the absence of a decision, the default choice sticks. Choice architects can pick defaults that benefit their constituents — even while protecting their ability to choose another option.

Second, intentionally use sense cues like color, sound, and light. This cue could take the simple form of yellow highlighting or bold type in a document. Or it might be the default volume setting on an audio system. Or it could extend to a multisensory art project or advertising campaign. Keep in mind the ethical dimension here: cue design can be put to nefarious use. Consider the fact that most casinos are windowless. Windows offer cues to the passing of time outside. Casinos want you to keep gambling so they remove one type of cues and replace them with another.

Third, simple checklists can reduce errors in many contexts. Atul Gawande, in

"All your neurons are firing at various rates all the time. What are they doing? Busily making predictions. In every moment, your brain uses all its available information (your memory, your situation, the state of your body) to take guesses about what will happen in the next moment."

Lisa Feldman Barrett[132]

his book *The Checklist Manifesto*, shows how these cues function as a critical tool in his own work as a surgeon. The use of checklists can help across the work of social change. This might be logistical (conference planning), ethical (checklists to make sure all voices are heard in a meeting), or strategic (systematically analyzing the interests of all stakeholders).

Fourth, place social cues into a decision-making context so that user choices are shaped by positive peer pressure. This is what Opower did with such success in the Home Energy Report discussed earlier in this chapter. Their design accomplishes this peer pressure by showing the power company's customers' specific data about how their own energy use compares with that of their neighbors.

As you map out the context of a decision over both space and time, other interventions may reveal themselves. In each case, we should keep in mind the ethical element of decision design. The power to guide others' choices is not to a power to be taken lightly.

Incentive alignment

There are many ways to think about how incentives can influence behavior. In the **Institutions** chapter, we discuss the formal and informal incentives that operate within organizations — from financial compensation to cultural reinforcement. **Markets**, of course, are a core mechanism for aligning incentives across buyers and sellers.

In the 18th century, the British government created a series of prizes to spur the creation of more accurate shipboard chronometers. Such clocks allowed for much more precise navigation and were a priority for the Admiralty. Over the course of more than a century, these awards — managed by a newly created Board of Longitude — drove significant technological innovation and helped to cement British naval superiority. The longitude prizes were a multi-decade attempt to align incentives.

In recent years institutions like the X Prize Foundation, which has offered prizes totaling more than $140 million, have worked to apply similar logic to social problems and opportunities from coral reef restoration to job reskilling.[133] These efforts require a problem that is well-defined. Complex, multifaceted, or interdependent topics do not always lend themselves to clear "winner." But for certain technical challenges, prizes can be incredibly fruitful as a mechanism for inspiring activity and intention.

Of course, the inherently competitive frame of a prize does not always lend itself to cooperation. If poorly designed, a prize can lead to an immense amount of wasted effort on the part of the losers.[134]

There are other models of incentive alignment. In 2005, a group of anonymous donors in Kalamazoo, Michigan, pledged to cover 100% of college tuition for graduates of the Kalamazoo school system. The program had a significant effect on high school graduation rates, college enrollment, and college completion.[135] The "Kalamazoo Promise" fulfilled its promise: the creation of a clear incentive had a direct impact on behavior.

Importantly, incentives do not have to be financial to be effective. The community of Wikipedia editors provides labor because the work is fulfilling and influential. Other communities are driven by tiers of recognition and a desire for status. In other cases (e.g., community gardens) there can be an exchange of non-monetary assets. All these incentive systems work because their designers asked simple questions about what other people actually want, and how those desires might affect their behavior.

Different types of reasoning

The human mind works in various ways. By tapping a variety of methods, we can reason towards truth, even if we can never fully achieve it. Consider three broad types of reasoning:

Inductive	Deductive	Abductive
From systematic data to a hypothesis (may be true)	From premises to a conclusion (always true)	From non-systematic data to a guess (may be true)
example:	*example:*	*example:*
Data: Every day of my life, the sun has risen.	Premises: All men are mortal, and Socrates is a man.	Data: All the beans in this bag are white. This bean in my hand is white.
Therefore: Tomorrow the sun will rise.	Therefore: Socrates is mortal.	Therefore: This bean is probably from this bag.

Each of these forms can be used in combination to help us understand the world.

We may begin with a deduction about what we think is important. (Deductive reasoning: all human lives are valuable; therefore, I'm going to do work that saves as many human lives as I can.)

Where possible, we can use systematic data to explain what works. (Inductive reasoning: there is strong evidence that when nurses visit young mothers at home, the kids end up healthier.)

And, in the face of uncertainty, we can explicitly try different ways of thinking to see what is most useful. (Abductive reasoning: I'm not sure what will get people to come to my rally, but a lot of people like pizza — so I'll offer some free pizza and see if that works.)

It is possible to also grope through the world with our best guesses. As psychoanalyst Adam Phillips suggests, "The new way we should describe change is experimenting with beliefs. Perfection, from a pragmatic point of view, is a non-starter, because we can never experiment with it."[136] That stance is valuable for an uncertain world. The Design Thinking chapter addresses effective experimentation in social change. More broadly, decision-making is its own science — for further resources, see the notes.[137]

Bayes' Theorem

Abductive reasoning may seem imprecise, but it can be formally modeled as follows:

$$P(A \mid B) = \frac{P(B)\,P(A)}{P(B \mid A)}$$

P (A) = The probability of A occurring
P (B) = The probability of B occurring
P (A | B) = The probability of A given B
P (B | A) = The probability of B given A

We do not always have the data necessary to actually do this calculation. But Bayesian thinking offers some more general lessons.

First, it can be helpful to be explicit about your beliefs prior to a decision or analysis.

Second, it can be more honest to move away from an either/or belief and admit we are not sure. Instead, we can have a fractional confidence that something is true — a "credence" — that can and should change with new evidence. ■

Information vs attention

The availability of information about social and environmental outcomes is one of the most encouraging shifts in human society over the past century. Consumers, investors, and institutional leaders are now able to make decisions in the presence of a far richer data set. Information is a currency of our time, and now that currency can help guide us to better outcomes.

But it is as if we discovered a cursed treasure. Just as information is becoming more available, attention is becoming scarcer. We are cursed to have more information than we can possibly use.

Efforts to improve decision-making with better information will be a core part of social change strategies for many years to come. But it is essential that social change agents figure out how to present this information so people will absorb it. That's why designers — in particular visual designers — are so critical to social change in the 21st century.

Consider the "paradox of choice." Choice undoubtedly can create a kind of empowerment. But evidence suggests that there is such a thing as too much

"To pay attention to one thing is to resist paying attention to other things; it means constantly denying and thwarting provocations outside the sphere of one's attention. We contrast this with distraction, in which the mind is disassembled, pointing in many different directions at once and preventing meaningful action."

Jenny Odell[138]

choice. For example, experiments have shown that people are less likely to buy jam when given 12 options than when given three. The simple reason: making choices requires mental effort.[139]

The phrase "pay attention" is revealing: we have to use a resource to direct our focus. The same is true when making choices. Our constituents have a limited amount of mental resources. In the work of social change, it pays off to think about how we present information and offer options.

Power and intuition

Behavioral science raises a wide range of ethical issues. Choice architecture is a manifestation of power. It can protect existing biases or even magnify them. So, once again, we arrive at a fundamental lesson: pay attention to these dynamics with humility and kindness.

To close, I'd like to offer a defense of intuition.[140] It's easy to feel cynical about human behavior after studying the evidence gathered by cognitive scientists and behavioral economists. We see that our biases distort our choices. We come to see the unconscious mind as an enemy; intuition becomes suspect.

With that said, intuition is the unconscious aggregate of life experience. It is a kind of invisible genius that emerges from the whole of our experience and the grooves that life has carved into our minds.

Even Daniel Kahneman — who taught us so much about hidden biases — argues there are cases where we can trust our intuition. He and collaborator Gary Klein emphasized that intuition can develop over time if you repeatedly experience similar situations and get feedback on them.[141]

To close, let's look back at our elephant from a changemaker's point of view. The rider, our conscious, rational mind, is busy steering. The elephant, our unconscious, emotional mind, helps power us forward through uncertainty. Our path, our context, is full of opportunities to guide us along the way. Our job as changemakers is to be realistic about the workings of the human mind — and ambitious about its potential.

Behavioral Economics Takeaways

1. **Human biases make it hard for the rational mind to shift the beast of the emotional mind.** Changemakers need to understand how people actually behave and develop social change strategies accordingly.

2. **The brain navigates immense amounts of information in our complex world by using shortcuts, sometimes called "heuristics."** They are neither good nor bad, but recognizing the cognitive biases that result is essential for understanding human behavior.

3. **Cognitive biases arise from these mental shortcuts.** Some examples: feeling peer pressure, risk aversion, and overrating our competence.

4. **These biases add up to broader illusions, which social change agents can correct for or maneuver them to their advantage.** Some examples: isolated identity, the possibility of perfection, and the neutrality of language.

5. **"Nudges," according to Richard Thaler and Cass Sunstein, are conscious efforts to tilt behavior.** Nudges are cues in the context of decisions that gently push people towards good decisions without forcing them. People who design nudges are called "choice architects."

6. **Social change agents would be wise to develop a discipline that can counteract illusions and biases with mental clarity.** Discipline creates space for understanding and for control. As Tara Brach says, "There is a space between stimulus and response and in that space is freedom."

7. **Much social change work is to blaze the path for better future outcomes. We can design systems to guide human decisions without constraining choice.** Five ways to begin mapping out that system:

   - Defaults: Setting defaults can have a profound impact on behavior. People automatically opt in; they have to take action to opt out.
   - Language: The words we use, even subtle ones, can steer behavior. Look at what Congress names its bills to see this trick in action.
   - Cues: Lighting, color, bold type, sound volume, and other cues can focus attention and, thus, affect behavior. Since many casinos don't have windows, sunlight can't cue people about the passage of time.
   - Checklists: Checklists have been shown to reduce errors in many contexts. Surgery and other critical fields rely on them.
   - Social context: People shift their behavior when you put their decisions in a larger social context. They have been shown to save energy when their use is compared with homes nearby.

8. **The right incentives can spur social action.** For certain technical challenges, prizes can be an incredibly fruitful mechanism for inspiring activity and intention. But prizes are inherently competitive and, if poorly designed, can cost losers immense amounts of wasted effort.

9. **Three forms of reasoning — inductive, deductive, and abductive — help us understand the world.** As social change agents, we can intentionally match our type of reasoning with the situation we're trying to resolve.

10. **Information is becoming more available just as attention is becoming more precious.** Social change actors have to figure out how to present information so people can absorb it and avoid overwhelming people with too much choice.

11. **Our work as choice architects can be for good or for ill.** Behavioral economics can be manipulating or empowering. Changemakers must pay attention to these dynamics with humility and kindness.

12. **Don't underestimate the value of intuition.** Our unconscious aggregate of life experience shapes illusions and biases, but it also builds wisdom. There is no greater reason to celebrate the human mind than the genius of intuition.

Suggested reading

Daniel Kahneman
Thinking, Fast and Slow

Robert Chialdini
Influence: The Psychology of Persuasion

Robert Sapolsky
Behave: The Biology of Humans at Our Best and Worst

Chip and Dan Heath
Switch: How to Change Things When Change Is Hard

Design Thinking

In Chinese landscape painting, the proportions
fit people. The image invites the viewer to
rescale themselves and take a stroll through
the pathways of the scene. How might we design
situations, solutions, and processes that are fit
to human scale? "Landscape of the Four Seasons
in the Styles of Old Masters," Wei Zhike, 1625

Thou shalt not design for thyself

Vision is one of the prerequisites for social change. It is the mechanism by which we imagine a better future. But vision can be its own kind of ignorance; it can prevent us from acknowledging what is right before us. Accordingly, we need ways to protect against the arrogance of our own perspectives and to reveal the insights that might be hidden in the people and the world around us. That takes intention, and that intention is captured in the spirit of design thinking.

"Design" first referred to creating an object or work of art. But the process of design has been expanded, generalized, and refined into a discipline often called "design thinking" or "human-centered design." This discipline — at once ancient and modern — provides a way of thinking about solving problems in a complex world.

In this chapter we will explore seven design thinking techniques — from prototyping to ethnography to visualization. Throughout, we'll see how design thinking is rooted in three basic mindsets:

1. **Listening**: Ensuring that the voices of others inform our understanding.

2. **Empathy**: Orienting solutions around the people who will use them.

3. **Iteration**: A pattern of action that recognizes we won't get it right the first time.

First, a story. And in the spirit of design thinking, it is a story that is mid-process.

Redesigning substitute teaching

Each day substitute teachers take over one in every ten classrooms in the United States. The century-old system for finding them so undervalues "subs" that education officials sometimes refer to them as "bodies."[142]

Substitute teachers face low pay, limited training, sparse lesson plans, and few chances to connect with colleagues. Some unlucky schools find only a quarter of the subs they need. They scramble to fill the gaps while students and staff suffer in the chaos.

Through their national nonprofit, Substantial Classrooms, Amanda von Moos and Jill Vialet are tackling this almost invisible but consequential challenge. Von Moos calls it, "one of the most under-worked-on, under loved, under resourced parts of education." But undervalued doesn't mean cheap. Typically, America's schools spend $4 billion a year on substitute teachers.

Many education advocates would come to this problem with a ready-made solution. But von Moos and Vialet had a different framework; they "fell in love with the problem, not the solution." And they went through an intentional process — design thinking — to quickly test ideas, shelve the ones that don't work, and refine the ones that do.

Principals and human resource teams told von Moos and Vialet that subs weren't available when they needed them. So von Moos and Vialet asked the question, "How might we get more subs to these schools?" They tested ideas like recruitment flyers and social media. No response.

They knew many subs only came once, so their next iteration asked, "How might we get these subs to come back?" As they cycled through more experiments — and talked to more people — voices emerged that told a different, deeper story than school administrators. Subs felt unprepared because teachers left no lesson plans. Teachers left no plans because too often there were no subs to use them.

"So making it easier for the teachers to create the plan and formatting it so that it looked good, consistently, turned out to actually make a difference," von Moos said. "I never would have guessed that going in. Ever."

Substantial Classroom's SubPlans platform was born. Teachers could easily create a plan; subs loved it.

But the design process continued. Von Moos and Vialet worked on issues that surfaced in the pilot, like subs who couldn't use computers. They expected they'd have to periodically retool. But they couldn't expect the COVID-19 pandemic would stop in-person schooling altogether. Suddenly, teachers and administrators faced a new set of challenges.

Their plans disrupted, von Moos and Vialet dipped into two dozen ideas in their experiment portfolio. They designed SubSchools, which provides subs professional development opportunities such as online courses, small-group learning, and webinars.

"I think you celebrate, and then you go back to work," Vialet says. "I don't think there's really declaring victory." The design thinking process continues.

The elements of design thinking

The story of SubSchools is a story of process. It is not complete; it is exploratory. Von Moos and Vialet are in the middle of the work and always will be. As in so much of social impact work, they did not begin with a "blank slate." Instead, they faced the lived experience of real people in a real context.

In this example, we see all three of the core mindsets of design thinking: listening, empathy, and iteration. Below, I lay out these and other common elements of design thinking and how they connect to the work of social good.

Listening

"Listen" is the first word of the Benedictine monks' instructions. As novices prepare for a lifetime of contemplation, that very first word reminds them of the stance they are to take.

And it is wisdom that we can bring to the work of changing the world when we use listening for design thinking.

Listening is both a way to gather information and a way to gather allies. Listening is how we learn. If we want to find insights into the behavior of individuals or the nature of systems, we must be receptive to them.

But there is a deeper significance to listening when applied to social change: it inherently grants power to the people we are listening to. Attentive listeners signal respect; they show that they value what the speaker has to say. Authentic listening makes recruitment easier. (In the **Community Organizing** chapter, we discuss the process of recruiting others to an effort.)

One powerful technique is "active listening." You repeat back to the speaker in your own words what you heard the person say. It's powerful because it demonstrates to the speaker that you were, in fact, listening carefully. You have to internalize what the speaker is saying if you are to articulate it back. (Active listening also precludes the common — but sloppy and disrespectful — listening habit of silently rehearsing what you will say as soon as the other person stops talking.)[143]

Design thinking is iterative, so you might be coming back to the same people as you refine your work. Establishing a strong relationship from the start sets the groundwork for your own future success. (The Game Theory chapter goes into greater depth on the importance of repetition in building relationships.)

Listening is a form of attention, and I am not the first to note that attention is among the most valuable resources of the modern age. As we seek others' attention in the design process, one of our most powerful assets is our own.

Listening and mysticism

"You must be nothing but an ear."
Dov Baer
(18th century)

"Incline the ear of your heart."
Benedictine monks' instructions
(6th century)

"Absolute unmixed attention
is prayer."
Simone Weil
(20th century)

"Humility collects the soul
into a single point
by the power of silence."
Isaac of Nineveh
(6th century)

"(Such men) by their stillness
become sages
and by their movement, kings."
Chuang Tzu
(4th century BCE)[144]

"In the beginner's mind
there are many possibilities;
in the expert's there are few."
Shunryu Suzuki
(20th century)[145]

"Humility--the acknowldegement of one's limitations and the accurate perception of one's abilities and accomplishments--increases our openness to learning and boosts our altruism, generosity, and helpfulness."

Julie Battilana and Tiziana Casciaro[146]

"There is no one right tool for gaining insight into the customers or beneficiaries you hope to reach. What's important is to recognize the limitations of our own instincts and to understand the motivations that will drive customer adoption of any intervention. This usually involves a mix of quantitative data to capture what is happening and qualitative techniques to explain why."

Ann Mei Chang[147]

Empathy

Building your ideas around the people who will use them — a mindset of "user orientation" — is easier said than done. It asks that we live by Heather Fleming's Golden Rule of Design: "**Thou shalt not design for thyself.**"[148] But how can we get beyond our own limited vision of the best possible path?

Our secret weapon is empathy. Julie Battilana and Tiziana Casciaro explain, "Deep and lasting development of empathy requires more than temporarily seeing the world through someone else's eyes. It entails sustainably shifting from a focus on the self to an awareness and appreciation of interdependence...The self is malleable, and unsurprisingly, an interdependent view inspires greater empathy, more cooperation, and a collective orientation."[149]

This kind of awareness can be terrifying. Putting yourself in someone else's shoes can mean removing a layer of defense around your own experience. Witnessing another's empathy for us can feel like someone is looking inside our mind. Authentic empathy requires courage.

Design thinking requires an

rientation to the user and this, obviously, an be facilitated by empathy. It has he potential to bring out the best ingredients of social change: morality, respect, ignity, and compassion. Executive irector of the Stanford d.school, arah Stein Greenberg emphasizes "an mportant limit of empathy: it's not moral r immoral; it is amoral. Empathy doesn't utomatically put you on a path toward oing good or bad in the world."[150] Our hallenge, as with other tools, is to wield mpathy for good.

Madame L'Amic:
What are the boundaries of design?

Charles Eames:
What are the boundaries of the problem?

Madame L'Amic:
Is design a discipline that concerns itself with only one part of the environment?

Charles Eames:
No.

Madame L'Amic:
Does the creation of design admit constraints?

Charles Eames:
Design depends largely on constraints.

Madame L'Amic:
What constraints?

Charles Eames:
The sum of all constraints.

1969 interview for exhibition[151] at Musée des Arts Décoratifs in Paris.

"Design is a solution to a problem.
Art is a question to a problem."

John Maeda

Stanford University's Hasso Plattner Institute of Design, often known as the "d.school," has proposed "eight core abilities" of design thinking:[152]

Navigate Ambiguity:
The ability to recognize and persist in the discomfort of not knowing and develop tactics to overcome ambiguity when needed

Learn from Others (People and Contexts):
Empathizing with and embracing diverse viewpoints, testing new ideas with others, and observing and learning from unfamiliar contexts

Synthesize Information:
The ability to make sense of information and find insight and opportunity within.

Experiment Rapidly:
The ability to quickly generate ideas — whether written, drawn, or built.

Move Between Concrete and Abstract: Understanding stakeholders and purpose in order to define the product or service's features.

Build and Craft Intentionally:
The ability for thoughtful construction: showing work at the most appropriate level of resolution for the audience and feedback desired.

Communicate Deliberately:
The ability to form, capture, and relate stories, ideas, concepts, reflections, and learnings to the appropriate audiences.

Design Your Design Work:
The "meta" ability to recognize a project as a design problem and then decide on the people, tools, techniques, and processes needed to tackle it.

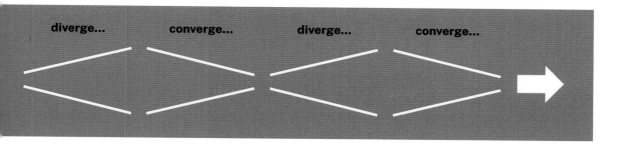

diverge...　　converge...　　diverge...　　converge...

rocess

esign thinking is a process, not an out-
ome. The best design thinking processes
end to have two critical characteristics.

- They are **intentional**. The designer
  or group will go through a deliberate
  series of steps which are articulated
  from the beginning.
- They are **iterative**. Instead of
  going through a process once, you
  might cycle through portions again
  and again.

his combination echoes one of the key
oints in the Strategy chapter, that
ffective strategy needs elements that
re both linear and cyclical. This overlap
 no coincidence: design thinking is
trategy made manifest in an intentional
rocess. Often, design thinkers frame
heir processes with questions that begin
ith "how might we...." This framing
ocuses participants on the goals at hand
hile opening the aperture of possibility.

There are different ways to iterate in
esign thinking. One common way is to
ternate between divergence and con-
ergence. Here's how it works: An initial
vergent stage might intentionally elicit
wide variety of potential options — say,

names for a new organization, strategic
frameworks, or recruitment tactics. A
subsequent convergent stage might then
home in on a subset of those possibilities
for further exploration.

This technique might sound like a
familiar brainstorming session, and
indeed, that can be a useful tactic. But
traditional brainstorming is often isolated
and ad hoc. The best design processes
go through a diverge-converge cycle
multiple times and filter them in different
ways (e.g. with external feedback, cost
analysis, or new questions.)

If structured properly, design thinking
processes are opportunities to strengthen
engagement through empathy. If a social
enterprise, say, wants to use design thinking techniques in an all-staff strategic
planning session, there is an opportunity
to build a positive relationship with the
staff. But for that to happen, the social
enterprise needs to be kind to them.
That consideration means laying out the
process in advance, setting timelines,
and having sufficiently forceful facili-
tation to ensure both attentive listening
and forward movement. You can see
similar dynamics in boards of directors,
coalitions, and business associations.

This kindness and clarity can set the stage for future iterations. First, by making an experience pleasant, you make people want to participate again in the future. Second, an isolated strategic planning process is not likely to yield much buy-in. But mapping out a set of moments when the plan will be revisited and revised offers participants a notion of the pathway forward, uncertain as it might be.

Prototyping

"The person who brings a prototype to a meeting gets all the attention."[153] The simple phrase distills a phenomenon we've all seen: *conversations are anchored by examples.*

A prototype is just an early working version of an idea. We typically think of prototypes as physical objects, but that's not always true. A prototype could be a draft of a strategic plan, a tentative mission statement, or the first take of a budget.

Prototypes, whatever their form, bring power. Even abstract thinkers find themselves using the concrete prototype as a reference point. It provides constraints that make the conversation manageable. If the prototype is completely rejected, it still has set the terms of the conversation; the next iteration will likely be discussed in opposition or relation to it. Prototypes serve both an internal and external purpose. Organizational insiders can use prototypes to determine what they wish to present to outsiders.

The concept of the prototype can be extended beyond internal strategy sessions. The most powerful feedback comes from users themselves. For this eason, many organizations seek to create what is known as a "minimum viable roduct (MVP)." The purpose of an MVP is earning. As the word "minimum" implies, the prototype should have as few features s possible — but still enough to enable earning. While software development s particularly conducive to the creation f an MVP, the concept can be used in hysical products or services as well.

Keep in mind that the MVP is part of a roader effort to better understand users. s Ann Mei Chang, says, "What is most nportant is to shift your mindset from ne of building to one of learning."[154]

Prototyping also brings dangers that an derail the value of design thinking. nce they're created, prototypes can take n a life of their own. That is why social hange agents would be wise to keep rototyping in its correct context — as a neans to an end, not an end in itself.

Improv comedy is an example of prototyping in action. In improv, a group of actors creates a story in real-time based on words or ideas offered by the audience. There's no planning or consultation, just action.

The core of successful improv is the philosophy of "yes, and...." That is, whatever the last person said — however absurd! — has to be built upon, not negated.

Improv is obviously not appropriate for many of the tasks of social change. (Can you imagine an improv comedy budget?) But it is an immensely useful technique for opening up possibilities and growing trust and connection within a group. ■

Physicality

Human experience is physically embodied. I am standing as I write this. Neuroscience research increasingly shows that we think with our bodies as well as our brains.[155]

If we are to design processes to build a better world, we have to take into account the actual bodies of humans.

Meeting agendas sometimes have a line or two labeled "bio break" — a time to stretch, get a snack, and use the bathroom. The idea is a kindness. But if we take that term literally, it suggests that breaks are the only time we are allowed to engage our full biological selves, to be fully alive.

So how might we design meetings, processes, and decision-making structures to maximize our "alive" time?

To start, let's intentionally build physicality into the decision-making experience so that both our brains and bodies can do the thinking. What does that look like? In human-centered design, this concept often takes the form of building physical prototypes. Many designers find that the mere process of building something physical helps clarify ideas. This can even work with abstract topics (at one workshop, I was once asked to build a physical representation of democracy reform!).

In part because the use of physicality is so rare, it can be a powerful way to turn concepts into experiences and experiences into memories. For example, one way to intentionally build physicality into discussions is to have people's bodies represent their beliefs about a topic. At a meeting I attended around platform neutrality, the presenters asked participants to place themselves on a continuum representing whether they thought neutrality was even possible. Everyone walked to different parts of a room to represent their opinions. Then, the facilitator took that moment to give people representing different beliefs a chance to share their perspective. Everyone then heard a range of perspectives in human surround-sound.

We can use physicality as a technique for communication, as well. I remember I was once unexpectedly asked to get up in front of a group of senior social sector leaders to explain the complex flow of information about nonprofit organizations. There was no screen and no projector. I had no choice but to "act ut the slide," to use my body to visually epresent information and its motion. 'or years afterwards, people would ome up to me and say they remembered hat moment — and, more importantly, hey remembered the ideas I was trying o convey.

Ethnography

Design thinking, as we have said, relies on listening. Anthropologists have listening down to a science called ethnography. Ethnography is the process of immersing yourself in a space, problem, and people. It is watching, listening, and participating — being there.

With time, that immersion may reveal patterns of behavior or essential details that might have been otherwise invisible. At best, ethnography can allow what anthropologist Clifford Geertz called "thick description" of a complex human situation.[157]

Wise ethnographers don't fool themselves that what they witness is exactly the same as what goes on in their absence. They must remain cognizant of the "observer effect." That is, people behave differently when they know they are being observed.

This limitation is unavoidable, but it can be mediated. Anthropologists often will embed themselves in a community, participating in its patterns even as they watch, listen, and learn. This kind of intentional, watchful presence has been called "participant-observation." As journalist and anthropologist Gillian Tett

157   Design Thinking

explains, "It pays to do intensive local and lateral studies that explore a situation in three dimensions, ask open-ended questions, and ponder what people are not talking about. There is value in becoming 'embodied' in somebody else's world — to gain empathy. That worm's eye approach does not usually produce neat power points or flashy spreadsheets. But it can be sometimes more revealing than any bird's eye or Big Data view."[158]

Ethnography is just one methodology of qualitative research that is used in design thinking. Other examples include interviews, focus groups, or textual analysis.

Qualitative research can help to reveal insights from subjects that don't easily lend themselves to the tidy mathematical and statistical models and measurements of quantitative analysis.

These research methodologies can be just as sophisticated as those of quantitative research. It is possible to impose rigor upon each stage of the process: thoughtfulness about research design, consistency in execution, and specificity in interpretation of the resulting data.

Consider the case of interviews. A first step might be a process of choosing questions that might expose hidden assumptions of the interviewer. That insight can then lead to the creation of an interview guide that provides a consistent structure for the interviews. Then, the data (in the form of interview transcripts) can be formally coded to help reveal patterns. The lessons that emerge can then serve to structure further iterations and exploration.[159]

All types of listening — such as interviews, surveys, and ethnography — offer an opportunity for dignity and deeper learning if you take one more step and close the loop. By reflecting what you have heard or witnessed back to those you heard from, you offer a chance for reactions, corrections, and expansion. This reflection helps build reciprocal relationships, not extractive ones.

In this way, listening itself is iterative. In a broader process of listening, you affirm the value of the group's time, create ownership, and may uncover more of your own hidden assumptions.

Biomimicry

Evolution is a method of design, and nature is a museum of design.

Artists and engineers have looked to nature for design inspiration for millennia. In the emerging discipline of biomimicry, product designers and industrial engineers are consciously copying the lessons they find in nature to build systems that not only work better but are more sustainable.

Biomimicry pioneer Janine Beynus has offered a summary of the design lessons of nature. She says that living beings in mature ecosystems:

1. Use waste as a resource
2. Diversify and cooperate to fully use the habitat
3. Gather and use energy efficiently
4. Optimize rather than maximize
5. Use materials sparingly
6. Don't foul their nests
7. Don't draw down resources
8. Remain in balance with the biosphere
9. Run on information
10. Shop locally[160]

Visualization

People think about the world in different ways: some in words, some in numbers, others in stories, and yet others in images. The design philosophy of this very book reflects this multiplicity.

Design thinking is itself rooted in the visual; many of the pioneers of design thinking were artists and visual designers. But the connection is deeper than history. In visualization, we can move across dimensions, so new ideas can come to life.

Spoken language, where one word comes after another, is inherently one-dimensional.

When you move to paper or the whiteboard, you shift into two dimensions.

With a physical prototype, you move into three dimensions.

Dance or other forms of physical movement add a fourth dimension: time.

Visualization will be a gift to some of your participants and a burden to others. Since some people feel less comfortable with visual thinking, I recommend keeping visuals clear and simple. This is one place where specific tactics may be worth sharing:

1. When representing a person, draw them. A quick stick figure is fine. Represent their thoughts with a thought bubble. It is easier to understand someone's context (and thoughts) when we see it represented visually.
2. If a question has more than one dimension, draw perpendicular lines and name the dimensions. If it makes sense, create quadrants and name each one.
3. Visualize stories with a timeline. If there are parallel stories, visualize them as parallel timelines. This reminds your audience of sequence (some things may have to happen before others) and interconnection (different entities may operate on different timelines).
4. Use color, especially to denote different categories. This serves as a gift to the viewer to help them mentally sort information and allows you an opportunity to highlight what you think is important.
5. Crowd size permitting, print out your visualization. (Make sure to recycle the paper!) If you have a visual that captures a proposal, tension, or problem, give each participant a copy so they can experience its physicality. Encourage them to write over it, to add notes, and to scratch things out.
6. When something gets a big positive reaction from the group, write it. Allow those words to absorb space in the room and in the visual field of the participants.
7. If there's a list of ideas, see if you can cluster them. Optimally, try to limit the number of categories (at any level) to seven.[161]

Test everything; hold fast to what is good."

Thessalonians 5:21

Ever tried.
Ever failed.
No matter.
Try again.
Fail again.
Fail better.

Samuel Beckett[162]

Lean Impact

For years Silicon Valley entrepreneurs have followed the philosophy of the "lean startup," fully articulated by Eric Ries in his book by the same name.

Build. Measure. Learn. Repeat. That's what you do over and over when you use the lean startup methodology. This sequence is closely related to what software developers call the "Agile" methodology. Agile breaks up software development — really any complex process — into shorter chunks called "sprints." Each sprint, which typically lasts two weeks, must end with a concrete output, even if small, and a "sprint review" of progress made and adjustments needed to move forward. Thus, Agile creates a cadence of prototyping (the concrete output) and reflection (sprint review).

Measurement drives learning, so all lean methodologies take data seriously. Absolute numbers like website visits give a sense of scale, but they can easily end up counting irrelevant activity and become what are derisively called "vanity metrics" that are more about feeding our arrogance than learning. In contrast, percentages and ratios can be more useful because, as a measure of proportion, they can often better capture the quality or stickiness of an interaction.

Candid CEO Ann Mei Chang systematically applied these ideas to social change in her book, *Lean Impact*. She emphasized that changemakers applying design thinking principles need to stay oriented toward a much more ambitious long-term social goal. Chang summarizes the application of lean principles to social change as follows: (1) think big, (2) start small, and (3) relentlessly seek impact. This trio captures the spirit of design thinking as applied to social change. With *intention* and *attention*, it is possible to seek immense impact one small step at a time.

1. **Vision can be its own kind of ignorance.** That's why we need the spirit of design thinking. It intentionally reveals insights that might be hidden in the people and the world around us.

2. **At its heart, design thinking is about two things: listening and iteration.** Listening ensures that the voices of others guide our decisions. Iteration provides a pattern of action that recognizes we won't get it right the first time. There are different ways to iterate in design thinking.

3. **When you design solutions for social good, you celebrate your triumphs and then get back to work.** Innovator Jill Vialet says, "I don't think there's really declaring victory." It is a constant cycle of learning and action.

4. **Build your ideas around the people who will use them — a mindset called "user orientation."** That's easier said than done. Heather Fleming's Golden Rule of Design is: "Thou shalt not design for thyself." Understanding other people takes empathy and active listening.

5. **The design cycle moves through a deliberate series of steps, typically more than once.** Designers cycle through portions of that process again and again to refine their idea over time.

6. **Prototypes, whether they are concrete or abstract, bring power to design conversations.** But prototypes can be dangerous if designers are too wedded to their creations.

7. **Neuroscience shows that we think with our whole bodies.** We can create design processes and decision-making structures that incorporate physicality.

search can be qualitative, quan-
ative, or both. Ethnography, the
ocess of watching and listening
th a group over time, is a valuable
ualitative research technique for
ocial change agents.

sualization helps bring new ideas
 life. There are basic techniques for
elping people see your ideas.

ocial changemakers can achieve
reat results with the cutting-edge
xperimental techniques of "lean
npact" design. Ann Mei Chang says
ne key is to stay oriented toward
nore ambitious long-term goals. Her
hree rules: Think big, start small, and
elentlessly seek impact.

Gillian Tett
Anthro-Vision

Sarah Stein Greenberg
Creative Acts for Curious People

John Maeda
The Laws of Simplicity

Tim Brown
*Change by Design: How Design
Thinking Transforms Organizations
and Inspires Innovation*

Community Organizing

In 2014, the People's Climate March brought
hundreds of thousands of people to the streets
of New York City. The gathering did not solve the
climate crisis. But it was a signal moment in a
growing social movement. Time will tell if that
movement can wield enough collective power to
bend the carbon curve.
Photo by Julie Dermansky

I am
because we are

The very phrase "community organizing" reveals a paradox. "Community" is that most ineffable and human of substances: entwined threads of place, language, and history. Yet "organizing" suggests rigid lattices and strict hierarchies; it describes attempts to impose order upon disorder.

At its best, community organizing does both. It is the art of finding order in the common interests, angers, and hopes of a group of human beings. It is not the only such discipline. Others do the same in different contexts, such as management, teaching, and coaching.

What separates community organizing is its focus on power.

Frederick Douglass said, "Power concedes nothing without a demand. It never did and it never will."[163] Community organizing begins with recognizing the need to grapple with the power of those whose decisions matter to us.

But, as Mario Lugay of Movement Commons emphasizes, organizing requires a next step: to acknowledge that *you* also have power.[164] Without that next step, we are liable to fall into strategies that fail to leverage (or expand) our power.

Community organizing takes many forms, and you don't have to be Nelson

Mandela or Cesar Chavez to do it. When neighborhood members come together to ask the park director to keep the local park open later, they are organizing a community. Indeed, when corporate executives come together in a group to lobby a state legislature, they are organizing a community. They are grappling with lawmakers whose decisions matter to them.

Let's begin with a story of expressing power amidst repression.

The women of Liberia

Charles Taylor's rebel army entered Liberia in 1989, ushering in an era of violence and ruin. More than a dozen peace agreements collapsed. Women saw their sons snatched to become child soldiers. Along with gunfire, death, rape, hunger, and looting, the women endured abusive marriages and too many children. Charles Taylor's authoritarian regime controlled Liberia's media. He banned street marches. Pedestrians who faced his motorcade could be shot as suspected assassins.

But Taylor couldn't control Liberia's women. Their stories wove together the rage, despair, dislocation, and dehumanization of women — no matter if they were rich or poor, Christian or Muslim, educated or illiterate.

"The movement we called the 'Mass Action for Peace' would later appear to be a spontaneous uprising...It was prompted by emotion — by women's exhaustion and desperation — but there was nothing spontaneous about it; managing a huge daily public protest was a complicated task and we planned every move we made," wrote Leymah Gbowee, who shared the Nobel Peace

Prize for helping to end 14 years of civil war and oust Taylor in 2003.[165]

It started with 20 women gathering weekly to pray and fast. Over the coming months, a movement bloomed in mosques, markets, and churches. Market women spread the word when they bought produce in the countryside and spoke to customers at their stalls. They hung flyers, illustrated for women who couldn't read.

"We worked in a world inhabited by women," Gbowee wrote in her memoir, "and we used women's networks to communicate."

Circumventing state media through allies like Christian radio, the movement defied the marching ban, bringing as many as a thousand women, dressed in white, to city hall. Month after month, women walked miles from internally displaced persons camps or came by the truckload to sit, sing, pray, and protest in clear view of Taylor's daily commute.

When peace talks finally began in Ghana, Gbowee's group brought Liberian women from refugee camps to protest at the site. She saw rebel negotiators basking like vacationers in the comforts of their four-star hotel, so she sat

hundreds of women at the conference room doors, threatening a siege. The festive atmosphere stopped.

With Taylor ousted, the movement registered women voters and helped elect his female successor, Ellen Johnson Sirleaf. Their tactics reached women in Africa and conflict zones around the world.

Gbowee founded and heads an education and development foundation for West African women and girls.

"We are building," she wrote, "a new generation of us."

The first pillar of organizing: Power

Power, as we have said, is what distinguishes community organizing from other disciplines that build common bonds among people. The revolutionary women of Liberia faced a profound, in fact life-threatening, power imbalance. It was only through tireless and courageous community organizing that they could aggregate their influence in such a way as to force change.

What is power? The scholars Julie Battilana and Tiziana Casciaro define it as the ability to influence the behavior of others.[166] They emphasize that power itself is morally neutral. It may be held by those with good or evil intentions; it may be wielded for good or evil ends. No matter how moral its purpose, power may achieve good or evil outcomes.

In the context of social change, power is an essential currency of decision-making, and community organizing is intentional engagement with power. This section describes power dynamics between community organizers and the people who will make the decisions they care about. The next section looks at a different power dynamic: relationships among organizers and their allies.

In community organizing, there is typically a "target," a person or group with decision-making power. We do not need to see targets as opponents; they may be relatively neutral decision makers. But in community organizing, we aim to change that target's behavior.

To change a target's behavior, you need to understand who and what might influence them. Community organizers can start this process with a "power map" — a diagram that shows which people or organizations influence a target. This exercise is sometimes simple, other times not. From the power map, you can begin to identify a pathway of influence.

A politician might care about voters or donors. A company might care about customers, shareholders, or employees. Then you can add layers or nuance. Are there swing voters who are authentically undecided about a particular election? Are there certain customers that the company cares about most? From this map, you can articulate a pathway of influence to guide the steps you will take to influence the decision maker and the measurements you will use to track your success.

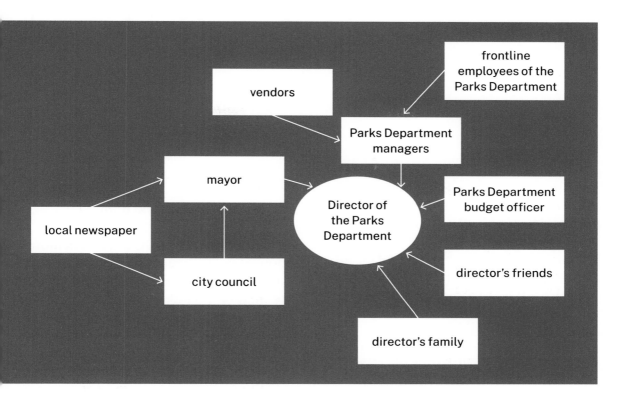

Let's explore a simple example. Imagine you want to expand the hours your neighborhood park stays open. You've identified that the Director of the Parks Department will make the decision.

The above power map suggests a range of different strategies. Let's consider two nearly opposite approaches. The first approach is aggressive: launch a pressure campaign on the Director. She reports to the Mayor, so our secondary target could be the Mayor. And if we need to get the Mayor's attention, we might do that that directly or through the local newspaper or the City Council.

The second approach is collaborative. What if the Director is actually not opposed to keeping the parks open — she's only concerned about the budget? That might suggest a simpler, different strategy: working with the Budget Officer to figure out how to keep costs low.

The example above highlights two essential points about community organizing strategy. First is the need to focus on a particular target. You might use multiple techniques to influence the target. After a victory — or defeat — you might change targets. The target might be an individual or a group. But in every case, you need a target. That clear strategic focus offers the best chance of success. Second is that you often have multiple options for influencing a target. Exploring the range of options may help you find one that is simply easier.

A note on electoral politics

Elections matter. Or, to speak more generally, it matters who holds the formal power of government — however it is they gained that power.

This chapter is focused on how to organize power to influence existing decision makers. But it is worth emphasizing that sometimes the best strategy is to become the decision maker.

Direct engagement in electoral politics — whether as a candidate or a supporter — is one of the purest forms of social change.[167] ■

Organizing, in the political sense, is to organize a social bloc into a political force. It is to name, frame, and narrate the trajectory of a group; to articulate its goals, grievances and targets; to move it into strategic collective action; to inspire other social forces to align in a common direction; and to leverage this force for political ends."

Jonathan Smucker[168]

The second pillar of organizing: Relationships

There's one character in the story of community organizing that's even more important than your target: your allies. It's not community organizing if you're alone.

Some helpful definitions are in order. I'm using the term "community organizing" as an umbrella term that encompasses multiple types of organizing. Let's consider two types:

1. "Advocacy organizing" seeks to gather and focus fragmented passion on a predetermined issue, giving people an opportunity to act on their beliefs to make change.
2. Another approach, which I will call "community-led organizing," focuses on building — and wielding — power within existing communities on issues of their choosing.

Both models derive their power from the set of people working for change, but they develop that power in different ways. I believe both models are essential for social change.

Advocacy organizing is a strategy for achieving a specific goal. It starts with a particular issue and builds the local, national, or global community of people and organizations who care about it. It is a force multiplier for existing advocacy organizations and campaigns.

Advocacy organizing is where my own career began. In 1999, for example, I worked with the Sierra Club on a national campaign to protect roadless areas in the U.S. national forest system. I was one of a dozen people sent out to organize students to pressure federal officials to permanently protect those areas. Collectively, the campaign gathered hundreds of thousands of signatures, organized hundreds of events, and defined the terms of the debate.

Our job was to take people's existing passion for forests, weave it together, wrap it up in a story, and demonstrate the power of that collective. That expression of power was an essential part of a multi-pronged strategy across many organizations. Two years later, the U.S. Forest Service announced the Roadless Rule, protecting 58.5 million acres from further road building and timber harvesting.

The people we organized already knew they cared about protecting nature, but it took an advocacy organizing campaign to turn their belief into action on a specific policy.

Community-led organizing is a deeper process of group-directed change. In this case, an organizer starts with an existing community and creates a process to elicit the issues that the community cares about. The organizer or organizers "holds space" for a community to lead itself.

This model is often used in chronically under-resourced areas — particularly Black and Brown communities — to give power to people who have been largely shut out of existing power structures. Communities explore needs, learn new skills, and develop mechanisms to make collective decisions. This type of organizing often includes a delicate balance of teaching and creating space for people to learn on their own.[169]

Ultimately, though, it is about building power to force change.

I saw this process growing up. For many years, my parents in Winston-Salem, N.C., were involved in an effort known as CHANGE. It was launched with an agenda of organizing and building power but — importantly — no pre-set agenda about which issue, policy, or opportunity to focus on.

The CHANGE initiative first organized religious institutions as a mechanism to pool funding and to bring people together. The newly gathered group did an audit of community needs, waiting to set goals until they had engaged with their neighbors. Then, the initiative began with a focus on very local issues like traffic safety in disinvested neighborhoods or ID cards for recent immigrants.

Notably, CHANGE represented a racial cross-section of the community, with membership including majority Black, Latino, and white houses of worship. This new coalition changed the political dynamics in the city: the mayor would regularly come to meetings, recognizing that CHANGE represented real power.

Over time, the initiative tackled larger questions of political power and won victories in criminal justice reform. The CHANGE initiative provides another common lesson in the value of community organizing: relationships are more important than formal organizations. CHANGE (the organization) formally disbanded after a decade of work, but CHANGE (the network of relationships) continues to this day.

The techniques of community organizing

Below, I'll discuss seven important aspects of community organizing. This is not an exhaustive list, and every organizing effort need not involve each of these techniques. Organizers can draw as they need from these. I will, though, highlight that almost every successful organizing effort will draw on two skills discussed in other chapters of this book: listening (see the Design Thinking chapter) and storytelling (see the Storytelling chapter).

Recruitment

Recruitment, an essential dimension of community organizing, plays out in different ways for the two strategies presented above.

Recruitment in community-led organizing relies on intense listening to identify the right goals and to keep communities motivated during the change process. Advocacy organizing, in contrast, starts with the issue and builds the community; you have to find people and convince them to join you.

I'll share an advocacy recruitment example from my own experience in Green Corps. One common strategy was to go to a college campus to organize students around specific environmental issues. To do that, we needed to find students willing to take action on them. To do that, we needed to get the students to come to a meeting. And to do that, we had to find and convince them to come.

Our technique was often as simple as talking to people at a table we set up outside the main student center. Green Corps taught us a very useful trick: "The Rule of Halves." Imagine that you want 30 people to come to your first meeting. How many people do you need to talk to at the table? Think of it like this:

- Half the people you talk to will be interested.
- Half of those will sign up for more information.
- Half of those will respond to a follow-up note that asks them to come to meeting.
- Half of those will actually show up.

So the Rule of Halves means you have to talk to 480 people to get 30 of them to show up to your meeting. That's no small number, but it can be reached within a week of setting up a table and talking with students.

The exact ratios depend on countless factors, but the math of the Rule of Halves shows us an essential finding about recruitment: it is possible to organize some subset of those who agree with you. And recruitment is possible with an infrastructure as simple as a well-placed table and chairs.

But it takes work and time.

Empowerment

Community organizing is built upon empowerment. To empower, first you give and then you give away. Let me explain.

In my time at Green Corps, some of my fellow organizers would intentionally choose a room for their first meeting that was a bit too small. The meeting would be densely packed, exciting, and exceeding expectations from the beginning.

Campaigns do not have to start with a big, in-person meeting. The first collective conversation might be virtual, or it might be a small meeting in a local café. Whatever the context, the organizer has to give something to the group: energy, purpose, information, and hope. Ultimately, the gift is inspiration, a desire to participate. And that inspiration is a necessary ingredient in organizing.

Then, having given inspiration, the organizer also has to give away something: their own power. People are the force multipliers for community organizing campaigns. An organizer will not engage as many people if they horde control for themselves.

Think about the meeting above with 30 people. Imagine that 10 become active volunteers. Then imagine that each of those 10 volunteers shares the passion you nurtured in them and gathers 10 more. Perhaps the process would take them longer. Perhaps some would recruit better than others. But you will have shifted the math of organizing from *addition* to *multiplication*.

This dynamic is not limited to volunteer-driven campaigns. Similar processes can be seen when organizing professionals or institutions. The simple act of giving up power — of trusting others to multiply shared purpose — captures the spirit of community organizing. **To build up collective power, organizers need to give up some of their own power.**

Demonstrating power

To use power, we must demonstrate it. Let's start by discussing literal "demonstrations" — gathering multiple people in one place at one time. The most famous grassroots political gathering in U.S. history, the 1963 March on Washington for Jobs and Freedom, was far more than a march. It was a demonstration of power.[170]

Demonstrations force decision makers to see what they are up against. This visual (and temporal) character can help to reset the framing of a given issue. For example, demonstrations can be a way to regain momentum after a setback — the largest demonstration in U.S. history, the 2017 Women's March, followed an electoral defeat. And demonstrations can build shared identity and commitment among participants. You get a visceral sense of power and community when surrounded by others who feel the same way you do.

It is worth acknowledging here that humans are not always their best in groups, which places special responsibility on the organizers who bring the groups together. The simple word "mob" evokes the ways that human emotions can be magnified toward evil ends.

So it is the responsibility of the community, and of an organizer, to design demonstrations in a way that lifts up the participants and even that lifts up the targets. Demonstrations with dignity are typically more effective than those without. The 1990 Capitol Crawl, described in the Storytelling chapter, is a classic example of a superbly designed demonstration. It had everything you would ask of a successful demonstration: a clear ask, compelling images, and a gripping story.

Organizing a morally powerful and politically effective demonstration is no small task. And it is not the only way to demonstrate power. There are other techniques that can be used by communities to influence the target behavior: petitions, fundraisers, lobbying, and more. The particular approach will depend on the circumstances. In all cases the key strategic question is this: will this approach actually influence decision makers?

> "Righteousness exalts a nation.
> Hate just makes people miserable."

Fannie Lou Hamer

Civil disobedience

Perhaps the single most powerful tool in the community organizer's toolbox is civil disobedience.[171] It has played a critical role in movements throughout history — from the comic farce *Lysistrata* to the civil rights movement in the United States to youth climate activists boycotting school to fight for their own future.

Many books (including those recommended at the end of this chapter) detail particular techniques of civil disobedience, their philosophical implications, and their political ramifications. The essence of what they say is this: civil disobedience serves as a reminder of moral choices. It highlights tensions in society and, when done well, makes them unignorable. When those tensions reveal paradoxes, it is much harder for people in power to maintain a contradiction that is seen as unjust.

The Salt March led by Mahatma Gandhi in March and April of 1930 is a perfect example. The Mahatma led a crowd 240 miles to the shore of the Arabian Sea. When the crowd arrived, they reached down and picked up crusts of salt from the beach. That simple act broke the law. At that time, it was illegal under the Salt Act of 1882 for Indians to collect their own salt. The law the crowd was breaking was clearly unjust; their act highlighted the contradictions of the British Raj and strengthened the moral argument of the Indian independence movement.

A direct historic line connects that movement with the U.S. civil rights movement; Martin Luther King Jr. said he drew inspiration from the Salt March.

Civil disobedience doesn't only target unjust laws. Martin Luther King Jr. forthrightly acknowledged (while sitting in jail), "there is nothing wrong in having an ordinance which requires a permit for a parade."[172] In this case, the political strategy in this type of civil disobedience is not about the law being broken, but about another injustice. The just law serves as a vehicle for highlighting the injustice that is being challenged.

Over the course of the civil rights movement, civil disobedience served as a consistent, dignified, and effective leverage point. It was not the only technique: grassroots educational campaigns, litigation, electoral politics, and legal demonstrations all contributed to the eventual — though still incomplete — victories of the movement.

Effective civil disobedience typically requires an immense amount of planning. It is generally not wise to simply fall into illegal activity. Since much civil disobedience is, in fact, against the law, it is important to understand the legal consequences of your actions and prepare ahead of time for legal support. When I was in jail after civil disobedience I counted my legal blessings: in addition to the unjust privileges afforded by my skin color, I knew that lawyers outside were working to protect me.

In all cases, it is crucial to have a narrative — simple is best — that the act of civil disobedience fits within and a logic to support the particular act. I'll offer an example from my own experience. In 1984, a leak at a Union Carbide plant in Bhopal, India, exposed half a million people to methyl isocyanate gas. Thousands died. Decades later, the site had still not been cleaned up.

In 2003, as part of a civil disobedience action organized by Greenpeace, I chained myself to a fence outside of a Dow Chemical facility in Houston, Tex. (Dow had owned Union Carbide since 2001.) Our chains were only one piece of the plan. At the same time, we "delivered"

Peaceful protest requires extraordinary discipline. In this 1960 photo by James Karales, activists in the Student Nonviolent Coordinating Committee (SNCC) train each other to maintain dignity in the face of brutal attack.

barrels of still-polluted ground water brought from Bhopal on Greenpeace's ship, *Rainbow Warrior*. The water was so polluted that it was treated as toxic material by the police.

The civil disobedience was explicitly tied to the delivery of the toxic water. The reporters present had a clear story to tell about the issue, not just the act of civil disobedience.

This work takes planning. Consider the famous example of Rosa Parks. Her refusal to give up her bus seat on Dec. 5, 1955, touched off the Montgomery, Ala., bus boycott. At the time, Parks explained that she was tired. And she was; she was tired of injustice.

But her act of sitting in the front of a racially segregated bus was not spontaneous or merely inspired by a sore back. Parks had worked within the NAACP for years. Just a few months before, in August of 1955, she had undergone thorough training in strategic civil disobedience at the Highlander Folk School in Tennessee. (The careful forethought behind her act includes its own weighty detail: some argue Parks was chosen for the role in part because she was a Black woman with relatively light skin, which made her less threatening to the local white population.[173])

The most morally powerful characteristic of civil disobedience is nonviolence. In fact, civil disobedience arguably is by definition nonviolent. In that nonviolence, it retains an intense moral authority. Not for the faint of heart — or for every situation — civil disobedience offers the potential to be the single most powerful social change strategy.

"The utilitarian argument against fiestas, parades, carnivals, and general public merriment is that they produce nothing.
But they do: they produce society."

Rebecca Solnit[174]

-•WE THE PEOPLE•-
ARE GREATER THAN FEAR

oster by Shepard Fairey commissioned
y art and activism group Amplifier

Art

Art provides an essential fuel for social change. References to a more hopeful future, a foreboding danger, and even the martyrs of the past can provide the emotional energy that is at the heart of every community organizing effort. Art can crystallize a sense of new possibilities, of a future that is different, better, more just, and more beautiful.

An individual poster or song may be a tactic, but sometimes art rises to the level of being core to a strategy. A single powerful image — a peace symbol, a raised Black fist, or a yellow ribbon tied around a tree — can instantly imprint a cause into someone's consciousness.

A song like "We Shall Overcome" can connect today's action with a powerful historical chain of activism. And it has practical implications in the sometimes-terrifying moments of political conflict. As physician and trauma expert Bessel van der Kolk explains, "Music binds together people who might individually be terrified but who collectively become powerful advocates for themselves and others...dancing, marching, and singing are uniquely human ways to install a sense of hope and courage."[175]

More generally, art can help people talk about change by introducing new language and symbols to the broader discourse. The movie *The Matrix* has served as an invaluable shortcut in societal conversations about virtual reality and the metaverse. Margaret Atwood's novel *The Handmaid's Tale* offered advocates a visual language to represent a future without basic reproductive rights.

Art tends to follow a circuitous path toward impact. We cannot always trace the ways that a song, painting, opera, or dance altered perceptions or beliefs. Sometimes art functions simply as a mechanism to create hope. That hope may not be for any particular outcome. But it builds human capacity to imagine things in a different way and to persist in striving for change.

The more that art has a political purpose, the more it will be susceptible to the critique that it is mere propaganda. Humor, authenticity, and consistency are antidotes to charges of propaganda.

There is no shame in a visual that lacks artistic quality or a song that is sung off key. The beauty is, first and foremost, in the act of participation.

Grasstops organizing

The fact that organizing, by its very definition, deals with power does not mean you can only organize the powerless. In fact, some of the most consequential organizing is of the powerful.

When an environmental group organizes admirals and generals to call attention to the challenges of climate change, that is organizing. When business leaders are convened to discuss human rights challenges, that is organizing.

This sort of work is sometimes known as "grasstops" organizing, an obvious pun on "grassroots." (It is not the only such pun; fake "grassroots" activity manufactured by corporate lobbyists is sometimes known as "astroturf" organizing.)

Community organizers can find a useful insight in these terms. Real grass is different from fake grass, but at first glance, they can be hard to tell apart. Grass grows in layers. Roots ground it, blades gather light, but all is grass. Every layer counts.

There are two delusions to avoid in grasstops organizing. The first delusion is that only those with power matter. We can quickly become seduced by those who can act with the snap of a finger.

hat type of power matters, but it is not he only kind. The second delusion is the etishization of powerlessness. When you evote your life to rectifying inequities f power, it can be all too easy to see the owerless as good solely because of their owerlessness.

No community needs help like that. ou cannot hope to channel people's ommon interests, angers, and hopes into eaningful change if you cease to view hem in their full humanity.

Canvassing

Lois Gibbs was a mother in Niagara Falls in 1978. Her neighborhood was built on a toxic waste dump, her kids were getting sick, and she wanted to do something about it. One day, she got a clipboard and walked towards a neighbor's house. Overwhelmed with fear and uncertainty, she turned around and went home. Luckily for her neighbors, she gathered her courage and went back the next day.

Over the next few years, Gibbs and her neighbors organized themselves into a force that won restitution and clean-up for her neighborhood, Love Canal, and launched the modern environmental health movement.[176]

Organizing began as a physical act. Before the age of telephones, emails, or social media, the only way to align people toward a common cause was to talk to them in person. In the next section, we'll explore some of the modern techniques of connection. But first, let's consider the basic, no-tech art of canvassing: walking up to a door, knocking, and talking to another human being.

Many people are familiar with election-related canvassing. There are three basic types of election canvassing. First, voter ID canvassing simply attempts to understand the likely voters for a particular candidate or ballot measure. Second, closer to the election, that tactic switches to what is known as GOTV, an acronym for "get out the vote," canvassing. This effort simply ensures that voters who favor your cause actually go to the polls.

Neither of these first two types of canvassing is fundamentally designed to change minds. Instead, they seek immediate impact at scale. This approach can be contrasted with a third type, "deep canvassing," which has no deadline like a looming election. Canvassers can spend as much time as they need at a given house, talk through issues, get to know people, and even attempt to change minds. Deep canvassing is one of the rare ways to break out of the traps of political polarization, but it is undoubtedly time-consuming.

Canvassing does not need to be explicitly electoral — or even political. My friend, a real estate developer, was trying to launch an eco-friendly, mixed-use housing project in a wealthy neighborhood in San Francisco. There was opposition from neighbors who feared change. She could have sent mailers to the neighbors or ignored their concerns. Instead, she simply walked up and down the streets, knocked on doors, and talked to them. It worked. Human connection enabled a commercially successful transaction that ultimately benefited the community.

Canvassing is serious work. Like civil disobedience, it takes courage: Lois Gibbs felt that emotional challenge when she first stepped outside her door.

And systematic canvassing takes systematic planning: recruitment, training, route design, and record keeping. Poor planning can turn off canvassers — if for example, they are sent to doors that have already been visited — and thus hurt the work in the long term.

The biggest lesson here is the power of one human talking to another. It does not scale like a website or podcast. But that personal touch is why it works.

Four puzzles for 21st-century community organizing

Community organizing is ancient. For thousands of years, it has evolved to match the characteristics of its era. Given the unique context of the 21st century, organizing must continue to evolve. Below, we'll go through four puzzles (or tensions) facing community organizing in an age when collective action is increasingly important.

Technology

Ultimately, organizing is about human connection, and the nature of human contact has changed as the nature of our society has evolved. Technology has made it possible to connect across vast distances and to do so quickly and at very low cost.

We can leverage the broad and shallow connection made possible by technology.[177] And we should recognize that authentic human relationships can happen through a screen. But through a screen we cannot replicate the human richness of being in the same room, of commonality rooted in place, and of blood spilled together. There is no simple solution to this tension. To navigate it, we ought to at least recognize it.

We have seen many examples of the power of social media as a mechanism for organizing. The Arab Spring famously relied upon social media for the bulk of its organizing. But that historic moment is also a cautionary tale.

Many of the dramatic changes spurred on by the Arab Spring turned out to be fleeting. Only one country — Tunisia — emerged from the Arab Spring with a democracy, and that success story is under constant pressure. Autocrats across the globe have come to understand that it is possible to turn off the Internet in a given geographic area. The economic consequences for such an act may be profound, but but can strangle a movement reliant on social media. Other regimes have developed techniques to limit the capacity of social media as a mechanism for grassroots political power — from censorship to systematic propaganda.

Technology-driven community organizing campaigns can — if they aren't careful — damage their own efforts without any interference from autocrats or opponents. For example, generous citizens often find themselves inundated with fundraising emails. Organizer Mario Lugay has called email blasts, "the most narcissistic form of communication."[178] It is supremely one-directional, from the center out. The short-term incentives are for each message to maximize its financial return.

This short-sightedness leads to multiple negative long-term consequences.

First, it creates an extractive relationship between an organization and its community. If all the emails are fundraising emails, donors feel they are perceived as nothing more than a bank account.

Second, this dynamic has been exacerbated by new techniques that baldly prey on human emotion and cognitive bias. (Think of approaches such as "This one trick may surprise you..."; "Last chance! Your offer expires in 24 hours!"; and "Five things you should know about....")

Sophisticated analytical and targeting techniques have undoubted short-term benefits for many organizations. But their long-term consequence has been to dissolve the sense of meaningful relationship between the organization and the supporter.

So we have a multi-layered cautionary tale. Donors may feel sucked dry and that their relationship is purely transactional. And these dynamics have the potential to erode a supporter's sense of agency that is so critical to community organizing.

We run the risk of cultivating cynicism instead of engagement. As we use technology for organizing, we need to think beyond a single interaction toward a lasting relationship.

Labor organizing

Much of the most consequential organizing in human history has been labor organizing.

The basic principles are the same as with community organizing, though there are notable differences.

First, labor organizing can offer direct benefits for those organized (versus the manifestation of general altruism or community interests). Second, in countries with strong labor laws, there is a specific legal format labor organizing happens within. Third, labor organizing can be much more difficult because the opposition will often be very well-organized and well-funded.

Many successful labor organizing campaigns leave a lasting institutional legacy: labor unions. Collectively, unions play an essential role in balancing political power in society. But they are as diverse as their memberships. Some unions focus only on the short-term interests of their narrow membership (e.g., a prison guards' union lobbying for more prisons); others are beacons of justice, advancing dignity for all working people (e.g., the Service Employees International Union's living wage campaigns.)

New campaigns like Fight for 15 (discussed in the **Strategy** chapter) are reimagining labor organizing for the 21st century. As the nature of work changes, so will the nature of labor organizing. ■

Decision-making

The way an organizer structures decision-making can make or break a campaign or an organization. Good decisions yield more impact, and fast decisions can be important in a changing environment. But in community organizing, decision-making is inherently complicated because you are trying to empower others, to model a better society in the way everyone works together to create one.

In the **Strategy** chapter, we considered the strategic effectiveness of the Occupy Wall Street (OWS) movement. Now, let's look at the way that movement made decisions. OWS was radically democratic in its operations. There was a deliberate effort to not bury the ideas of collective action, common purpose, and community resilience beneath a narrative of single leaders. This decision had strategic consequences, because the public and the media, lacking individual protagonists to follow through their journey, had a harder time wrapping their minds around the OWS story.

At the same time, the movement was a remarkable experiment in a different way of running a society. A "General Assembly" that included all participants made the decisions. OWS showed it was possible to make decisions, maintain a community, and influence the world around them without resorting to hierarchical structures. But there was a cost to that experiment. One OWS organizer, Jonathan Smucker, has written, "General Assemblies were not functional forums for actual decision making. Because they were so cumbersome and easily derailed, many of the most active OWS organizers, myself included, eventually stopped going to them."[179]

Occupy Wall Street will, I believe, echo through history as a pivot moment in the quest for a fair economy. But their experiment showed that — under certain circumstances — pure democracy can yield less participation. The decision-making structure succeeded in the short term and failed in the long term. In the end, all leaders — community organizers included — have to balance efficiency and participation.

Movements that consume themselves

Social movements have long reserved their bitterest vitriol for themselves. Fine-grained slices of ideology are often the source of the worst in-fighting. Monty Python mocked this phenomenon in their biblical film spoof, *The Life of Brian*. The leader of an anti-Roman activist group, the People's Front of Judea, explains, "Listen. The only people we hate more than the Romans are the fucking Judean People's Front."

Some degree of internal debate is, of course, necessary and healthy. But it a shocking historical fact that those devoted to changing the world seem to channel enormous energy into infighting instead of the work itself.

I see two ways to adjust our mindsets to escape this puzzle.

First, recognize that a variety of different perspectives can make a coalition or organization stronger. This is an instrumental view, not an ethical one; it simply more strategic to have a range of perspectives allied together.

Second, there will be times when we can't accommodate every point of view, but we need to acknowledge the human-ity of those with whom we disagree.

The way we engage with others should reflect the world we want to build.

Loretta J. Ross suggests an approach that is relevant for intra-movement conflict: when someone does something hurtful, "call in" rather than "call out."[180] Ross argues that it is more effective to start by creating space for private conversations that explain how an action might have caused harm instead of defaulting to public attacks on character. This same idea can be applied when trying to shift the behavior of a strategic target. If you don't like what someone is doing, try to tell them in private before attacking them in public

More generally, this narcissism of small differences can consume movements. It distracts attention and causes great pain to those trying to build a better world.[181] We can do better than trashing, cancellation, and struggle sessions. Instead, we can build an ethic of social movement accountability that is rooted in learning, forgiveness, and diversity.

Political power and cultural respect

In this third decade of the 21st century, it is unclear how political power will rise out of the next generation of social movements. Recent movements like Black Lives Matter have transformed discourse but (thus far) made only a modest impact on policy. Transformed discourse is a beginning, not an end.

We simply do not know what changes await. Grassroots uprisings against authoritarianism around the world have seen immense scale and meaningful impact. They have transformed government behavior and, in some cases, toppled dictators. But in others, their victories have been fleeting. We should be under no illusions that entrenched power will easily yield.

And in an era of political polarization, organizing has also become entangled in cultural politics. It is now difficult to distinguish issue organizing from labor organizing from electoral organizing. This blur quickly breeds cynicism, as false stories of "crisis actors" and "paid protestors" deny the authenticity of the challenges we face and the efforts to address them.

So, what to do? Lasting change happens when a collective can demonstrate enough power to knock the old world off its axis. We can gather that power over time. I'll suggest three ways.

First, organizing at a local level or within specific communities can create a stable political and communal foundation. It enables concrete changes (small as they may be) that changemakers like us can build on. Local work wins victories, builds power, and creates a kind of cultural momentum that can sustain itself over time.

Second, encouraging new narratives can transform conversations and plant the seeds of change. The narrative victories of Occupy Wall Street and Black Lives Matter have only begun to play out. We've seen a new generation of extraordinary leaders like Greta Thunberg, Vanessa Nakate, and Malala Yousafzai. Indeed, there are millions of new characters in our shared story. Every day, at street protests and in basement meetings, people discover a new spark of identity and of purpose. And on the pathways ahead, they'll create new ways to organize the human experience.

Third, we can ensure that our organizing is rooted in the best of humanity. We transform ourselves best when living with hope, sensing the possibility of a better world, demonstrating the highest states of moral character, and manifesting connection between daily lives and broader systems. Whether for a vast social movement or a small community project, these are the fires that power community organizing.

Community Organizing Takeaways

1. **Community organizing is the art of finding order in a group of people's common interests, angers, and hopes.** Other disciplines such as management, teaching, and electoral politics do the same. What separates community organizing is its focus on power.

2. **In the context of social change, power is the essential currency of decision-making.** Community organizing is intentional about engaging with power. It typically targets a decision maker and is clear about the desire to change that target's behavior. People working collectively are many times more powerful than individuals in forcing change.

3. **Power mapping is a fundamental tool that maps out those who influence a decision maker.** From this map you can articulate a strategy, determine how you will influence your target, and track your success.

4. **Two approaches to grassroots organizing are advocacy organizing and community-led organizing.** Advocacy organizing starts with a particular issue and builds the local, national, or global community of people and organizations who care about it. Community-led organizing starts with an existing community and creates a process to elicit the issues that the community cares about.

5. **Recruitment is an essential dimension, but how you recruit depends on your approach.** Community-led organizing relies intensely on listening so you can identify the right goals and keep communities motivated. In advocacy organizing, you have to find people, attend to their emotional state, and convince them to join you.

6. **Volunteers are the force multipliers for most community organizing campaigns.** Community organizing is a kind of multiplication, an attempt to magnify the power of an individual through a network of others.

7. **Community organizers use a variety of approaches to collect and focus people power.** Among them are demonstrations, civil disobedience, canvassing, art, and grasstops organizing.

8. **Technology can magnify people power, but it also can also weaken relationships.** Many modern movements are knit together by social media, but this approach runs the danger of creating shallow relationships that do not translate into lasting power.

9. **The way an organizer structures decision-making can make or break a campaign or an organization.** Good decisions yield more impact, and fast decisions yield more dynamism. But decision-making in a political context is inherently trickier; you are trying — authentically, one hopes — to empower others, to model a better society in the way everyone works together to create one.

0. **Lasting change happens when a collective can demonstrate enough power to knock the old world off its axis. We can gather that power over time.** Three pillars of lasting change: Organize at a local level or within specific communities to build a stable foundation from concrete changes, even small ones.
Encourage new narratives. They can transform conversations and plant the seeds of change.
Ensure that our organizing is rooted in the best of humanity.

Suggested reading

Saul Alinsky
Rules for Radicals

Jonathan Smucker
Hegemony How-to

Paulo Friere
Pedagogy of the Oppressed

Charles Payne
I've Got the Light of Freedom

Rebecca Solnit
Hope in the Dark

Game Theory

"Follow the Leaders" art installation popularly
known as "Politicians Discussing Global Warming"
by Isaac Cordal. Montreal, Canada, 2015.

Win-win

We will not win alone. Much of this book has been about the building blocks of collaboration, such as transparency, kindness, logic, humility, adaptability, trust, and clear communication. Collaboration is a necessary ingredient of social change.

Accordingly, we should be sobered by the fact that human history is littered with failed collaboration and unnecessary conflict.

During the Cold War, the U.S. military hired mathematicians to parse the tragic logic of the nuclear standoff. Thinkers like John Von Neumann built the new discipline of game theory to precisely illuminate the terrible decisions facing political leaders. Game theory was used to explain market behavior and political conflict.

Over time, the discipline grew and evolved. Elinor Ostrom won a Nobel Prize in economics for showing how people can, in fact, work together to find creative solutions for common resources that they'd otherwise deplete if they only pursued their own selfish interests.[182]

Social change agents like us can similarly benefit from game theory to explain — and potentially avoid — shortsighted and selfish behavior that limits our individual and collective success.[183]

193   Game Theory

This chapter starts with three of the basic dilemmas of game theory. Then we'll look at five ways to transcend these dilemmas. We'll find lessons from nature, agriculture, and ice cream. Throughout, we'll explore how these tools can help us chart a path to the social good the right way, the only way — together.

Three dilemmas

We'll start with the most famous problem in game theory, the "prisoner's dilemma." Imagine two suspects held in separate cells. The prosecutor asks each to declare the other guilty. They can't communicate with each other.

- If neither declares the other guilty (the two prisoners "cooperate"), each faces a light sentence — 30 days.
- If both say the other one is guilty (the two prisoners "defect"), each faces a serious sentence — 3 years.
- If one defects and the other does not, the defector is rewarded with freedom. The other gets the heaviest sentence — 10 years.

When we consider the two prisoners as a pair, their best choice is clear: each should keep quiet and take the light sentence. But individuals acting in isolation feel the incentive to defect. No matter what the first prisoner believes the second will do, they may perceive that they will get a better deal through declaring the other guilty. That clouded perception favors an outcome that is actually against their best interest.

While the prisoner's dilemma is the most famous of the models of game theory, it is not the only one. There are two other models worth noting here — "chicken" and the "stag hunt" — which offer further insight into the snares that prevent collaboration. Below I've laid out all three models as an interaction between two players, Antonio and Beatriz.

"All I have to do is divine from what I know of you: are you the sort of man who would put the poison into his own goblet or his enemy's?"

Vizzini, *The Princess Bride*

Prisoner's Dilemma

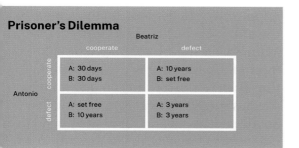

Beatriz

	cooperate	defect
cooperate	A: 30 days B: 30 days	A: 10 years B: set free
defect	A: set free B: 10 years	A: 3 years B: 3 years

Antonio

Chicken

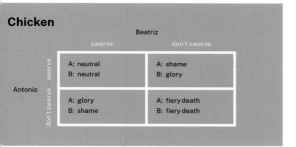

Beatriz

	swerve	don't swerve
swerve	A: neutral B: neutral	A: shame B: glory
don't swerve	A: glory B: shame	A: fiery death B: fiery death

Antonio

Stag Hunt

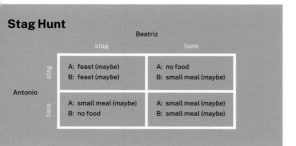

Beatriz

	stag	hare
stag	A: feast (*maybe*) B: feast (*maybe*)	A: no food B: small meal (*maybe*)
hare	A: small meal (*maybe*) B: no food	A: small meal (*maybe*) B: small meal (*maybe*)

Antonio

The next model is the game of chicken. Chicken is like an abstract version of *The Fast and the Furious* action film franchise. Imagine two drivers barreling directly towards each other. The first to swerve is scorned as a cowardly "chicken," and the other hailed as having nerves of steel. Of course, bravery has its drawbacks; if neither driver swerves, they're both dead. Chicken is, of course, an absurd game. But, as we'll soon see, it captures very real human behavior.

A third model is the stag hunt. The stag hunt is a game of probabilities. Two hunters are out in the same woods with an opportunity to collaborate. Each can choose to hunt either a stag or a hare. Hares are easier to snare, but they are small game. Stags are more difficult; they require the attention of both hunters. Even working together, the hunters have no guarantee of success; the probabilities are simply higher. Any two collaborators — people or organizations — will face a version of the stag hunt. How will each divide their precious attention? Both Jean-Jacques Rousseau and David Hume used the stag hunt to describe the dynamics of the social contract.

Collective tragedy
from individual dilemmas

Life, of course, is not a game. But all-too-real tragedy emerges from the dynamics captured in these models.

Why has humanity filled the sky with greenhouse gases? Because climate change is a global prisoner's dilemma. Nations, companies, and individuals don't trust that others will act for the collective good. So they — we — defect from a common purpose. And we all bear the sentence handed down by the sky. This is the "tragedy of the commons" — a collective manifestation of the prisoner's dilemma.

Much of the history of human warfare is a history of leaders playing chicken with nations. This game reached a kind of rational absurdity in the Cold War with the concept of mutual assured destruction — aptly known by its acronym, "MAD." Retaliatory murders among warring drug cartels have a tragic rationality when viewed in isolation. All too often, societal violence is a collective consequence of the game of chicken, where pride eclipses self-interest.

Societies fragment into lonely and undernourished souls because so many people choose to focus on the hare, not the stag. It is not an epic betrayal that leads to jail time, like the prisoner's dilemma. Instead, it is the lost opportunity for deeper engagement. It is the microwaved dinner at home when you could pool skills and resources to make a meaningful meal with your family, friends or neighbors. Individuals lack the necessary faith — perhaps the rationality — to invest with others in something bigger. Instead of choosing community, they choose isolation.

These tragic outcomes can be demonstrated mathematically and seem inevitable when looked at through cold, rational calculus. And yet the world is in fact full of collaboration. Every partnership is evidence of the ability of humans to work together, every exchange is evidence of the possibility of trust, and every compromise is proof that we are not, in fact, chickens.

It turns out that game theory models provide us with clues for how to escape their traps. But before we explore them, let's discuss what happens when we — knowingly or not — settle into a pattern.

Equilibrium

So much of social change is about trying to break out of a situation that seems stuck. It is worth pausing to ask: how do situations settle? What really is an equilibrium?

Let's look at a simple but revealing example. Imagine a long beach with people happily spread across it, soaking in the sun and ocean breeze. There are two ice cream vendors on the beach. Each is proud of their ice cream and wants to serve it to as many people as possible. Where do they set up? One at either end or both in the middle? Something else?

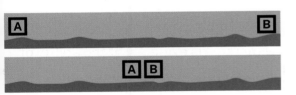

It turns out that — assuming they're trying to maximize their share of the territory — both will end up in the middle. If they start on opposite ends, either could move towards the middle and, therefore, take over more than half of the "territory." (This territory is nothing formal, simply the area from which it is fastest to walk to a given ice cream stand.)

This is an equilibrium. Once the vendors have both set up shop in middle of the beach, they'll stay there. And hopefully they'll become friends and maybe even trade hints so they each become more successful. But we also can't deny this arrangement is worse for the beach-goers at the far ends of the beach.

The mathematician John Nash, famously portrayed in the film *A Beautiful Mind*, formalized a way to think about this type of situation, later called the "Nash equilibrium." When a group of players interacts over time, they are prone to settle into specific behaviors. These behaviors reach an equilibrium when no individual wants to unilaterally change, given their knowledge of how everyone else behaves. That equilibrium may or may not be optimal for the group as a whole.

These balanced equilibriums, optimal or not, are by nature "sticky" but not permanent. What if a third vendor arrives on our ice-cream–laden beach? All game-theoretical hell breaks loose. The third vendor can join the first two in a cluster in the center — but then anyone could nudge just a bit to either side and capture half the market. They could spread out, but they'd face constant incentive to move. There is no equilibrium. The situation is unsettled and ripe for something new.

This is a trivial example of ice cream vendors. But in the real world — especially in unsettled times — there is an opportunity to break loose and find something better.

In the Age of Flux chapter, we considered the notion of a "plastic hour," the realization that today's complex, rapidly changing world may offer an opportunity for agents of change. The equilibriums of the moment seem ripe for transformation.

Transcending the dilemmas

Each of the models above is what we might call a "toy model" — an intentional oversimplification. It does not capture every nuance of a real situation. It isn't meant to. Instead, these models focus our attention on the most important aspects of each actor's choice.

So while we can't confuse the models with reality, we can recognize the power of play. Thinking through games allows us to experiment, to explore, and to find joy in the search for better outcomes.

Scholars and practitioners have spent countless years looking for opportunity in these games. Below, we look at five lessons that games have taught us about how to achieve better outcomes together. In each case, it turns out that the solution to successful collaboration can be found by understanding the limitations of the model itself:

1. **Information**: Information can help to remedy the pathologies of these dilemmas.
2. **Repetition**: Our interactions usually are not isolated instances but links in a chain; over time we can build trust.
3. **Institutions**: We can build structures to help facilitate shared purpose.
4. **Virtue**: Kindness and generosity can transcend the temptation to defect.
5. **Abundance**: Seeing sacrifice and gain through an abundance mindset brings more options to the table.

Information

Sometimes, lack of access to information is a feature of a situation. It's true that prosecutors will offer one suspect a deal without the other suspect knowing of it. But when facing decisions, we usually have access to more information than the characters in these simplified games: we share a lawyer with the other prisoner, we know the proclivities of the other driver, or we had breakfast with the other hunter.

The good news is that changemakers are rarely working in isolation. We are not making decisions in complete ignorance of others. In the modern world, we have immense access to information. A web search can help us get the information we need. We also have access to each other; we can have a conversation.

Sometimes getting the right information requires structural changes. Making information visible, and therefore valuable, requires transparency — the willingness (or legal requirement) to openly share details about your work with the rest of society. Public capital markets rely on information. That is why Michael Bloomberg is a billionaire; he created a media empire by carefully tailoring financial information for his customers' needs.

The open flow of information makes a market more fair. Insider trading is illegal because it relies on insider information and thus betrays the supposed logic of the overall market. Even free samples at a farmers' market provide transparency; customers get an idea of the quality of the food they're buying.

Information flow enables collaboration and alignment among social change organizations. The United Nations' 17 Sustainable Development Goals (SDGs) are an attempt to align our global efforts and track our collective progress.[184] The SDGs have become a common anchor across corporate, government, and philanthropic efforts, highlighting shared purpose and enabling shared measurement.

Transparency is a key weapon in the battle against corruption. Too often, public funding meant to provide relief to society is siphoned off by those corrupt few who control the money. Research shows that publishing data — especially about financial flows — curtails corruption. Data might be shared online, in the media, or even on a big poster in the middle of the village square.

Such strategies do not prevent small-time graft or every misdirection of funds. But transparent financial information creates a basic shared understanding of where the resources are and limits the ability of nefarious actors to take advantage of their community. And it gives the effective power of accountability to people who crave it.[185]

My own work has been built upon my deep conviction that transparency of information holds transformative power in the work of social good. GuideStar's founding purpose was to provide information to donors to help them make good decisions. I joined the organization out of the belief that, collectively, civil society would be stronger if information flowed easily throughout the nonprofit sector. Not only would donors make better decisions, but nonprofits could better learn from each other, and the rest of society could better understand the purpose, value, and operations of nonprofit organizations.

A colleague organization, Foundation Center was started in 1956 in response to (false) accusations that foundations were funding communist infiltration. The solution was radical transparency: opening a library in New York City where

> "Interdependence is iterative."
>
> adrienne maree brown

foundations freely shared information about the grants they were making. Over time, nonprofits began using that information to find out who might give them funding and who else was working on the same issues. And funders could use the information to discover others who shared their passion.

These two organizations were opposite sides of the same coin. So we got married. The merger of GuideStar and Foundation Center in 2019 to form Candid was a double victory against the prisoner's dilemma. First, the two parent organizations had to overcome their own narrow interests to execute the merger itself. Second, the combined entity was better positioned to help donors and nonprofits collaborate. The information infrastructure was finally aligned with common purpose.

Repetition

In the simple versions of the prisoner's dilemma, stag hunt, and chicken models there is a single interaction. The reality is that human society is built upon repeated interactions. Over and over, we find ourselves confronted with the same people. Our reputation with those individuals matters.

The best way to gain trust is to show trust. Those who put their trust in others typically earn it back many times. Conversely, just as a reputation for trustworthiness and for trusting is valuable, a reputation for being a sucker is not.

Accordingly, repeated games require balancing the power of trust with the need for accountability. As a changemaker, you must be willing to stand up for yourself.

The simplification of these games lends itself to computer modeling and rigorous experiment. Over the decades, researchers have explored countless strategies in repeated prisoner's dilemma games.[186] And, after billions of experimental iterations, the evidence is clear: there's one strategy that works best. That strategy is known as "tit-for-tat."

One can think of "tit-for-tat" as a strategy of (1) generosity, (2) accountability, and (3) forgiveness. You begin by cooperating (generosity) and stay there as long as your partner does the same. If you are betrayed — as we all are likely to be at some point — you switch to a "defect" strategy (accountability). Once — if — your partner cooperates again, you return to cooperation (forgiveness).[187]

In real life, we will not find ourselves in such a consistent, one-dimensional situation. But the underlying lesson is clear: kindness can be a good strategy — when it is tempered with accountability and clarity.

Institutions

The economist Elinor Ostrom has analyzed scale examples from around the world where people have collaborated to share limited resources and protect their future livelihoods. The secret of collective action, Ostrom says, is the time-consuming work of "getting institutions right." If all institutions are games with sequences of available options, information, rewards, and punishments, then successful institutions make people want to play. They clearly define who can play and give them a voice in shaping the rules together. Players pool knowledge, trust each other to keep their word, and monitor themselves to make sure they do.

Ostrom's book, *Governing the Commons: The Evolution of Institutions for Collective Action*, provides a number of examples of these concepts at work. Below are two that both involve mobilizing labor and resources for irrigation. The first one, in the Philippines, is a federation that formally incorporated in 1978 with antecedents dating to the 19th century. The second, in Sri Lanka, is a new institution that grew up to resolve long-standing water disputes in the territory.

Irrigation and Institutions

Farming requires water. Irrigation projects often do more than bring water; they create corruption and conflict. So, in farming communities around the world, agricultural thirst has demanded collective creativity. Let's look at two examples.

A small federation of tenant farmers on the northwest tip of the Philippine island of Luzon faced a puzzle: landowners granted them the use of land in exchange for maintaining their irrigation system. The federation and its member communities had to figure out how to pry thousands of hours of difficult labor from tenant farmers to maintain a dams made of bamboo, banana leaves, rocks, and sand.

The federation and member communities built in many institutional incentives to make farmers want to play their game. Members have shares with equal voting rights, and they elect their leadership. Their responsibilities are clearly defined. Water is distributed roughly in proportion to how much work and materials each community supplies. In extremely dry times, members take care to water the neediest parcels first and send people from downstream to make sure upstream farmers comply. They have a system for rule breakers but seldom need to use it. The result is almost full compliance, with each member averaging about 39 days of communal work per year.

Consider another example from 3000 miles away. In the 1970s, on the left bank of the Gal Oya irrigation project in southeast Sri Lanka, the irrigation system had fallen into nightmarish disrepair. At first, the government proposed stricter discipline and enforcement for the area's 19,000 farmers. But a small pilot project followed a trust-building approach. It trained organizers to help small groups of farmers identify maintenance problems and strategies to solve them. The farmers discovered they could successfully cooperate, and government officials discovered that the farmers, who they'd seen only as problems, were actually partners in rehabilitating the irrigation system.

With the seed of communal problem-solving firmly planted, the farmers grew a larger organization to handle bigger problems. By consensus, each group chose a representative to share their ideas and report back on the big-picture issues. They eventually developed four tiers of institutions to address the gamut of problems from clearing local field channels to developing policy. The change meant that by the 1980s, 300 families enjoyed two rice harvests each year, with 1,000 more acres under cultivation. Three quarters of the farmers saw no water conflicts. Perverse incentives had given way to mutual trust. ■

"By bein' kind to strangers
you run the risk
of them bein' kind to you."

Jeff Daniels

Virtue

Kindness, cooperation, sacrifice, and
vision are more than just pretty words on
a cross-stitch embroidery sampler. They
are genuine solutions for changemakers
who want to avoid or escape the trap of
unproductive games.

When I was in business school, my
professor shared the challenges of the
prisoner's dilemma and asked the class
to do a series of experiments to try it out
ourselves. I distinctly recall his bemused
frustration that we were not nearly so
greedy as he expected business students
to be. Or more precisely, we were not
rational in the way he had assumed.

For most of us, our inclination was to
cooperate. Our decision made sense in
the broader theoretical framework of
game theory. Students like me were in
the middle of a repeated game; this was
not the last time we would be interacting
with a given classmate. It was in our
rational interests to collaborate, not to
betray or defect. And, well, some people
are just nice.

I do not want to deny the brutality of
life and the fact that sometimes harsh
calculus is necessary. There is evil in the
world; though perhaps more relevantly,

there is fear that leads to selfishness on
the part of those with whom we interact.
We'd be fools to ignore that.

Game theory gives us permission to
default to virtue. The "tit-for-tat" strategy
is a kind of summary of virtue: start with
kindness, show discipline when presented
with bad behavior, and offer forgiveness
when others show their best selves.

Abundance

If I eat the last slice of mushroom pizza, you'll get none. If investors demand 75% of the equity in a new startup, there's only 25% left for the founders.

Cases like these are "zero-sum games." There is a single pool of spoils; benefit for one is loss for another.

But here's the good news: life tends to be multidimensional. I might actually want more salad and be happy to give you the last slice of pizza. The founders of a social enterprise might gladly yield ownership control if they can better achieve their mission by meeting the investors' equity demand. With a broader view, we turn a "zero-sum" situation into a generative "non-zero sum" moment.

The abundance mindset shows up in negotiations. One useful tool to keep in mind is your "BATNA" — "best alternative to negotiated agreement." Knowing your BATNA helps you if there is no agreement. That baseline can create a sense of confidence going into a negotiation.

When I led GuideStar in the merger negotiations that would eventually create Candid, I knew that we had a strong BATNA: no matter what happened, we could maintain our work with the confidence that we were creating sustainable impact. That baseline of confidence allowed space for creativity to find something even better for our people and our work.

There are times when one person's gain is in fact another's loss. As we discuss in the Ethics chapter, it's the right moral and strategic choice to be honest about those consequences. And, as discussed in the **Behavioral Economics** chapter, there are even cases where human irrationality leads to a "negative-sum game" where people sacrifice solely so that others suffer.

But as social change agents, we have an opportunity to expand the aperture of possibility beyond the zero-sum and negative-sum mindsets. At best, we can imagine and articulate broader options as we work with others to solve shared problems. Our interactions themselves can yield abundance.

"There are at least two kinds of games. One could be called finite; the other infinite. A finite game is played for the purpose of winning, an infinite game for the purpose of continuing the play."

"Infinite play resounds throughout with a kind of laughter. It is not laughter at others who have come to an unexpected end...it is laughter with others with whom we have discovered that the end we thought we were coming to has unexpectedly opened."

James P. Carse[188]

Game theory in the natural world

The natural world has a simple but powerful lesson for changemakers: life is more than the survival of the fittest. There is no doubt that brutal calculus exists in life. Predation is a zero-sum game. But evolution teaches us that there are reasons to seek solace in cooperation, in the sharing of information, and in the unpredictability of it all.

Charles Darwin argued that natural selection was a primary mechanism for the evolution of life, but he never claimed evolution was solely a question of "survival of the fittest." Over the past century, scientists have discovered that there are multiple mechanisms of evolution.

Most schoolchildren learn about the concept of symbiosis. A bee gathers nectar from a flower and in turn spreads the flower's pollen. A remora cleans off a shark's skin while benefiting from the defense provided by the mere presence of the great predator. Common lichen is not even its own species; it is the emergent property of interacting colonies of algae and fungi. As Merlin Sheldrake explains, "Lichens are a product less of their parts than of the exchanges between those parts. Lichens are stabilized networks of relationships; they never stop lichenizing; they are verbs as well as nouns."[189]

And symbiosis can be nested: 40 trillion microorganisms live in the average human body.[190] If we rely on the bacteria inside us to survive (and we do), can we really think of ourselves only as a single, independent entity? Organisms even become permanent parts of each other through a process known as endosymbiosis. Billions of years ago, bacteria captured within the walls of ancient cells evolved to become mitochondria and chloroplasts — the power stations of animal and plant cells, respectively.

With another mechanism, horizontal gene transfer, cells simply trade genetic information with each other like baseball cards. That capability is central to why viruses can adapt so quickly and how life has evolved.

Cooperation operates at the ecosystem level. Recent research by Suzanne Simard and others has helped reveal the extraordinary mutuality of the natural world with a focus on trees.[191] Trees may seem to be lone towers silently asserting their independence, but they are, in fact, woven into a mighty web with their neighbors. In some species, tress will signal to others — using pheromones — when a new parasite has arrived, giving their neighbors time to prepare defenses. In others, stronger trees will send extra nutrients to weaker ones in a kind of arboreal progressive taxation. This even can happen across tree species. Perhaps most remarkably, the sharing happens via networks of fungus that tie the trees' roots together.

Nature is full of self-sacrifice. Lewis Thomas, former president of Memorial Sloan-Kettering Institute, speaks of a species of coral, Gorgonaceae: "Even when circumstances require that there be winners and losers, the transaction is not necessarily a combat...when two individuals of the same species are in close contact, the smaller of the two will always begin to disintegrate...He is not thrown out, not outgamed, not outgunned; he simply chooses to bow out."[192]

In the **Design Thinking** chapter, we looked at how the discipline of "biomimicry" draws inspiration from biological design when building products for humans. Social change strategists have an opportunity for a deeper kind of biomimicry: emulating the explicit interdependence of the natural world. ◼

Game theory and social change organizations

You don't have to look far to see how we in the world of social change can get caught in the snares described by game theory. Social change organizations might dream of the benefits of cooperation, but they are usually oriented towards their own familiar funding streams, staffing models, programmatic strategies, and organizational cultures. It can be easy to let an existing equilibrium prevail over the prospect of a partnership.

Let's consider a hypothetical example. Imagine two complementary human services nonprofits. One offers mental health programs in local high schools, and the other provides services to homeless youth. Each receives $100,000 a year from the same local community foundation. Both nonprofits know the foundation seeks opportunity for greater impact through collaboration; in fact, it will provide $300,000 in total funding for a well-designed collaborative effort to provide wrap-around services.

The community foundation has presented a possibility in such a way that the best interests seem clear. But both nonprofits are nervous. If the collaboration does not work out, will the community foundation cut their core funding? Might one organization betray the other and tell the community foundation it could provide both types of services on its own for just $250,000?

To that worry and distrust, add uncertainty and short-term costs: Even if, for example, the executive directors of the two organizations want to collaborate, staff members may resist. They might say the partnership will force them to restructure the program, redo internal systems, abandon their unique culture, or — horrors! — admit the weakness of their organization.

These two nonprofits are missing a prime opportunity to better serve the young people they care about. Both nonprofit leaders, by understanding that they are in the grip of the dilemma, can transcend their natural reluctance and pursue their true best interests.

New conditions, like our interdependent, globalized world, require new ideas. Dividing people into 'us' and 'them' is out of date."

Tenzin Gyatso, the 14th Dalai Lama[193]

Enabling collaboration through communication

Collaboration can challenge social change leaders' sense of identity. We would be wise to respect how emotionally and intellectually difficult it can be for social change practitioners to acknowledge that they cannot succeed alone. So how might we transcend those barriers? Below, I'll suggest eight strategies to help enable collaboration. The first four are techniques of communication.

Define the community.

Collaborations are more likely within the boundaries of a shared identity. Sometimes that identity has to first be articulated. The first step is to identify what the groups have in common: "We are defenders of tropical rainforests" or "We serve people without housing in Miami." Overwhelming evidence suggests that a sense of community plays a central role in human decisions.[194] Collaboration requires a sense of commonality, and when that commonality is described, it becomes actionable.

Celebrate each other.

The short-term incentives for organizations are to take credit for wins and to seek as many resources as possible. But the long-term interests of common purpose require others winning, too. This dynamic becomes most acute around fundraising (whether for donations or investments), where there is often a perception that it is a zero-sum game. Some organizations transcend this, though. Movement Commons has built cohorts of nonprofit fundraisers that explicitly and systematically ask their donors to also donate to partner organizations. By doing so, they are creating an opportunity for funders to broaden their impact on an issue they care about.

Name your weakness.

Introductions at Alcoholics Anonymous (AA) meetings often begin with, "My name is X, and I am an alcoholic." This statement shows trust and humility on the part of the speaker. Similarly, social change organizations can open themselves to collaboration by acknowledging their limitations as independent actors. Naming the problem need not create a pessimistic atmosphere; indeed, the next phrase at an AA meeting is often something along the lines of, "... and I've been sober for five years." And its power extends to the listener, making them more likely to admit their own weaknesses. Then, explore opportunity upon a foundation of honesty and humility.

Show successful examples.

One powerful human tendency, as we discuss in the Behavioral Economics chapter, is to do what we see others doing. Organizations are far more likely to collaborate if they see relatable examples of other successful collaborations. This process can create a virtuous circle of sharing simple examples, building confidence, bringing in new data, and making larger steps possible.

Make explicit the implicit division of labor.

Over time, organizations tend to differentiate themselves. Consider nonprofit service providers in a medium-sized city. One organization takes the west side of a town, another the east; or one handles middle-school students, another high-school students. Once potential collaborators acknowledge those differences, they can capitalize on them. But for that differentiation to translate to collaboration, someone needs to say explicitly what implicit division of labor may have developed over time. Without that openness, participants may hesitate to speak clearly or act decisively, afraid to offend or stereotype. When the division of labor is discussed openly, conflicts or differing perceptions can be addressed directly.

For example, in 2003 I was tasked at Rainforest Action Network (RAN) with leading a campaign to pressure Ford Motor Company to accelerate the transition to clean vehicles.

The Sierra Club was involved in similar campaign and was seen by Ford as more moderate. The executives at Ford would talk to the Sierra Club but ignore us. As best we could tell, Ford saw us as too radical to even talk to. Then, a ew organization called Bluewater Network came into the campaign and engaged in even more aggressive tactics, posting a full-page ad in the *New York Times* with a picture of Bill Ford with Pinocchio's nose. Ford's attention immediately swung to us. We were able to engage with them because Bluewater had opened space that allowed us to no longer seem quite so radical.

Four Network Principles for Collaboration Success[195]
Jane Wei-Skillern and Norah Silver

- Principle 1:
  Strategy Is Determined by Mission Impact Before Organizational Growth
- Principle 2:
  Build Partnerships Based on Trust, Not Control
- Principle 3:
  Promote Others Rather Than Yourself
- Principle 4: Build Constellations, Not Stars

Enabling collaboration through structure

Organizational ecosystems have a structure. There could be one large organization or many small ones; they might all be for-profit businesses, all nonprofits, all government agencies, or a mixture. In a collaboration, some subset of those organizations works together for common purpose. The arrangement of that collaboration is critical.

Here, I offer some suggestions on how to optimize impact through structure.

Identify the guide.

Multilateral collaboration greatly benefits from a guide — a person or organization — to manage the process, provide encouragement, and help solidify a shared vision.[196] Without this structure, the short-term incentives of the individual participants will tend to prevail, and the collaboration will dissolve. Pure top-down management will not work; if nonprofit participants feel a foundation is forcing them to engage, the partnership will not be authentic. Ideally, participants can identify a facilitator who is aligned with the shared purpose but is

seen as neutral relative to the specific interests of individual participants. Like a guide leading a group of climbers up a mountain, this facilitator is both a participant and a leader. They bear costs and reap shared rewards.

Reassess the formal structure.

Collaboration does not necessarily require formal restructuring. You do not need to merge with your partners, have a formal legal contract, acquire your vendors, or even set up a formal network. But any of those alternatives might, under the right circumstances, be the right choice. In the Institutions chapter, we will examine broader questions of institutional structure. But at the very least, consideration of collaboration is also a moment to consider structural change.

...esign collective systems.

...ormalized systems for knowledge ...haring, governance, and external ...ommunications not only create value; ...ey also reinforce collective identity ...nd incentivize organizations to remain ... the group. This design makes it more ...kely that the collaboration will last long ...hough to achieve the desired change.

...e intentional about transparency ...discretion.

... general, collaboration is most effective ...hen it is forthright and transparent. ...hat builds trust on the part of those ...utside of the actual negotiations. With ...hat said, in politically fraught contexts, ...here can be exceptions. We may not want ... work together in smoke-filled rooms, ...ut sometimes collaboration behind the ...cenes can yield the best results. Secrecy ...an be appropriate at times — but should ...e an exception, not the rule.

Game theory highlights some of the consequences of human weakness. But it also offers us a pathway towards collaboration. Ultimately, the recipe is simply: generosity, accountability, and forgiveness.

1. **Figuring out how to align our work with others is so complex and important that it deserves its own science. That science is game theory.** The consequences of our actions are partly determined by other people's simultaneous decisions.

2. **The "prisoner's dilemma," the most famous game theory thought experiment, demonstrates how people choose betrayal even though mutual trust is in their best shared interest.** A decision that seems narrowly rational is often the product of greed or fear.

3. **Even when changemakers dream about cooperation, we can act against our best interests.** Our own cozily familiar funding streams, staffing models, programmatic strategies, and organizational cultures often favor stability over the prospect of partnership. Game theory teaches us how to overcome those traps.

4. **The natural world has a simple but powerful lesson for changemakers: life is more than a game of the survival of the fittest.** Mutual support is a successful strategy for adaptation and change in a complex and fast-changing world.

5. **With just one pool of spoils, one person's gain is another's loss. But life is more complex: in almost every situation, there are many dimensions to consider.** Social change agents can develop an abundance mindset that imagines broader options to solve shared problems.

6. **We find ourselves continually confronted with the same people. Generosity is a good strategy for these repeated interactions.** The highly successful "tit-for-tat" strategy begins from a stance of generosity and stays there as long as one's partner cooperates. But as soon as you are betrayed, you respond in kind and then wait until your partner cooperates again. Then, in perpetuity if possible, you continue to be generous.

Information flow is another way to avoid the traps of game theory dilemmas. Changemakers like us rarely work in isolation. We have access to information and to each other. Information isn't always enough; mechanisms to make information both useful and visible create accountability and structure for conversation.

The secret of collective action, according to Elinor Ostrom, is the time-consuming work of "getting institutions right." If all institutions are games with sequences of available options, information, rewards, and punishments, then successful institutions make people want to play. Well-structured collaborations maximize impact and are more likely to last long enough to achieve the desired change.

9. **The right attitude opens space for collaboration. It is emotionally and intellectually difficult for social change practitioners to acknowledge that they cannot succeed alone.** Among the techniques to surmount these sentiments: describing your common ground, speaking honestly about your weaknesses, and sharing successful examples of similar collaborations.

10. **Kindness, cooperation, sacrifice, and vision are genuine solutions for changemakers who want to avoid the traps of unproductive games.** Game theory shows that in long-term relationships, cooperation is, quite simply, a good strategy.

Markets

Man Controlling Trade," a statue outside of the headquarters of the Federal Trade Commission in Washington, DC
Photo by Tom Shearer

The visible hand

Markets organize much of human exchange. There are those who proclaim that markets are the engine of prosperity, a magical machine of exchange and growth. Other counter that markets are an amoral fount of inequality and environmental destruction.

The evidence would suggest that both are correct. Over the past century, billions of people have emerged from extreme poverty thanks — in large part — to the market. Over the same period, we have devastated our biosphere thanks — in large part — to the market.

Like it or not, we exist within markets. We have to understand them if we wish to be effective in building a better world. And, of course, money is essential for our organizations, whether for-profit, nonprofit, or government — as GuideStar founder Buzz Schmidt put it, "Financial capital is the universally necessary ingredient for the care and feeding of all enterprises."[197]

In this chapter, we will look at how market mechanisms can be tuned for good and how social change agents can tap into that power. And, importantly, we'll explore how markets can fail us and how much of the work of social change is cleaning up the messes left behind by the wild horses of the market.

First, a story about power, money, and trees.

In the 1990s, Rainforest Action Network (RAN) sought to understand the underlying forces that led to deforestation. What could they do to drive sustainable forestry practices? Logging companies seemed impervious to protest; they appeared ready to ignore or outlast the activists. To oversimplify, they were not susceptible to public pressure because they didn't have retail customers. A power mapping exercise revealed two potential leverage points: corporate customers and financiers.

The logging companies might have been able to ignore protestors, but a retail outlet like Home Depot could not. Over time, targeted public pressure on logging company corporate customers translated into influence on the logging companies themselves.

Similarly, deforestation was fueled by investments from major banks. After years of campaigning, banks like Goldman Sachs and Citigroup made major changes in their lending policies.

It was one step among many to tilt the capital markets towards sustainability. Upon securing commitments, RAN immediately shifted from "pressure" mode to "praise" mode, going out of its way to celebrate the steps made by these banks.

Timber companies can no longer ignore sustainability; external pressure has, fundamentally restructured the logging business. This has been a key input to a broader reassessment in how financial flows impact forest health. According to corporate disclosure platform CDP, investors with assets totaling more than $100 trillion are now integrating information about forestry practices into their analyses.[198]

A market's-eye–view can offer strategic insight for campaigners, and their success can offer a new narrative frame for telling the story of how to build a better world. Over decades, environmental campaigners took a destructive market system and used its mechanisms to tilt it towards a sustainable future.

Economist Milton Friedman said that the social responsibility of business is to make a profit. The company's profits can, if the owners so choose, be reinvested

"...ike money, limited liability corporations, and human rights, nations and consumer tribes are intersubjective realities. They exist only in our collective imagination, yet their power is immense."

Yuval Noah Hariri[199]

...society as charitable activity. There is something to be said for this concept, and that something is that it's wrong.

At its heart, Friedman's argument assumes there are two forms of activity: pure capitalism and pure philanthropy. The reality is far more complex. The broader marketplace is composed of a variety of sub-markets composed of countless players. Some create value, others destroy it. Some build dignity, others sow injustice. Some return to the Earth as much as they take, others steal from the accounts of the future. Most players have both devil and angel inside them.

Society has responded to this complexity with a thrilling multiplicity of goals, strategies, and business models. Countless innovators have created models that blend markets and morality. I believe that this hybrid view represents a maturation of the human species. It is a sign that we not only recognize the need to attend to the market, but we can, in fact, guide it.

No doubt, we have a lot of work ahead. Markets remain only partly oriented towards the common good. Below we will explore eight aspects of markets and

how social change agents can turn them towards impact. We'll start by looking at three aspects that primarily operate at the organizational level: business models, net impact, and finance. Then we'll explore broader marketplace dynamics: pricing, information, market infrastructure, division of labor, and value over time.

The "Fearless Girl" statue was installed in front of the famous Wall Street bull on March 7, 2017. She radiates courage in the face of the raw power of the market. In a notable irony, the statue was sponsored by financial giant State Street Global Advisors.
Photo by Richard Zinken

Business models

Every organization has a business model. It may or may not be intentional (or even conscious), but the pattern of money coming in and out of the organization is a business model. It is the inteface between the organization and the market.

Consider Milton Friedman's isolated poles of pure profit and pure charity. These two points can be connected to form a line, a continuum representing the economics of social change. On to this line we can map a wide variety of both marketplaces and business models.

For example, think about the "market" for watching ballet performance. Patrons are willing to pay for tickets to see the ballet; but they aren't generally willing to pay enough to cover the full costs of putting on a ballet. Aggregate ticket sales might cover, say, cover 40% of the organization's budget. Ballet organizatio business models reflect this reality and rely on donations to round out their business model.

Other organizations find themselves at different places on the continuum. A health clinic may find that Medicaid payments cover 95% of costs; an additiona sliver of donations is necessary to round out the business model. A homebuilder committed to working in poor communities may make a modest profit. A venture capital firm may make a fortune investin, in renewable energy companies.

The truth is that that most social issues — and thus, most social organizations — are right in the muddy middle. Much of the hard work of social change is managing business models that can operate in that messy space in between pure donations and pure profits.[201]

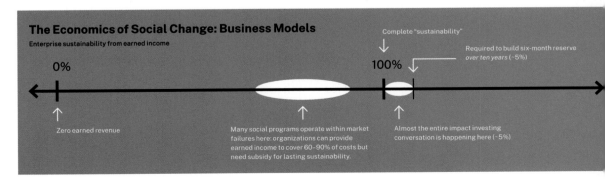

The Economics of Social Change: Business Models

Enterprise sustainability from earned income

Complete "sustainability"

Required to build six-month reserve over ten years (~5%)

0%

100%

Zero earned revenue

Many social programs operate within market failures here: organizations can provide earned income to cover 60–90% of costs but need subsidy for lasting sustainability.

Almost the entire impact investing conversation is happening here (~5%)

Luckily, even messy business models come down to basic arithmetic: revenue minus costs. Let's consider aspects of each.

Revenue mix

Mission-based organizations face a fundamental tension over the best revenue strategy: focus or diversity? Evidence from both the business world and the nonprofit sector would suggest that organizations that are able to grow rapidly do so because of the power of one dominant revenue line.

The tension is this: revenue diversification, when it can be created, is a powerful hedge against uncertainty. If one revenue line collapses, others can maintain the baseline revenue. Grantmakers often push for revenue diversification in nonprofit business models. Yet true revenue diversification is rare — and, indeed, attention might be better focused on strengthening the core of a business model. Ultimately, despite its proliferation of products and services, Google is an ad company. The Sierra Club may offer guided trips into the mountains and sell beautiful calendars, but its business model relies on the generosity of its donors.[202]

Cost structure:

The costs associated with a given strategy may scale in different ways. Labor-intensive interventions like regular one-on-one counseling can be extremely effective, but each new client brings additional costs.

Contrasts that model with automated online education, where the primary costs are upfront in the creation of educational materials. The "marginal cost" — that is, the cost to serve each additional beneficiary — is close to zero.

Business models can reflect the tensions between quality and quantity discussed in the **Mathematical Modeling** chapter. Effective interventions with low marginal cost are rare but they tend to be much easier to take to scale. However, there are cases where high marginal cost interventions are the only ones that work. Sometimes, creating impact is expensive.

Revenue, cost, and the business model continuum represent key dimensions of the organizational economics of social change. The coming sections on Net Impact and Finance represent others.

Net impact

The F.B. Heron Foundation has long aspired to something simple yet radical: they wish to understand the *total* impact of their activities. Historically, most foundations have focused their attention on the impact of their grantmaking. Heron has sought to also systematically consider the impact of *all* of its investments and *all* of its operations.

The team at Heron came up with a framework they described as "net contribution." In this framework, every enterpise can be seen as creating impact across four dimensions: human capital, natural capital, civic capital, and financial capital. Impact on a given dimension may be positive, negative, or both. The Foundation's net contribution reflected the sum of the contributions of its grants, investments, and contracts.

This type of exercise is not easy: it takes time, thought, and a lot of data collection. But it can offer profound insights. For example, the staff at Heron noticed that a real estate trust in their investment portfolio was providing thousands of jobs. That data point led them to explore more deeply. They discovered that this real estate trust was, in fact, the Corrections Corporation of America (CCA) — one of the largest operators of private prisons. The employment numbers were accurate but obscured a much bleaker truth.

Heron's consideration of net contribution led them to disinvest from CCA and p their capital to higher use. The foundatior explained, "Based on those risks, both soci and financial, Heron decided to divest fro CCA and began organically thinking abou the overall impact of enterprises rather than just their jobs. Being focused too narrowly on the number of jobs provided would have led us to miss the larger impac of these enterprises on the people and co munities about whom we care…our goal i: to continuously improve the data informir our investment choices, so that Heron wil be better positioned to optimize the portf lio for social and financial performance.":

Heron is not alone in this kind of thinking. Related frameworks like "blend value" or "multiple bottom lines" similarly bring together multiple aspects of enter- prise performance.

But the systems for supporting those organizations are all too often misalignec with the sheer variety of business model: markets, and market failures. To take the ideas behind net contribution to societal scale, we need to think about *information* in a new way.

Information

Markets thrive on information. Buyers and sellers (generally) want to make informed decisions. Countless platforms — from Consumer Reports to Bloomberg to GiveWell — have emerged to provide information to inform decisions.

Consumers can use certification schemes for chocolate, clothing, household appliances, and countless other goods. Investors large and small have access to immense amounts of data about the environmental, social, and governance performance of individual companies. Donors have access to detailed information about nonprofits and their programs. (You will not be surprised that I am partial to Candid's Seals of Transparency.)

The availability of this information is made possible by entire ecosystems of organizations that prepare, collect, organize, and distribute it. Government documents often provide a standardized baseline, such as nonprofits' Forms 990 and public companies' 10-Ks in the U.S. Historically, such forms have tended to focus primarily on financial information.

That baseline information requires work — often a lot of work — to ensure that it is put in appropriate social and environmental context. There are many efforts to improve the ecosystem of information — from standards to taxonomies to unique IDs to goal frameworks — so that it can be compared and crunched in meaningful ways. In the chart on the next page, you can see some examples of where that hard work happens.

type of information	example	hosting organization
standards	Sustainable Accounting Standards Board	Value Reporting Foundation
taxonomies	Philanthropy Classification System	Candid
unique identifiers	Legal Entity Identifier	Global LEI Foundation
goals	Sustainable Development Goals	United Nations
protocols	Nutrition labels	U.S. Food and Drug Administration
certifications	FSC Recycled (wood products)	Forest Stewardship Council

The integration of this kind of information into global marketplaces makes it easier to include social and environmental considerations in consumer, business, and government decisions. It increases pressure on specific entities to reform their practices. It highlights the interconnection across systems, geographies, and markets. And, importantly, it sets the stage for learning across people, organizations, and geographies. But the challenges are legion. It can be a lifetime of work to oragnize information about one single aspect of human activity. The information envioronment for social change decision-making is rapidly getting better, but it will never be perfect.

swath not thine heart in thine horde, for thou art become a steward of the endowment of God."

Instructions of Ptah-Hotep, c. 2350 BCE[205]

Finance

Finance sits at the intersection of time and risk. What is investment but money spent now with the hope of a future return? What is a loan but a way of putting a number on trust?

This can go terribly wrong. The financial crisis of 2007 and 2008 was a case of risk shifted from private investors to the public as a whole. The industry of fossil fuel finance is a shift across time of financial burden from present generations to future ones.

But the tools of finance can be put to a higher purpose. A multi-year grant is an expression of trust over time. An investment in a new cleantech startup is not just a bet on a company, it's a bet on behalf of the common good.

Social finance — broadly defined — is now a multi-trillion-dollar industry. Environmental, social, and governance considerations have been integrated across finance. We see as investors providing equity finance for social enterprises, foundations reimagining how to support nonprofit financial health, and government agencies orienting their funding around results through social impact bonds.

The term "financial engineering" is often used with disdain. But smart finance can be engineering in the best sense of the word: an attempt to solve a problem. Social finance in fact offers an opportunity for creativity. I will briefly highlight six lessons on the financing of social good.

First, acknowledge the "messy middle" of social change business models. Many social organizations will require a mix of different types of financing to match up with the specific structure of their market.

Second, orient finance towards impact. This may seem obvious, but too often financial structures reflect a capital provider's past internal processes, not the actual needs of the recipient. Unleash creativity on a problem, not a process.

Third, remember that financial relationships tend to reflect power dynamics (as also discussed in the **Ethics** chapter). For example, the process of applying for for foundation grants is rife with bureaucracy that reflects power imbalances. Accordingly, nonprofits are forced to think about the "net grant," or the financial value of a grant minus the the costs of staff time to apply for and manage it. There are, alas, grants with a negative net value.

Fourth, where possible, stretch time horizons. Social impact almost always takes longer than expected. The best financing arrangements are aligned with the time horizon of the issue or solution.

Fifth, balance operational considerations with financial ones. Some early social impact bonds had a brilliant theoretical structure but were simply too operationally complex to implement.

Sixth, remember that outcomes require enterprises. Financing structured solely around the per-unit cost of delivering a given outcome can work in isolation — but it assumes others have invested in the enterprise itself.

The world of social finance is vast and growing, offering a critical tool for mediating across the complexity of different markets, different business models, and different social issues. All of us working for a better world have to wrestle with risk and time. Finance is doing it on purpose.[206]

Acronyms bringing good to the marketplace

SRI: Socially Responsible Investing
Public-market Investments filtered to either avoid destructive companies ("negative screen") or focus capital to productive ones ("positive screen").

CSR: Corporate Social Responsibility
Conscious efforts to ensure companies minimize negative effects and — at best — maximize positive ones.

ESG: Environmental/Social/ Governance
The three main categories of considerations when analyzing the non-financial impact of a company or security.

SIB: Social Impact Bonds
Financial security that pays a return dependent on the results of social programs paid for by the bond.

PRI: Program-Related Investments
Socially oriented investments made by U.S.-based foundations (typically debt, sometimes equity) that count towards a foundation's legally required annual payout.

> "No market can exist for long without underlying public institutions to support it."
>
> Elinor Ostrom[207]

Pricing

Markets are a dance of prices. Prices convey information and, at times, are an expression of power. Let's consider some elements of pricing that bear on the work of social change.

Many people, rightly or not, value things that they have spent money on. That's why it can be strategic to charge for a product or service that exists for fundamentally pro-social reasons. Consider efforts to provide water pumps to farmers in the Global South. Studies have showed that those who pay for their pump are more likely to invest in ongoing maintenance than those who got a pump for free.

There are other cases, however, where the greatest impact comes from offering something for free. Imagine if Wikipedia charged one penny to view each entry. Despite the incredibly low price, the friction created in that transaction would undoubtedly cause usage to plummet. Sometimes, free is the only price that will work.

Social change actors can consider variation in willingness and ability to pay. Outright price discrimination where you charge one group more than another is rightly illegal. But there are ways to capture more value with differential pricing: coupons, periodic discounts, service tiers, and more. If well structured, differential pricing can advance both financial and impact goals.

There can be significant equity implications of differential pricing. It can drive equity (high tuition for wealthy students paired with full need-based scholarships) or inequity (medical debt collection procedures).[208]

Price does not equal impact. In the section below on market failures, we'll discuss externalities: cases where a price may under-or over-estimate the total value created by a given transaction. Sometimes, optimal social good can be created when products become more expensive (consider taxes on cigarettes); other times a subsidy can help to support nonfinancial outcomes (consider incentives to install solar panels).

Market infrastructure

Changing the behavior of a market as a whole is sometimes possible. Successful shifts in market behavior are often sticky — that is, they create a new equilibrium.

Consider, for example, efforts to transform the market for coffee to better reflect broader considerations such as the labor of those who grow it. This "fair-trade" coffee market has indeed transformed over the past few decades, reaching billions of dollars and millions of farmers. To get there, though, required interventions across the marketplace. Each of three elements had to be recalibrated over time to build the flywheel that turns today. The three elements are supply, demand, and what I have called "architecture."

In the case of fair-trade coffee, the *supply* is simply the availability of beans that have been grown in a way that respects the dignity of the laborers.

The *demand* is the portion of the marketplace that wishes to spend additional money to ensure the fairness of the coffee that they purchase.

The *architecture* links supply and demand. It is not one thing but a cluster of multiple elements. In the case of fair-trade coffee, a certification process checks to ensure that a given grower is, in fact, meeting certification standards. Those certifications must be standardized and licensed to the companies selling packaged goods. Consumers need to be educated about what the certification means. And a physical supply chain must get the goods from the producer to the processor to the consumer.

In my work, I saw firsthand how these three elements work together to change market behavior. From 2006 to 2021, during my time at the Hewlett Foundation, GuideStar, and Candid, one of my primary goals was to build a marketplace for donations that was better informed by data. The number of organizations providing this data in a standardized way went from essentially zero to more than 200,000 over the course of a decade.

To do this, we had to continuously refine the architecture that brought together those supplying the information with those demanding it. (See further discussion of this work in the **Complex Systems** chapter.) The growth in organizations providing performance data was in part enabled by the creation of an architecture for collecting and disseminating this information that included data standards, training programs, incentives, and so on.

I'll offer two essential lessons that we learned over the course of this work.

First, changing market behavior often takes longer than you might think. Markets have their own inertia, and that inertia involves a set of self-reinforcing feedback loops. Building or refining a marketplace takes financial support, humility, stamina, and creativity.

Second, success requires considering all three of the marketplace elements at once and nudging them up bit by bit. You cannot simply create the supply and hope that the demand will emerge. If you invest in the demand in the absence of the supply, that demand will be frustrated and evaporate over time. You might build the most elegant architecture, but it will lie unused without the supply and demand.

Division of labor

More than a century after its introduction in 1913, the assembly line — where each worker specializes in a particular task — remains a quintessential illustration of division of labor. The resulting efficiencies helped drive the Industrial Revolution, bringing extraordinary economic growth and profound human suffering. Can changemakers tap into the power of division of labor without succumbing to its dangers?[209]

Functional division of labor among organizations can improve aggregate impact. Consider a set of independent nonprofits that serve the distinct needs of one individual. One organization may be better at providing housing, another at job training, and a third at health care. But for this system to work best, the organizations need open channels of communication. Otherwise, the client will suffer — think cross-scheduled sessions, contradictory messages, and misaligned timelines.

A related set of benefits can arise from the geographic division of labor by mapping to the distribution of need across space. In this case, physical proximity is the start of efficiency but not the end. One place may simply have different needs from another. Communities can and will adapt their approaches accordingly. A remote village served by a single healer will deliver maternal and child health services differently than an urban clinic.

The presence of a given division of labor does not mean that arrangement is permanent. It can and should change as circumstances demand. Sometimes market mechanisms themselves drive changes in the division of labor, like when homeless shelters might be forced to consider consolidation when faced with funding cuts. Alternately, when additional philanthropic capital flows into a given issue area, it can create an opportunity for new models to emerge.[210]

This all takes work. The Game Theory chapter introduces techniques for structuring organizational collaboration. Changemakers need to be flexible about organizational identity, steadfast about what is best for their mission, and honest about how market dynamics affect each individual player in the arrangement.

A well-run factory has common procedures, clear communication, shared goals, and systems to empower workers. Organizations similarly in sync can reap the benefits of organizational diversity and independence while best serving their beneficiaries.

Economies of scale

Arithmetic matters. A nonprofit organization renting a large office space pays less per square foot than one subletting a few cubicles.

But more importantly, economies of scale matter because they can increase social impact. Large advocacy groups across like the Sierra Club can mobilize people quickly and cost-effectively due to their immense size. A single email can go to millions of members and be reinforced through local chapters, social media, and events.

Other times, though, small is beautiful. Neighborhood groups need to be rooted in neighborhoods. Sometimes a niche topic is best addressed by a small, niche organization.

The dynamics of scale may vary within a single organization. Consider a network of daycare providers. By centralizing certain administrative functions, they may indeed be able to achieve enterprise-level economies of scale. But the same strategy would collapse if applied in the classroom: higher student-to-teacher ratios tend to hurt educational outcomes.

Indeed, there are cases of diseconomies of scale, most obviously when

If the mind releases its fiduciary grip on time, does not dole it out in a fretful way like a valued commodity but regards it as undifferentiated, like the flatness of the landscape, it is possible to transcend distance — to travel very far without anxiety, to not be defeated by the great reach of the land."

Barry Lopez[212]

institutions become large and bureaucratic. If decision-making is slowed by size, effectiveness will suffer. Other cases are more subtle. For example, at GuideStar, we discovered that malicious cyberattacks increased nonlinearly as we grew — we faced a diseconomy of scale when it came to cybersecurity.

Scale can allow us to do more good with limited resources. But social change agents should recognize that scale can distance them from the complex realities on the front lines of the work. The Game Theory and Institutions chapters offer ways to navigate the puzzles of scale through collaboration. And, as we saw in the Complex Systems chapter, we explore the relationship between scale and diversity will always be with us.

Value over time

Experiments have consistently shown that most people prefer to get something immediately rather than wait for it. They "discount" the uncertain future versus the certain present. The value of something now is different from its value later. In purely financial terms, this discount can be approximated by interest rates on debt.

Economists speak of a "social discount rate" (SDR) that represents how we make trade-offs between the present and the future. An SDR represents how much we "discount" (that is, reduce, assuming a positive SDR) a cost or benefit one year in the future. A high SDR focuses our attention on present considerations because it places a lower value on future considerations. An SDR of zero implies that future financial interests are equally important to present ones. In this way, the social discount rate is not just an analytical tool, it is also a moral statement. (See the discussion on time in the Ethics chapter.)

How might this idea can be applied more broadly? Social problems evolve differently over time. Some issues like pandemics or climate change are "compounding" — they grow worse if not addressed. Action now is more effective than action later because it prevents the issue from getting worse. Other issues — e.g., ensuring that ballet endures as an art form — are "conserving" issues. In such cases, it may make sense to set aside resources for future use.

Capital held by a foundation dedicated to addressing "compounding" issues has a high SDR because will be less "useful" in the future than it is now. Capital devoted to "conserving" issues might have a low SDR; it makes sense to save this money.[213]

It is not easy — indeed it might be impossible — to determine precise discount rates for different social issues. But, at the very least, we can take the time to think about how value might change over time, make approximations, and be willing to act accordingly. I beleive that far more capital would be devoted to the social good if more donors and investors thought carefully about discount rates. Urgency takes on new meaning when you give it a number.

Complaint to My Empty Purse

To yow, my purse, and to noon other wight
Complaine I, for ye be my lady dere.
I am so sory now that ye be light,
For certes but if ye make me hevy chere,
Me were as leef be leyd upon my bere,
For which unto your mercy thus I crye
Beth hevy ageyn or elles mot I dye.

Geoffrey Chaucer

The invisible hand never picks up the check."

Kim Stanley Robinson[214]

Market failures

Throughout this chapter, we've spoken of the power of markets. That power can be leveraged for good or ill. Accordingly, it is worth time to explicitly talk about three ways that markets can fail.

Externalities:

Markets are organized around price. Price is an agreement between a buyer and the seller on how much will be exchanged for a given product or service. Economic theory would suggest that it rises from the interaction of supply and demand, achieving a certain type of equilibrium. All that is mostly true.[215]

Price is not a full reflection of the cost to make a product or provide a service. Those costs may well be invisible to the buyer or the seller. They may be borne by those who are not a party to the transaction. Those costs (or benefits!) outside of price are called "externalities."

The fate of the world may well hinge on how well humanity can deal with externalities. The energy economy is a powerful example of what's at stake. The price of a gallon of gasoline reflects, if inconsistently, the costs of drilling, refining, and delivery. But it does not reflect the costs of the polluted stream down the road from the drilling site, the lung disease borne by the disadvantaged neighborhood near the refinery, or the dangers faced by the cashier behind the bulletproof glass of the gas station. And, perhaps most urgently for humankind, the price of a gallon of gasoline does not reflect the costs of a changing climate.

Inequality:

Markets tend to drive unequal outcomes. Let's consider two mechanisms. The first is a matter of simple arithmetic. Consider two people. One makes $20,000 year. The other makes $200,000 year. Each gets a 3% raise. For the first person, that is an extra $600 each year. For the second person, it is an additional $6,000 each year. While the proportionate difference between these two people stayed the same, the absolute difference has changed.

The opposite is also true, a loss of 3% is more significant in absolute terms for a high-income person, though it likely has greater practical implications for a lower-income person who suddenly has $50 a month less to spend in an already pinched budget.

This mathematical phenomenon is compounded by a second mechanism: the advantages that policy, law, and culture confer on people with more money. Differentials in wealth become embedded in institutions and patterns of life. A simple and powerful historical inequality captures these phenomena: r>g. This simply means that the rate of return on capital (r) has consistently been greater than the economic growth rate (g). Economists Thomas Piketty, Emmanuel Saez, and others have exhaustively shown this equation to have been generally true over the course of centuries — with, of course, many exceptions and complexities.

Mechanisms exist that work against the inequality produced by markets. Among them: progressive taxation, labor unions, and the social safety net. And, in a classic — and ethically fraught — irony, it is the immense fortunes enabled by inequality that often fund the most significant non-governmental campaigns to address inequality.[216] The wise wealthy recognize this dynamic. As MacKenzie Scott has said, "There's no question in my mind that anyone's personal wealth is the product of a collective effort, and of social structures which present opportunities to some people, and obstacles to countless others."

Power:

Markets have immediate consequences for politics. Money represents power, even if that power is not always visible on the surface. Campaign contributions are the most obvious example, but as political scientist Lee Drutman has shown, there are more subtle mechanisms that wield even greater influence.[217] For example, lobbyists end up essentially serving as outsourced political staff for under-resourced members of Congress — a role especially influential on technical issues.

Similarly, the employment pattern known as the "revolving door" creates a cozy club for financial power as senior political leaders move into the private sector and back. Often regulators' previous jobs were within the industry they are regulating.

The market influences the distribution of power in other ways, too. Wealthy people have greater cultural and intellectual influence. Poverty brings a range of psychological burdens. Markets are engines that spew inequality if they are not well-tuned.

Wrestling the market

My professor Frederic Jameson once remarked that it was easier to imagine the end of the world than the end of capitalism. Perhaps someday our collective imagination will prove him wrong. But even if we never contain the great forces of the market — like those statues outside the Federal Trade Commission building — we can harness them to do good.

Social change agents can now tap into a variety of different economic models. In the consumer market, considerations beyond price and personal value are now commonplace in everyday buying decisions. The capital markets are now infused with new kinds of information and new incentives that guide stakeholders towards better outcomes. The philanthropic markets grow in scale and in scope.

Taken together, these forces at least offer the potential to carve an amoral marketplace into something that works in the best interest of the planet and the people who live here.

The humble shipping container transformed the world economy by creating a unit of standardization.

Markets Takeaways

1. **Like it or not, we exist within markets.** They are how we organize the bulk of human exchange. We must understand them and seek to guide them if we wish to be effective in building a better world.

2. **Markets can fail us, but they can also be a force for good.** Much of the work of social change is cleaning up the messes the market leaves behind. But social change agents can tap into the power of market mechanisms.

3. **Price is not a full reflection of the cost of a product or service; the world's fate might hinge on how well humanity addresses that misalignment.** Costs outside of price are called "externalities." More complete pricing to reflect externalities is at least a partial solution to some of today's challenges.

4. **Markets drive unequal outcomes.** Hard work and talent aren't the only explanations. Policy, law, and the system confer other advantages on people with more money.

5. **Finance is the art of wrestling with two profound dynamics of human experience: risk and time.** Finance can be detrimental, concealing true costs by shifting financial burdens from the present to the future. Or it can support the creation of social good through smart finance.

6. **Economies of scale can increase social impact.** Scale can reduce per-unit costs and change the dynamics of a market. But it also risks blinding you to the complexities of the work on the ground.

7. **Changing the behavior of the market as a whole is sometimes possible.** Getting there requires simultaneous incremental interventions in supply, demand, and the "architecture" of the market, which includes elements such as certification standards or information platforms.

3. **The pattern of money coming in and out of the organization is its business model.** Every enterprise should take time to think about its impact on the world holistically; exploring consequences can sometimes reveal unpleasant truths. Evidence suggests that organizations grow rapidly because of the power of one dominant revenue line. Costs are equally important and may scale in different ways.

Antony Bugg-Levine
Impact Investing:
Transforming How We Make Money
While Making a Difference

Ronald Cohen
Impact: Reshaping Capitalism
to Drive Real Change

9. **Markets, including for social good, thrive on information. Buyers and sellers generally want to make informed decisions.** Entire ecosystems of organizations prepare, collect, organize, and distribute information. There are many efforts to improve the ecosystem of information — from standards to taxonomies to unique IDs to goal frameworks — so that it can be compared and crunched in meaningful ways.

Brent Copen,
Lester Olmstead-Rose,
David La Piana
The Nonprofit Business Plan:
The Leader's Guide to Creating a
Successful Business Model

Thomas Piketty
Capital in the 21st Century

Complex Systems

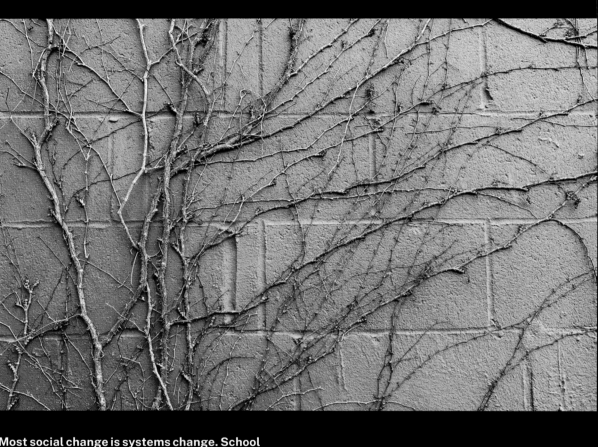

Most social change is systems change. School system reform is — literally — about reforming a *system* of schools. Confronting climate change is about addressing how economic systems impact ecological systems. The very concept of structural racism rises from a recognition that injustice is built into systems.

would not give a fig for the simplicity
his side of complexity,
but I would give my life for the simplicity
of the other side of complexity."

Oliver Wendell Holmes

A whole greater than the sum of its parts

In this chapter, we'll address how changemakers can think about systems. That may sound abstract, so let's take a moment for to ground ourselves in a concrete example. Let's talk about ants.

Ants are small, but their scale is extraordinary. There are tens of trillions of ants in the world. Individual leaf cutter ant colonies can reach 8 million individuals.[218] In those colonies, we see the emergence of extraordinarily sophisticated behavior: agriculture, democracy, rebellion, and diplomacy.[219] Somehow, millions of ants act as one. The colony is the individual: a whole greater than the sum of its ants.

Scientists have begun to tease out the way that individual ants add up to something so much more. For example, when a foraging ant discovers food, it will release pheromones to attract its siblings. As those new ants come, they release more pheromones, attracting more ants. This is known as a **positive feedback loop**.

But the presence of many ants may then attract an ant-eating predator, leading the ants to release different pheromones to signal retreat, a **negative feedback loop**. Simple mechanisms of communication allow ants to collectively act across space, time, and threats.

"For any problem, the more you can zoom out and embrace complexity, the better chance you have of zooming in on the simple details that matter most."

Eric Berlow[221]

Those working for a better world would be wise to pause and learn. These are not just cute examples of cool animal behavior. Ants operate as systems, and so does the world.

The science of systems is relevant for us in two ways. First, if we want to change the behavior of systems, we need to understand them. Second, we — people and organizations devoted to the public good — are ourselves a system. But we are fragmented; arguably we remain less than the sum of our part.[220] If ants can add up to something greater, why can't we?

This chapter explores many dimensions of systems, interaction, and complexity. We will start with a simple question: *what is a system?* Then we'll look at the elements of systems and the characteristics of complex systems. Throughout, we'll see how we might change the existing systems of the world and also build new ones.

What is a system?

In simple terms, a system is a set of components interacting within a boundary. We experience systems throughout our lives: the parts of a car engine, a pack of dogs in a park, and even our own consciousness.

In 1948, Warren Weaver, a mathematician based at the Rockefeller Foundation, offered a basic categorization of systems: simple, complicated, and complex.

| simple | complicated | complex |

Two billiard balls colliding on a table is a **simple** system; we can use basic Newtonian mechanics to understand their motion.[222]

A thousand billiard balls thrown into an empty swimming pool form a **complicated** system. Weaver called this "disorganized complexity." Science can use statistics to describe the collective behavior of a complicated system — the variance among individual elements tends to average out. As those balls

"The systems people target for change
are causal architectures that have social problems
as their effect."

Christian Seelos and Johnna Mair[223]

ettle in the bottom of the empty pool,
hey reach a static equilibrium. It may be
nessy, but by looking at the individual
arts of a complicated system we can —
ventually — understand it.

In contrast, **complex** systems operate
ifferently at the group level than at
he individual level. These systems
emonstrate what Weaver described as
organized complexity." A single water
molecule does not freeze, boil, or exhibit
urface tension — it is only a collection of
vater molecules that exhibits those prop-
rties. Similarly, the swings of a market
annot be predicted solely by the beliefs
f individual investors. Consciousness
annot be explained simply by the behav-
or of individual neurons.

This higher-level order is called
n "emergent property." By definition,
mergent properties cannot be
redicted solely by the behavior of
ndividual components. Instead, these
atterns *emerge from the collective
ehavior of the entire system.*

This is, then, the essential lesson of
his chapter: the whole matters. When
ve look at a situation, an institution, or
community holistically, we can see
atterns and behaviors that are invisible

when we only look at the parts. Human
language reflects the centrality of wholeness to human experience. English words
for central human concepts like "health"
and "holy" trace to the Proto-Indo-
European root *kailo*, meaning "whole" or
"intact." Intuitively, we see the importance
of wholeness. But we need more than just
intuition to tease apart the behavior of
many complex systems.

Systems and social change

Just about every aggregation relevant for
social change is some kind of a system.
Health care delivery, higher education,
and criminal justice are systems. The
energy economy and the political
environment are systems. Sometimes big
change happens when we restructure the
order of the system itself: labor unions
restructured labor markets, social media
restructured the public conversation
about gender identity, and organic certification restructured entire supply chains.

When considering social systems, we
can start by looking for a simple explanation by mapping out the components and
interactions of a system. If we're lucky,
we might identify a simple intervention.
Maybe we just need to put more money

History is fractured & fractal.
Even when we've succumbed
We have not surrendered.

Amanda Gorman

"Assuming stability
is one of the ways ruins get made."

John Lewis Gaddis[232]

into social media advertising to get people to come to our art fair. Maybe the best way to help people without resources is to give them money.

Other times, the system may be understandable — it's just really complicated. In a complicated system, it may in fact be possible to disentangle all its parts. But it will take patience and resources to address those parts one at a time.

Most of the time, though, the systems we care about are complex. The whole is fundamentally different from the sum of its parts. We can't just rebuild a system from scratch to match our perfect vision. What we can do is tend to, alter, and care for the system. Or, to put it another way: even if we cannot be architects of a complex system, we can be gardeners.

Over the past century, scholars across disciplines have transformed our understanding of systems. We've seen profound insights from physics,[224] mathematics,[225] engineering,[226] biology,[227] computer science,[228] economics,[229] sociology,[230] and more.[231] Scientists have shown how complex systems can adapt, learn, and respond to external stress. Mathematicians have uncovered extraordinary patterns: the self-similarity of fractals, the infinite variety of the Mandelbrot set, even the "Six Degrees of Kevin Bacon." Beneath complexity you find math.[233]

Here's the good news: we don't need to understand the math behind complex systems science to draw lessons for social change. Even a basic language and some common patterns can help us be smart gardeners for good.

What makes a system complex?

Scientists are far from unraveling the mysteries of complexity. Still, the academic literature does suggest a set of common characteristics for complex systems.[234] These characteristics offer hints for anyone thinking about how to change the behavior of a system.

The components are connected to each other. For example, the brain is a set of neurons connected to each other by synapses. The connections themselves can vary in strength; the links among neurons in the brain vary significantly. The structure of the connections may exhibit hierarchy, clustering, or other types of order.[235] And what are relationships — the substance of so much of social change — but connections among humans?

The interactions among components follow rules.[236] For example, the Internet works because the interactions among routers are standardized. There are rules to determine how to break up a message into packets and send them via different pathways. Without standardized rules, the Internet would collapse into a muddle of incoherence.

3. **The interactions among components include both negative and positive feedback loops.** Above I described feedback loops used by ants to communicate with each other. Another example of a negative (balancing) feedback loop is a thermostat: If the temperature gets too hot, the thermostat turns on the air conditioning. Markets are a tangle of negative and positive feedback loops — from price to reviews to investment. They often yield an unjust pattern: the rich get richer (a positive or "reinforcing" feedback loop.)[237] Importantly, feedback loops can be either internal (among components) or external (between components with forces outside the boundary).

4. **The components optimize.** Consider the structure of a river system. Individual droplets of water follow gravity and roll downhill. This individual optimization creates the branching patterns of the system as each droplet follows its own best pathway. It is worth noting here that for a component to optimize, it need not exhibit consciousness: a bacteria might move towards food and an algorithmic trading platform seeks profit, yet neither requires a conscious goal.

5. **The system interacts with the world outside of its boundaries.**[238] Consider a genome. It is only meaningful in interaction with the world around it. For genetic code to unfold into a living being, it has to extract energy from its surroundings provided by, for example, a gestating mother or sunlight on a plant. Moreover, the genome itself only changes over time because it interacts with the world through natural selection. Institutions of all sizes — from a bodega to a hospital to a U.N. agency — interact with the world outside their boundaries. The blurring boundaries of the modern world can make it difficult to explicitly identify where a system ends and where its context begins.

6. **The system processes information.**[239] For example, in a market, prices convey information about value, supply, and demand. That information may change as the market interacts with the world around it and, indeed, may change the system's behavior over time. Similarly, the position of a bird in a flock or the gradient of ant pheromones conveys information to animals around it. The beliefs and choices made by people in a system are embedded information. The arts ecosystem processes the emotional engagement of audiences, critics, and the general public.

7. **Components enter and exit the system over time.** When you see a fallen log covered with mushrooms, you are seeing the cycling of nutrients through a system. The mushrooms enter the ecosystem through the use of the nutrients of the tree that is exiting that same ecosystem. Put another way, there is both birth and death in a dynamic system. We see this in business as well: start-ups threaten established players; the sale of distressed assets creates opportunities for new entrants; new government agencies are born and others fade away.[240]

Phenomena

Equilibrium is when a system has "settled" into a certain steady state (see the Game Theory chapter for a detailed discussion).

Tipping points are when a system reaches a certain threshold that radically changes its structure or behavior.

Collapse occurs when the connections within a system break and emergent properties disappear.

Resilience is the ability of a system to avoid collapse even under stress. Systems with multiple interacting feedback loops and additional resources ("slack") are often more resilient against collapse.

Fractals are patterns that exhibit "self-similarity," where it looks the same at different scales. These patterns often emerge within complex systems.

Network effects occur when the addition of new components scales the value of the network exponentially.

> "You cannot control complex systems, only disturb them. And even a small disturbance, artfully designed, can have large systemic effects. We call this 'social acupuncture.'"
>
> Graham Leicester and Maureen O'Hara[241]

Lessons for social change

Systems analysis is relevant from both the inside and the outside. Consider a police department with a history of discriminatory practices. Activists might be trying to change the department from the outside — just as a new police chief is trying to change it from within. People inside and outside a dysfunctional legislature may wish to transform its procedures. Both activists and pharmacists may wish to transform the system for funding prescription drugs.

In general, we want a system to show the emergent characteristics of complexity: learning, responsiveness, adaptation, resilience, and efficiency. Below, I'll suggest seven ways to build — or renovate — high-performing systems.

This might seem abstract, so I'll try to ground this in a concrete example that is close to my heart. Over the past two decades, many people — myself included — have worked to make the system of philanthropic giving function better for nonprofits and the world.

Already, that system has seen significant changes. Consider, for example, the proportion of American givers who actively chose from among multiple organizations instead of simply saying yes or no to individual requests. That proportion tripled from 2010 to 2015.[242] If extrapolated to the country as a whole — admittedly a big "if" — this finding would suggest a change in how 12 million people give away $15 billion each year. Additional evidence suggests that increased transparency can bring huge increases in donations — as much as a 50% increase — to nonprofit organizations.[243]

No matter how we choose to interpret the quantitative data, there's been a clear shift in the public discourse about giving. There are rising expectations for transparency and results reporting from donors, government officials, and the media. And, as importantly, there's been an unmistakable call for all stakeholders — notably nonprofits and their beneficiaries — to be treated with dignity throughout the process.

So, below, I offer seven general lessons for interacting with complex systems. In each case, I show how this played out in the work to improve the system of philanthropy.

Be intentional about connectivity. The relatively weak connectivity of many systems dampens the ability to respond to the needs of the outside world. To increase connectivity, perhaps the simplest thing to do is to increase the ease of connection — or, in simple terms, the convenience for the end user.

In philanthropy, we sought to do this by (a) standardizing interactions (e.g., providing donors information in a predictable format) and (b) making information available near where actors are already operating (e.g., adding information about nonprofits into donors' online finance interfaces).

Simplify the rules. If all interactions among components follow their own separate rules, it is hard to achieve any systems-level efficiency (i.e., there are no economies of scale) or cumulative learning (i.e., components are constantly reinventing the wheel).

In philanthropy, we sought to simplify rules by (a) creating and adopting common standards for information transfer (e.g., grant applications and reporting) and (b) removing barriers to the transfer of money.

3. **Support feedback loops.** Feedback is a prerequisite for learning: try something, see what happens, and adjust. Weak feedback loops make for weak learning.

   In philanthropy, we worked to build feedback loops between (a) foundations and grantees (e.g., through surveys like the Center for Effective Philanthropy's Grantee Perception Report) and (b) nonprofits and beneficiaries (e.g. through the Fund for Shared Insight).

4. **Encourage goal orientation.** When components in a system have clear goal orientation, they are more likely to adjust behavior and optimize goal achievement. This also can — consciously and unconsciously — make it easier for components (people, organizations, or ants) to align and aggregate behavior.

   In philanthropy, (a) advisory groups like Bridgespan worked to support nonprofit strategy processes,[244] and (b) Candid sought to gently guide nonprofits towards goal orientation by prominently highlighting organizations' goals, strategies, and metrics on the GuideStar platform.

5. **Embrace a common identity.** In social change, the parts of a system are often people, and those people may or may not see themselves as part of a community. To get people to engage in a shared purpose or common protocols, you may first have to address what people mean when they say, "we." At its best, "community building" can be far more than a feel-good activity. It can have critical strategic consequences if it clarifies a constituency's identity and shared goals.

In philanthropy, (a) we began with a recognition that the tax code offered a "boundary" that defined the group for both legal reasons and shared identity, which provided a very useful initial frame, and (b) we also recognized the blurring boundaries across sectors, so we engaged with partners in business and government who did not share the same legal status. In an age of multiple bottom lines, we needed an expansive and explicit sense of shared identity: the common purpose of building a better world.[245]

6. **Enhance the flow of information through the system.** For people to work together, they each have to know what the others are doing. Often, there is an opportunity to improve the flow of information among different nodes in a given system.

In philanthropy, much of our focus was on flow of data about nonprofit organizations. We sought to (a) build on existing data (the financial information available from the Form 990) with new data (questions about programs, operations, and governance) while also (b) supporting the flow of that data through data standards, new pricing models, and technology like APIs (application programming interfaces).

> "A social body that can't concentrate or communicate with itself is like a person who can't think and act."
>
> Jenny Odell[246]

Embrace exit and recombination.
Organizations that step aside, merge, or seek acquisition deserve to be celebrated. They are contributing to the potential of our entire system.

In philanthropy, (a) we sought to provide cultural support for the more dynamic recombination of organizational resources — whether money, people, or ideas; (b) actively show that recombination could work — as with the merger of GuideStar and Foundation Center to form Candid.

Tensions

Social change agents face a number of tensions when engaging with complex systems. The four ethical and strategic dilemmas below are likely to come up in any systems-level work.

A flock of starlings — known as a "murmuration" —
over the ruins of Brighton's West Pier on the south
coast of England. In complex systems, we sometimes see holistic behavior emerge organically
from a seemingly rigid latticework of connection.
Photo by Doug Scarr

ature has taught me that a storm
an be used to clear out branches that are dying,
 let go of that which was keeping us
om growing in new directions."

alidah Imarisha[247]

tandardization vs diversity

iversity, rightly, has a fundamentally
ositive connotation when talking about
uman beings. Most of us working for
better world imagine one in which
versity is celebrated, where different
entities and perspectives flourish.

But one of the ironies of complex
ystems science is this it takes a degree
 standardization to enable the emer-
ence of diversity. The mosaic of human
oetry is made possible by standardized
nguage. The flowering of the Internet
as made possible by the TCP/IP proto-
ol. Or consider how a farmers' market
built upon standards. It takes shared
greement about place and time, regular
acing, and common booth structure
 create a framework that ultimately
veals the diversity of the fruits, vegeta-
es, and flowers.

Standardization can be essential
r one of the most powerful forces of
e modern economy: network effects.
onsider email addresses. They were not
ry useful when only a few people had
em. But as more people got and used
nail, the tool became more and more
owerful. Social media companies are
ilt upon network effects. The power (or

value) of a network scales rapidly with the
number of nodes in the network.[248] The
concept is relevant beyond technology.
Language is powered by network effects.
Even the most abstract ideas can gain
power as they are adopted by others.
As philosopher Kwame Anthony Appiah
remarked, "a value is like a fax machine:
it's not much use if you're the only one who
has one."[249]

In my work at GuideStar and Candid,
we were confronted with the standardiza-
tion/diversity tension on a regular basis.
We standardized how nonprofits could
tell their story by creating a common
reporting protocol. That standardization
had the explicit purpose of revealing
diversity through an easy-to-use search
capability. We made every possible
effort to structure the questions to allow
nonprofits to share their specific circumstances, approach, and results.

But the standardization of common
questions was only possible because
nonprofits share a core set of characteristics. Efforts for standardization should
stop if and when they begin to flatten
essential diversity.

Big vs small

Any analysis of a system should look at the sizes of its component parts. Do entities of different sizes play different roles in the system? Do larger entities have access to more resources? Are smaller entities more likely to be connected to each other?

These are analytical questions, but they can quickly become ethically fraught. We see this in the nonprofit sector. There are those who argue that, for example, large nonprofit organizations are more effective because they've achieved economies of scale; their size makes them more efficient.

Others argue that small nonprofit organizations are more effective because they are less bloated with bureaucracy and tend to be closer to the lives of those they are trying to help.

I believe both arguments are correct. A healthy system will have some degree of diversity in terms of size. But the benefits of size diversity can be drowned out if the larger entities look down upon the smaller ones and the smaller ones resent the larger ones.

An Entrance

If you want to give thanks
but this time not to the labyrinth
Of cause and effect —
Give thanks to the plain sweetness of a day
when it's as if everywhere you turn
there is an entrance —
When it's as if even the air is a door —

And your child is a door
afloat on invisible hinges.
"The world is a house," he says,
over lunch as if to give you a clue —
And before the words dissolve
above his plate of eggs and rice
you suddenly see how we are in it —
How everywhere the air
is holding hands with the air —
How everyone is connected
to everyone else by breathing.

Malena Mörling

tock vs flow

eople often confuse two quantities: what
s currently in a system (the "stock") ver-
us what travels through the system (the
flow"). Consider a bathtub. The amount of
ater in the tub at a given moment is the
tock of water. Water coming in from the
pigot or going out the drain is a flow. And
et flow is the amount of water coming in
ninus the amount of water going out over
given time.

This distinction is surprisingly
rofound and relevant. For example,
onfusion between stock and flow hides
ne extent of inequality in our society. Too
nany people focus on income inequality
flow) instead of the accumulated
ulf represented by wealth inequality
stock). Operationally, this distinction
auses endless confusion in discussions
f organizational finances (assets are
tocks; profit is a flow).

Being able to distinguish between
tock and flow can yield insights.
onsider statistics about the size of the
opulation without housing in a given
ommunity. If the population stays the
ame over time, does that mean organiza-
ons fighting homelessness are failing?
laybe it simply means that any newly

homeless individuals are quickly provided
housing and wrap-around services,
removing them from the population.

In such a case, we would see that
the problem is not with the set of
organizations addressing the housing
problem, but with the broader society
that continues to push people onto the
streets. This insight might then inspire
organizations to shift attention towards
identifying those on the brink of losing
housing; in this case, the best strategy
is to focus on changing the flow into
the system while trusting the existing
work on the flow out of the system.

Enumerate the parts of a carriage,
And you still have not explained what a carriage is.

Tao Te Ching

Unpredictability

When intervening in a system, we can have a directional sense of how we hope it will behave. But we should prepare ourselves for unintended consequences. Complex systems are morally neutral. Emergent properties are not inherently good. And even good consequences can emerge unexpectedly.

Consider, for example, social media. It is its own kind of ecosystem, and it has led to countless emergent phenomena (social media virality), tools (hashtags), roles (online influencers), and behaviors (trolling). These elements change over time. At the time of the Arab Spring, many commentators (rightly, in my view) celebrated the democratizing, empowering nature of social media. But with the rise of online conspiracy theories and misinformation campaigns, we have been forced to reassess the consequences of social media for society.

Such is the nature of complex systems. We must hold in tension the positive potential of the creation of new systems or the evolution of old ones with the possibility that things could go terribly wrong. And, through it all, we must remember that in complex systems, change can multiply in unpredictable ways.

The community of social change

The community of social change is growing in scale, impact, and complexity. With insights from complex systems science, we can think clearly about how we — members of a global community driven to shape a better world — might become greater than the sum of our parts. For that to happen, we need to move beyond a view of only our individual parts and see our collective efforts as a single, immensely complex organism.

By its very nature, emergence is a bottom-up process. Above, I highlighted a set of field-level strategies for the social change community to achieve our shared potential. There are many actions that leading institutions of the field — large foundations, major business networks, and key government agencies — can do to enable bottom-up power. These larger institutions are a part of our ecosystem that can provide the right nutrients to unleash vitality and resilience in the larger community.

I emphasize that, ultimately, capturing the systems-level potential of the social sector requires distributed action. Each player in the community of social change can make individual choices that build

ause-and-effect assumes history marches
orward, but history is not an army. It is a crab
cuttling sideways, a drip of soft water
earing away stone, an earthquake breaking
enturies of tension."

ebecca Solnit[251]

hared power. Activists can enhance
heir own goal orientation by forcing
hemselves to articulate specific goals.
nvestors and foundations can share
ata about their use of capital through
ommon data standards. Governments
nd social enterprises can build ways
> fold structured feedback from their
onstituents into their decision-making.

    We are all connected — as humans
nd as changemakers. It is up to all of us
> determine whether we will become
reater than the sum of our parts.

1. **We have a lot to learn from ants.**
An ant colony is a complex system.
It acts like a single, sophisticated
organism far greater than the sum of
its ants.

2. **In a complex system, behavior at the
level of the group is fundamentally
different from the behavior at the
level of the individual.** You can't
predict how the whole system will
work based on the behavior of isolated
components. That system-wide,
higher-level order is called an emergent property.

3. **Just about everything that is inter-
esting for social change is a complex
system.** Some examples: health care
delivery, the energy economy, and the
electricity grid.

4. **Changemakers need to understand
how complex systems work.**
We can and should look for simple,
linear interventions. But, often, major
change is only possible through the
restructuring of a system.

5. **Complexity is morally neutral.**
Just because a given system is more
than the sum of its parts doesn't mea
that sum is positive. We must bring
values to our gardening.

6. **Changemakers need to think of their
contribution in terms of the system a
a whole and not just the component
they represent.** Working through
that puzzle will reveal diversity and
unleash new behavior across the
system and its component parts.

7. **Pay attention to the distinction
between "stock" and "flow."** Failure
to distinguish the two arguably
hides the extent of inequality in our
society — for example, people focus o
income inequality (a flow) instead of
the accumulated gulf represented by
wealth inequality (a stock).

Many leaders in social change want the field to show more character-istics of a complex system such as learning, adaptation, resilience, and systems-level efficiency. Some steps the field can take include being intentional about connectivity, simplifying the rules, enhancing information flow, and embracing closures and recombination.

One of the ironies of complex systems science is that it takes a degree of standardization to enable the emergence of diversity. The mosaic of human poetry is made possible by standardized language. Network effects emerge from standardization when a product or service gains additional value with every new user.

). We have a sense of how we hope the system will behave but must prepare ourselves for unintended consequences. That said, the lessons of complex systems science offer us hope for a philanthropic sector that mirrors the best of life: creation, vitality, and richness.

adrienne maree brown
Emergent Strategy

Donella Meadows
Thinking in Systems

Melanie MItchell
Complexity: A Guided Tour

Eric Beinhocker
Origin of Wealth: Evolution, Complexity, and the Radical Remaking of Economics

Peter Senge
The Fifth Discipline: The Art & Practice of The Learning Organization

Institutions

The Nishiyama Onsen Keiunkan is a hotel near Japan's Mount Fuji. It has 35 rooms nestled among trees on the east bank of the Haya River. Each one of us could learn from this hotel. Why? It was founded in 705 C.E. and has been managed by the same family for 52 generations. Hardly any of its wood, stone, or glass is original. But Keiunkan remains, a lasting pattern made of people.

Patterns of people

Institutions are patterns of relationship. They are lasting structures for how people connect, conflict, align, and entwine. We can think about them in two categories.

- *Behavioral institutions* reflect patterns in how people act over time. Consider marriage, high school reunions, or neighborhood barbeques.
- *Organizations* are the institutions that provide structure to collective activity. They are the companies, agencies, teams, and schools.

In the work of social change, we find ourselves in constant interaction with both types of institutions. They are an essential context for our work. We have to work within and through them. Sometimes they are a target for our work; we are trying to change the behavior of an organization or a group of people. And very often, they are a vehicle for our work; they provide the structure for what we do.

The term "institution" can conjure images of stultified bureaucracies and stuffy social patterns. But like many essential terms in this book, the concept of "institution" is itself neutral. There can be good institutions and bad institutions. There can be effective institutions and ineffective Institutions. Our challenge as change agents is to take institutions as they are, even as we work to change them.

One the most remarkable institutions of the modern era is Wikipedia. Technically, it is housed within a nonprofit organization, the Wikimedia Foundation. But its legal structure is less important than the pattern of behavior of its users. That community has built a system of writing, editing, and organizing that operates across 326 languages.[252] Wikipedia has achieved a remarkable scale — 6.1 billion monthly visits — making it the fifth most-visited website in the world.[253] But even those immense numbers do not capture the power of a new way of organizing human knowledge.

Thriving institutions don't need cutting-edge technology or global prominence. Consider the simple power of a village cooperative. Across the world, these organizations aggregate farmers' resources and risks. The cooperative might help to store and process the community's crops, pooling funds to buy equipment that no single farmer could afford. It creates bargaining power for the farmers and provides a cushion to absorb a bad harvest.

Behavioral patterns create a cultural identity with tactical and cultural advantages: a structure of relationships in which to ask questions, offer tips, and work together towards shared goals.

This chapter looks at the role institutions play in social change and explores how to best tilt them towards a better world. We'll start with the metaphor of organizations as organisms to understand their general tendencies. Then we'll explore nine key dimensions of organizational behavior and how they intersect with the work of social change. Finally, a discussion of the evolving social contract looks at the societal expectations of organizations and the individuals who lead them.

Organizations as organisms

We can think of organizations as organisms. It is no coincidence that in English the two words are so similar. Both trace their roots to the Greek ὀργανισμός, meaning "instrument, implement, tool, or organ of sense."[254] Organizations are tools made by people.

Like organisms, organizations tend to protect their existence and seek their own continuity. You won't find some little homunculus hidden in the founding documents of a nonprofit or a company that demands to live forever. Instead, the organization's structure, systems, and processes — and, of course, its people — will tend to favor decisions to keep the organization going. Logistical and legal hurdles might keep it from dissolving.

Human behavior also feeds the self-preservation dynamic. Staff wish to keep their salary and benefits. Leaders may feel a sense of responsibility or perhaps pride or shame.

In social change, this impulse towards self-preservation is both a weakness and a strength. It is tempting for social change agents to inadvertently prioritize their presence over their purpose. This tendency is especially dangerous in the nonprofit sector, since these organizations are founded expressly for the purpose of building a better world. There's a saying in the social sector, "nonprofits exist to put themselves out of business." It's one thing to pivot to a new purpose, like the March of Dimes did after the development of the polio vaccine in 1955.[255] It is another to linger for your own sake.

It's important to note, though, that investing in an institution is not inherently selfish. There is nothing shameful in a nonprofit spending money to build up its accounting system, for a social business to celebrate a milestone, or for a government agency to advertise the programs it offers to the community. Organizations simply need to do such things greater purpose, not their own glory. Shame is only justified if we forget that organizations are means to an end, not ends in themselves.

Organizations, like organisms, can seem to have their own consciousness. Lewis Thomas described the legendary Marine Biological Laboratory at Woods Hole as, "a human institution possessed of a life of its own, self-regenerating, touched all around by human meddle but constantly improved, embellished by it...it seems to have a mind of its own, which it makes up in its own way."[256] Indeed, the laboratory paralleled the organisms it studied.

Just as the brain of an organism shows up on an anatomical drawing but its "mind" does not, the "mind" of an organization does not appear on its tidy, well-structured flow chart. Every new entrant to an organization faces that puzzle: how do I fit in with the way decisions are made here? Each organization is its own mystery, and its behavior is constrained by history, culture, and processes.

It is possible to identify a set of factors that are important to how most organizations function. As social change agents, we can use those insights to help guide our own organizations and to influence others.

Navigating organizations

If organizations are patterns of relationships among people, how do we influence those patterns?

This section will discuss nine different aspects of institutions: inertia, finances, culture, leadership, structure, information, incentives, regulation, and governance. Organizations weave these various aspects together into what is, itself, a type of pattern. These patterns tend to reinforce themselves over time, but they can be changed with intention and patience.

Inertia

A first predictor of an organization's future behavior is its past behavior. Existing patterns — whether resource allocation, communication, or decision-making — offer clues as to what to expect in the future.

Consider resource allocation. Intentionally or not, next year's budget will almost always be based upon this year's budget. It is possible to break the pattern. For example, in "zero-based budgeting," each department begins not with last year's budget, but with zero.

ach expense has to be justified, even if
 has been in place for years. But such
fforts require significant leadership
nd commitment. There is a weight to
pending patterns.

Systems and processes also feed
ertia. It's simply easier for a LIttle
eague coach to just copy-and-paste the
troductory email from last season. For
xample, if you are looking to influence
major corporation, its actions might
e locked in by a multimillion-dollar
ustomer relationship management
ystem. These patterns may be designed
tentionally or develop spontaneously.
uccessful organizations pay attention
) them and are intentional about which
atterns they wish to defend.

Now, obviously institutions can and
o change. Indeed, much of the work of
ocial impact is about shifting institu-
onal behavior. But it is usually fair to
tart your analysis with an assumption of
ertia. Then you can decide if and how
ou might seek to disrupt it.

Finances

Most organizations use money.
As we discussed in the **Ethics** and
Markets chapters, money and power
are deeply entwined. Money reflects
the distribution of power within
and around an organization.

Often, you can gauge how much power
people have within an organization in part
by how much money they control. In some
cases, the connection is direct: foundation
executives who oversee bigger grant
budgets have more resources to work with.
In other cases, the connection between
money and power is more subtle: a city
official who oversees a large administrative department might not wield as much
power as the head of the Mayor's small but
influential communications office.

As noted, the ethical dimensions of
finances are complicated and often problematic, but when seeking to understand
organizations, following the money provides essential information and a way of
thinking about strategic leverage points.

Consider, for example, advocacy
efforts that use an understanding of
financial vulnerabilities to change the
behavior of corporations. The **Markets**
chapter discusses how companies respond

263   Institutions

to financial incentives. Whether you are trying to influence an institution from the outside or guide it from the inside, one thing is for certain: money matters.

Culture

Culture is the set of norms that unconsciously guide actions within the organization. Is a company hard-partying or family-oriented? Do people tend to write down their ideas, or do they confront problems verbally? Is there a sense of deference to senior executives, or are they challenged by the rest of the staff? Is the budget seen as a loose guideline or a fixed plan?

These patterns are immensely important. They set the tone and standard for almost every interaction, decision, and action in an organization. And — to quote a saying that makes strategists groan — "Culture eats strategy for breakfast."[259]

Despite the power of cultural patterns, they can change. "We are what we repeatedly do" is a maxim that holds true for both individuals and organizations.[260] Just as repetition sets patterns, it can change them.

It is possible to shift organizational culture with conscious attention to what Rockefeller Foundation official Zia Khan refers to as "rules and rituals." He explains, "Rules speak to the head, and rituals speak to the heart. Our behaviors are driven by both."[261] Rules might include compensation policies or frameworks used for planning. Rituals might include a company's formal monthly "town hall meeting" or the accounting team's weekly donut run.

Language, ritual, and stories form the fabric of organizational culture. Intentional leaders repeat over and over in the present what they wish to see again in the future.

Leadership

In physics, a system needs energy to shift from one equilibrium to another. In organizations, breaking out of one way of doing things requires a specific type of energy: leadership.

Leaders can offer a story — recall our definition of leadership, "an invitation to a shared story" — about how an organization might behave in a different way. They then can invite others into these new behaviors. That invitation is more likely to be accepted and successful if th onhuman factors — systems, processes, nd finances — are aligned with this new tory.

That leader need not be the chief xecutive. Anyone can offer an invitation o a new, shared story. But it is far easier o make this invitation when it is aligned vith the organization's formal leadership.

Chief executives have an additional esponsibility for institutional change ecause people both inside and outside n organization will naturally look to them or the organization's story — and for lues as to how well the change is really oing. Often, the chief executive — rightly r wrongly — becomes a living symbol of ne organization.

A single vision imposed from above night work in a cult, but it is unlikely o lead to system-level creativity and ngagement. If employees do not have a ense of their own agency, the organiza-on may indeed be like an organism — a ead one.

Organizational leadership is nus a constant struggle between entralization, which brings order nd sometimes bureaucracy, and ecentralization, which brings mpowerment and sometimes chaos.

Social change is, in and of itself, an act of leadership. The ability to reshape institutional patterns of relationships can be magnified by the personal characteristics of good leadership. Those characteristics might or might not include charisma or vision, but they definitely include character, clarity, and compassion. Individual humans who can tell a story, organize an event, and inspire community are the motivative force behind much of social change.

The Nagyvásárcsarnok in Budapest is a marketplace designed to promote exchange.

The Tempodrom in Berlin is an event space
meant to focus attention.

"It is a lot easier to find an unorthodox person than an unorthodox organization."

Melissa Schilling[264]

Old power values	New power values
formal governance	informal, networked governance
competition, exclusivity, resource consolidation	collaboration, crowd wisdom, open-sourcing
confidentiality, discretion	radical transparency
expertise, professionalism, specialization	maker culture, DIY ethos
long-term affiliation and loyalty	short-term, conditional affiliation[263]

In *New Power*, Jeremy Heimans and Henry Timms offer a contrast between what they call "old power" values and "new power" values. While their inclination towards "new power" is clear, Heimans and Timms go to great pains to emphasize that old power approaches remain relevant.

Structure

Organizations naturally follow existing patterns, echoing those that came before. Big tech companies, city police departments, or community-based nonprofits tend to look like others in their category.

For some critics, this commonality is a shame: it constrains creativity and forces people to fit their organizations into a single box. There is much to be said for this critique. Indeed, many of the greatest innovations have come from imagining new types of organizations that break out of the iron cage of old models.[265] New structures such as L3C ("low-profit limited liability company" and DAO ("distributed autonomous organization") offer new ways to govern institutions with an eye toward broader purpose.

New strategies do not require new structures. Indeed, for an entrepreneur (whether socially oriented or not), it can be a relief to follow the templates that have come before. Each existing pattern invites questions: why is this organizational model common? Are there invisible forces that lead businesses to offer debt in the form of a bond, or teams to have coaches, or nonprofits to describe their work in terms of their mission statement?

sking questions like these helps you
to be intentional about the template you
choose and vigilant about whether it
helps or hinders your work.

Where possible, focus attention
on the content of the work, not on its
container. If there is a good model
available, use it and move on. New
solutions do not necessarily require new
organizations. At Candid, we often saw
social change agents with a good idea
who automatically defaulted to starting
a new nonprofit — instead of building on
the work of the 1.8 million U.S. nonprofit
organizations that already exist.[266]

The size distribution of a group
of organizations can have significant
implications for the effectiveness of
achieving social change. For example, the
U.S. environmental movement includes a
number of large nonprofit organizations
but no single dominant one. This situation
contrasts with the gun rights movement,
which is dominated by the National Rifle
Association (NRA). The environment
movement requires a degree of coordina-
tion across key organizational players to
wield its full power; the NRA doesn't.

A more diffuse structure can bring
advantages, too, including a division of
labor among different organizations and
closeness to diverse communities. But
balancing the needs and styles of many
organizations is never easy. See the Game
Theory chapter for more information on
successful collaboration and alignment.

Other structural questions can
seriously affect how well institutions
achieve their goals. One critical but
often ignored dimension is time. Many
companies are created with the full
intention of later being acquired. In the
world of institutional philanthropy, the
default assumption has long been the
opposite: foundations exist in perpetuity.
But this tradition has been — rightly, in
my view — challenged by those who argue
that some challenges and opportunities
in the present are too urgent to justify
saving money for the future.[267] (See the
discussion of the social discount rate in
the **Mathematical Modeling** chapter.)

Networks of local organizations can
link together — across *space* — under
a single brand as members, affiliates,
franchises, or subsidiaries. The governance of these networks can take many
forms, from strict centralization to full
decentralization. Optimally, the model
should reflect what is best to advance the

mission. If consistent branding and alignment is critical to the strategy, centralization may be justified. If local context varies significantly, a more decentralized model will probably be more effective.

We humans have encoded centuries of learning into our institutions. At their best, they represent our collective understanding of what works. But any system can get stuck and structural inertia cn be dangerous in a rapidly changing world.

The COVID-19 pandemic offered a powerful case study in how institutions can quickly become unstuck. In a matter of days, restaurants completely overhauled their operations. Health care providers finally overcame logistical and bureaucratic hurdles to offer remote visits. Countless organizations embraced remote work after years of resistance.

As we move forward into an uncertain future, we will have a chance to reimagine organizational structure across space, time, and scale.[268] Indeed, new patterns of interaction (e.g., swarms[269]), formal structures (e.g., DAOs[270]), and techniques (e.g., quadratic voting[271]) offer patterns of people that may well change the contours of our institutional future.

Information

If we think about organizations as organisms, we can imagine their resources as the nutrients they metabolize. Money, which we've already discussed, is one critical nutrient for organizational health Information is another. Leaders can align what people do across an institution in part by creating a flow of information tha constantly steers people back to organizational purpose and shared strategy.

Optimally, clear metrics track the progress of an organization. In general, the business world has an easier time measuring an organization's worth. The sale of a product or service is clearly important for the financial health of a business as a whole. Sales data provide an essential proxy for the value created b a business. Quite simply, people would nc buy the product or service if it were not useful to them. When you have a paying "customer," revenue can provide information about both the scale of your work and its quality.

These dynamics are more complex in the work of social change. In donation-funded nonprofit organizations, the "buyer" is often not the "user."[272] Leaders need to rely on multiple sources of formation to ensure not just the health f the organization, but, more importantly, he efficacy of the work.

Government agencies also need formation systems to run their operaons. Many public entities have the added urden — and opportunity — of providing formation used by the community s a whole. Data released by the U.S. epartment of Labor or the Federal eserve can yield trillion-dollar swings in he public markets.

In general, the best solution to this omplex information puzzle is to select small set of metrics. They can be esented as a "dashboard" — a regularly odated visual presentation on a single age that reflects different signals about n organization's progress.

Articulating a hierarchy among these etrics presents a clearer picture of rogress over time. For example, a group orking to reduce carbon emissions in he cement industry should have a single timate metric: tons of carbon reduced. ut that metric might *lag* by years. ther activities could serve as *leading* dicators: the development of new arbon-reduction technologies, programs share them with cement production

facilities, or progress in the adoption of new regulations. These interim metrics give the organization a sense of its progress towards its distant goal.

For this information to be meaningful and reliable, however, monitoring cannot be an isolated function; it will be most effective if built into the cadence and processes of an organization. This monitoring can begin with internal meetings and be supplemented with external ones.

For example, at GuideStar we had quarterly "impact calls" that were modeled on for-profit earnings calls. Every three months, we invited all of our stakeholders to hear our progress across a set of metrics in our dashboard. Over the years, thousands of people joined us. We had the luxury of emphasizing the long-term nature of our work. We could frame the discussion to show where we were heading and how we planned to get there. Importantly, we integrated the same metrics into the regular operations of GuideStar itself. We intentionally carved out time at regular internal meetings to review progress and periodically paused to ensure that these were, in fact, the right metrics to use. This reinforced a symmetry of information between internal and external stakeholders.

External information can provide essential context. For example, a job-training program can assess its programs in the context of the state of the broader labor market. A drop in placement rates might be explained by weak employer demand rather than poor program quality.

The successes and failures of other organizations can be an invaluable source of information. Particularly helpful are studies using formal research methodology of a particular problem-solving approach — an "intervention." Replicating a successful program isn't always possible, because context matters. But evidence showing that an intervention that works in a particular context is a strong inducement to try it in another. (See the discussion of randomized controlled trials in the **Mathematical Modeling** chapter.)

Incentives

The title of a seminal article says it all: "On the Folly of Rewarding A, While Hoping for B."[273] People respond to rewards and punishments. There is a reason that sales commissions are based on closed sales, not simply on outreach.

But incentive alignment is not always so easy. People's motivations are too complex to distill management down to a science of mechanical interactions. For example, research suggests that most employees are less motivated by the size of their paycheck and more focused on dignity, respect, or autonomy.

Thoughtfulness about incentive alignment is central to making institutions work. Ann Mei Chang, CEO of Candid, says, "Incentives are the substrate out of which culture emerges and takes hold over time."[274] Accordingly, incentives should be reassessed periodically to make sure they are working.

We no choice but to account for the realities of human behavior. Complex organizations are particularly subject to incentive misalignment, because the person making the decision doesn't always deal with the consequences. If you set up incentives incorrectly, you may find that one part of an institution is embittered about cleaning up the messes left by another. (See the "Incentive Alignment" section in the **Behavioral Economics** chapter.)

A particular kind of incentive misalignment can be seen in the principal-agent problem." A company's owners, for example, might have a set of interests that are different from the company's management. Businesses often try to solve this problem through performance-based compensation.

But the subprime mortgage collapse of the 2008–2009 financial crisis showed how this approach can provide perverse incentives for management to make decisions based on whatever measures will determine their compensation. Financial company executives, compensated on short-term performance, invented lucrative but risky subprime mortgage investment vehicles — at the expense of their company's long-term reputation and, thus, financial future.

Social finance must deal with this dynamic. As environmental, social, and governance metrics are integrated into investment decisions, they will face Campbell's Law: important metrics will be gamed.[275] As the head of the Global Reporting Initiative, Eelco van Enden, commented, "What gets measured gets managed. But what gets measured also gets manipulated." Without attention to incentives, we may indeed hit the target but miss the point.

We hope for	But we often reward
long-term growth	quarterly earnings
mission impact	financial results
teamwork	individual effort
challenging "stretch" objectives	meeting goals
Total quality	executing on schedule
surfacing bad news early	reporting good news[276]

> "Democracy is the worst form of government except all those other forms."
>
> Winston Churchill

Regulation and the role of government

Government is both a context for institutions and a collection of them. In the U.S., there is no monolithic "The Government." The United States government, for example, is formed of at least 90,000 separate organizations operating at the national, state, and local levels.[277] Government policy produced by all those organizations sets a basic context in which other individual and organizational decisions are made.

Leaders — whether nonprofit or for-profit — forget this reality if they say, "I just want to be left alone." They fail to acknowledge the essential role government plays in making the market possible at all — whether through the physical infrastructure of roads, the maintenance of currency, or the rule of law. As economist Rebecca Henderson says, "markets require adult supervision."[278] Belief that the market can thrive without government is, in my mind, a case of the illusion of independence that we discuss in the **Behavioral Economics** chapter.

Some readers of this book will be government leaders and policymakers. Your choices create the architecture in which others act. Regulation can be necessary to deal with market failure, but it imposes very real consequences on the regulated. Government activity can yield extraordinary benefits (public universities) and severe injustice (systems of mass incarceration). The **Markets** chapter discusses how much of the work of social change is cleaning up the messes markets leave behind. The same principle applies for the messes that government regulation can inflict on society. Thus, in the work of social change, regulation is both a tool and a target.

Sometimes nonprofits serve — in an unofficial sense — as regulators. At GuideStar and Candid, we found ourselves playing a quasi-regulatory role; the very structure of our databases and the questions we asked set the context in which many millions of people understood the nonprofit sector. Similarly, we realized that our choices were — at least partially — determining what data was viewed through donation platforms. While our role was not a legal one, it was embedded in the system.

Organizations would be both morally and strategically wise to admit when they are playing any kind of "regulatory" role. Arts organizations regulate culture by choosing which artists to highlight.[279] A fair-trade cooperative regulates farming processes.

More generally, social change is itself taking place in a new kind of regulatory environment. Major for-profit technology platforms find themselves mediating human communication. Many advocacy efforts use technology platforms to pressure not just governments but companies and nonprofit organizations.

Thus, the work of social change is itself in part regulated by choices made by these technology platforms. We can and should debate whether it is appropriate in society for unelected leaders who own and run these platforms to have such power, but we also have to acknowledge the reality of the context in which we work.

Let me close this section with a brief defense of government. It is all too easy for politicians to criticize government ineptitude. Consider Ronald Reagan's famous line, "the nine most terrifying words in the English language are 'I'm from the government and I'm here to help.'" His joke is both funny and wrong. Consider some of the great enablers of the modern networked economy: the internet, the World Wide Web, portable computing, and GPS. Every single one was developed by a government entity.[280] Blanket critiques of government undermine society's potential. As Mariana Mazucatto says, "the subtle and insidious effect of this widely held view is to constrain civil servants with an ideology that says they can as easily do harm as good and chip away at their confidence...Ethos and creativity are crushed. A government that lacks imagination will find it difficult to create value. In reality, value emerges from the interaction of the public and private sectors and civil society."[281]

Governance

All institutions need mechanisms to make decisions. They can take many forms, from purely hierarchical to entirely consensus-driven. These structures can and should reflect the different purposes and strategies of each organization.

Individual corporations — whether nonprofit or for-profit — tend to have a division between governance and management. *Management* is the day-to-day operation of the organization. That role is symbolically — and at times practically — manifested in the chief executive. *Governance*, ultimate responsibility for the organization, rests with a board.

Board members may represent different constituencies or viewpoints. U.S. for-profit company boards legally represent the owners. But a corporation need not have a governance model built solely on ownership. In Germany, employees are given formal representation on the corporate board. In a nonprofit, the "owners" are, in a sense, society itself. While the corporate division of labor between management and governance has come to seem "normal," it is worth pondering the arbitrariness of this arrangement. There are many other ways to allocate power.

Government entities, for example, are led by a mix of people who are elected, appointed, or hired — or, indeed, have taken power by force. The roles may be at will, for a fixed term, or lifetime appointments. Government actually offers a much greater variety of governing models than the business and nonprofit sectors. This variety reminds us that there are many possible models to govern our work — and the world.

Collective governance is one of humanity's greatest inventions. But the mechanisms of the past may not work in the future. We must continue inventing new ways to make decisions, together.

All actions are enveloped by flaws
As fire is enveloped by smoke

Bhagavad Gita

A changing social contract

Institutional context changes, and so must institutions. Every day, we see how society is reassessing the rights and responsibilities of our institutions. To what degree are businesses responsible for addressing social problems? Do foundations represent societal interests or the interests of the wealthy? Are corporations an extension of the national security interests of their home country? Should nonprofits be held to the same financial standards as businesses? Should governments address economic externalities through taxation, regulation, or neither?

There is no sign that societal expectations will settle into an equilibrium. These questions will stay with us, and organizational leaders will have to navigate the environment. But there may be behaviors that are more likely to succeed in this dynamic context. I'll suggest four.

First, successful institutions will default to transparency. If institutions expect the benefits of access to others' information, they must provide access to their own.

Second, successful institutions will track multiple bottom lines. Social and environmental issues are now central to decision-making, so institutions must know their status and impact.

Third, successful institutions will proactively engage with stakeholders. Engage with your stakeholders before they engage with you.

Fourth, successful institutions will collaborate to solve shared problems. The world is changing too quickly to rely on any one institution to solve big problems.

Those institutions that adapt may be positioned to build legitimacy, flexibility, and resilience. Indeed, these four behaviors might even be preliminary elements of a new organizational social contract.

1. **Institutions are patterns of relationship. Organizations are the institutions that provide structure to collective activity.** They are lasting structures for how people connect, conflict, align, and entwine.

2. **Institutions are an essential context for the work of social change; we work within and through them.** Institutions can be effective or ineffective. Our challenge as change agents is to take institutions as they are, while also working to change them.

3. **Organizations are a means to an end, not an end in themselves. But organizations, like organisms, seek to survive. They protect their own existence.** Social change agents can inadvertently prioritize the success of their organization over its very purpose.

4. **Decision-making is bound and constrained by the organization's history, culture, and processes.** By examining how organizations function, social change agents can find insights to guide our own organizations and influence others.

5. **Finances tell you how money reflects the distribution of power within and around an organization.** Following the money can also reveal strategic leverage points to help you bend an organization's behavior.

6. **Culture is a set of norms that unconsciously guide actions within an organization.** We are what we repeatedly do. If you wish to build a culture, the essential fact is that you must repeat — again and again — the behavior you wish to see.

7. **A leader has to offer a story about how an organization might behave in a different way and then invite others into these new behaviors.** That invitation is more likely to be accepted and successful if the nonhuman factors — systems, processes, and finances — align with this new story.

8. **Information is a critical nutrient for organizations to thrive.** Optimally, clear metrics track progress. Measuring progress is more difficult for social change organizations than for businesses. The best solution is a "dashboard," a visual presentation of a small set of metrics that regularly reflect different signals about progress.

Jim Collins
Good to Great in the Social Sectors

Cass Sunstein
Simpler: The Future of Government

Leslie Crutchfield and Heather Mcleod Grant
Forces for Good: The Six Practices of High-Impact Nonprofits

9. **Incentive alignment is central to effective institutions.** Ann Mei Chang, CEO of Candid, says, "Incentives are the substrate out of which culture emerges and takes hold over time."

Catherine Shaw
The Campaign Manager: Running and Winning Local Elections

An enormous iceberg looms over the village of Ilulissat in Greenland, bringing with it the threat of tsunamis and metaphors.
Photo by Ulrik Pedersen

Justice is calling."

Darren Walker

"We may be brothers after all. We shall see."

Si'ahl (aka Chief Seattle)

Our descendants will probably outnumber our ancestors. If we can manage to survive as a species for a few more centuries, tens of billions of new humans will walk this planet. If we think ahead across millennia, there might even be trillions.[282]

And here we sit in a plastic hour. Flux and danger are all around us. The ground shifts beneath our feet. And we still dream of acting towards something greater.

What lies ahead? I don't know, and neither do you. The future is open, uncertain. What I can do is close this book with some hypotheses for those of us trying to do good in this world.

First, we can stretch our time horizons. The Earth has five billion years before the sun explodes; the least we can do is try to think in decades and not years. The billions of people who are likely to follow us deserve nothing less.

Second, we can open ourselves to new ways of thinking. to be ready to expand our personal toolbox. We do not have to fully embrace a new framework; instead we can try it on and see what it has to teach us.

Third, we can zoom out of our own narrow views. When we take a broader view, we not only gain analytical insight, we build interpersonal empathy. As we zoom out from our isolated perspectives, let us also pull back from our screens. Even for a moment, we can set aside glowing rectangles and find roots in prayer, exercise, nature, or meditation.

Fourth, we can remember that the kind thing to do is the strategic thing to do. Our world is messy and complex and dangerous, but ultimately it is kindness that allows us to build up something better.

The world will not easily yield to our visions of perfection. But, in the end, we are constrained only by the laws of physics. So let us check to see if the ground is okay. Then, we can turn our attention to the hard work of doing good. Next to us is a box of tools awaiting use by a righteous hand.

Acknowledgments

This book was written on the ancestral lands of the Piscataway, Nacostan, and Manahoac peoples.

Many hands make heavy work. Collaboration and learning takes time and energy. And it is so very, very worth it.

I'm grateful to every author I've read, whether I agreed with them or not. I'm grateful to every practitioner I witnessed, whether they were successful or not. I'm grateful to the countless people throughout history who worked for something better. We all owe them our thanks.

My career has been guided and supported by too many mentors to list. But I'll mention several as formative for me: Susan Bell, Jeff Bradach, Mike Brune, Paul Brest, Hal Harvey, and Mari Kuraishi. I'm grateful to all of my teachers, especially Bill Meehan, Laura Arrillaga-Andreesen, Larry Goodwyn, Michael Hardt, Warren Hierl, and Hubert Decleer.

Many colleagues have directly supported me in writing this book — whether by providing feedback on manuscripts, title possibilities, stories, or poems. I received invaluable input from Christie George, Rodney Christopher, Sarah Hurwitz, Paul Brest, Henry Timms,

Lee Drutman, Elbert Ventura, Jeff Bradach, Alix Guerrier, Ben Harder, Jon Jacoby, Paula Goldman, Deena Rosen, Phil Buchanan, Asha Curran, Tony Curnes, Sarah Stein Greenberg, Gabe Cohen, Brian Trelstad, Kathy Reich, Minh-Thu Pham, Peter Tavernisi, Beowulf Sheehan, and others.

I had the immense privilege to write much of this book in residence at the Rockefeller Foundation's Bellagio Center on the shores of Italy's Lake Como. I'm grateful to Zia Khan and Sarah Geisenheimer for facilitating my residency there. And my warmest thanks to Pilar Palaciá, Alice Luperto, and the rest of the staff at the Villa Serbelloni for making my experience both productive and transcendently pleasant. And my fellow residents in Bellagio were of immense intellectual and emotional support. Here's to the pasta, Vitus Azeem, Josiane Sylvie Mbakop Noukeu, Gregory Mitchell, Taylor Royle, Shu Lea Chang, and Russell Lewis.

For shorter writing stints in various nooks of the Appalachians, I'm grateful to Alex Laskey, Rachel Farbiarz, Dennis Whittle, and Mari Kuraishi.

Thanks to my delightful agent Leah Spiro for shepherding me through the process. My editors at Wiley, Brian Neill, and Deborah Schindlar, have been great allies and anchors. Researcher Sara Rhodin Lechtenberg was most helpful as I got started. And I'm especially grateful to Barbara Cornell, research assistant, editor, and colleague extraordinaire for joining me on this particular safari.

Ultimately, this book is the product of family; I've dedicated it to my father, David Harold, and my late mother, Madeline Harold. They taught me to be, to see, and to love. My beloved sister, Rachel Harold, has been with me since the cornfields. My in-laws, Gerald and Janice Sufrin, have fueled this work with their enthusiasm, curiosity, and support.

Every day, my sons, Cyrus and Micah, remind me why it matters to care about the future. May you both find the tools you need to build a more beautiful world.

And none of this would be possible without my magnificent wife, Carolyn Sufrin. She has supported me with her heart, her time, and her intellect. Go buy her book, *Jailcare: Finding the Safety Net for Women Behind Bars*. As she will tell you, there is still work to be done.

Bibliography

Abraham, Ralph and Shaw, Christopher
Dynamics:
The Geometry of Behavior, Part 1
Aerial Press, 2016

Alexander, Christopher; Ishikawa, Sara;
Silverstein, Murray, et al.
A Pattern Language:
Towns, Buildings, Construction
Oxford University Press, 1977

Allinsky, Saul
Rules for Radicals:
A Practical Primer for Realistic Radicals
Vintage, 1989

Appiah, Kwame Anthony
Cosmopolitanism:
Ethics in a World of Strangers
W. W. Norton, 2006

Barabási, Albert-László
with Pósfai, Márton
Network Science
Cambridge University Press, 2019

Bateson, Gregory
Steps to an Ecology of Mind:
A Revolutionary Approach to Man's
Understanding of Himself
Ballantine Books, 1978

Battilana, Julie and Casciaro, Tiziana
Power for All:
How It Really Works and Why It's
Everyone's Business
Simon & Schuster, 2021

Baudrillard, Jean
The Agony of Power
Semiotext(e), 1997

Benyus, Janine M
Biomimicry:
Innovation Inspired by Nature
HarperPerennial, 2002

Boggs, Grace Lee with Kurashige, Scott
The Next American Revolution:
Sustainable Activism
for the Twenty-First Century
University of California Press, 2012

Boulton, Jean G; Allen, Peter M.;
and Bowman, Cliff
Embracing Complexity:
Strategic Perspectives for an
Age of Turbulence
Oxford University Press, 2015

Bourgeois III, L.J.; Eygenson, Serge;
and Namasondhi, Kanokrat
The Tao of Strategy:
How Seven Eastern Philosophies
Help Solve Twenty-First Century
Business Challenges
University of Virginia Press, 2021

Boyd, Andrew co-editor and
wrangler-in-chief; Mitchell, Dave Oswald
co-editor
Beautiful Trouble:
A Toolbox for Revolution
OR Books, 2012

Brand, Stewart
How Buildings Learn:
What Happens after They're Built
Penguin, 1994

Brest, Paul and Harvey, Hal
Money Well Spent:
A Strategic Plan for Smart Philanthropy
Bloomberg Press, 2008

Brest, Paul and Krieger, Linda Hamilton
Problem Solving, Decision Making,
and Professional Judgment:
A Guide for Lawyers and Policymakers
Oxford University Press, 2010

brown, adrienne maree
Emergent Strategy:
Shaping Change, Changing Worlds
AK Press, 2017

Brown, Tim
Change by Design:
How Design Thinking Transforms
Organizations and Inspires Innovation
Harper Business, 2009

Buchanan, Phil
Giving Done Right:
Effective Philanthropy
and Making Every Dollar Count
Public Affairs, 2019

Capra, Fritjof and Luisi, Pier Luigi
The Systems View of Life:
A Unifying Vision
Cambridge University Press, 2019

Carl Jung
The Red Book
Liber Novus, Philemon, 2009

Carse, James P.
Finite and Infinite Games:
A Vision of Life as Play and Possibility
Free Press, 2012

Chagnot, Annie and Emi Ikkanda, editors
How Lovely the Ruins:
Inspirational Poems and Words for
Difficult Times
Spiegel & Grau, 2017

Chakravorti, Bhaskar
The Slow Pace of Fast Change:
Bringing Innovations to Market in
a Connected World
Harvard Business School Press, 2003

Chang, Ann Mei
Lean Impact: How to Innovate for Radically
Greater Social Good
John Wiley & Sons, Inc., 2019

Chenoweth, Erica and Maria Stephan
Why Civil Resistance Works:
The Strategic Logic of Nonviolent Conflict
Columbia University Press, 2012

Cialdini, Robert B.
Influence: Science and Practice
Allyn and Bacon, 2001

Cohen, Ronald
Impact: Reshaping Capitalism
to Drive Real Change
Ebury Press, 2020

Collins, Jim
Good to Great in the Social Sectors:
Why Business Thinking Is Not the Answer
Harper Collins, 2005

Collins, Jim and Porras, Jerry I
Built to Last:
Successful Habits
of Visionary Companies
HarperBusiness, 2002

Crews, James editor
How to Love the World:
Poems of Gratitude and Hope
Storey Publishing, 2012

Cukier, Kenneth, Victor Mayer-
Schonberger, and Francis de Vericourt
Framers:
Human Advantage in an Age of
Technology and Turmoil
Dutton, 2021

Doerr, John
Measure What Matters
Penguin Business, 2018

Drutman, Lee
Breaking the Two-Party Doom Loop:
The Case for Multiparty Democracy
in America
Oxford University Press, 2020

Duncombe, Steve and Lambert, Steve
The Art of Activism:
Your All-Purpose Guide
to Making the Impossible Possible
OR Books, 2021

Ebrahim, Alnoor
Measuring Social Change:
Performance and Accountability
in a Complex World
Stanford Business Books: 2019

Ellenberg, Jordan
Shape: The Hidden Geometry of
Information, Biology, Strategy,
Democracy, and Everything Else
Penguin Press, 2021

Federal Reserve Bank of San Francisco
and Nonprofit Finance Fund
What Matters: Investing in Results
Federal Reserve Bank of San Francisco
and Nonprofit Finance Fund, 2017

Fleishman, Joel
The Foundation: A Great American
Secret; How Private Wealth Is Changing
the World
Public Affairs, 2009

Franklin, Ursula M.
The Real World of Technology
Anansi Press Inc. 2004

Freedman, Lawrence
Strategy: A History
Oxford University Press, 2013

Freire, Paolo
Translated by Myra Bergman Ramos
Pedagogy of the Oppressed
The Continuum International Publishing
Group Inc., 2003

Gaddis, John Lewis
On Grand Strategy
Penguin Books, 2019

Gawande, Atul
The Checklist Manifesto
Picador, 2011

Gbowee, Leymah with Mithers, Carol
Mighty Be Our Powers: How Sisterhood,
Prayer, and Sex Changed a Nation at War
Beast Books Kindle edition, 2011

Giridharadas, Anand
Winners Take All:
The Elite Charade of Chaging the World
Alfred A. Knopf, 2018

Gleick, James
The Information:
A History, a Theory, a Flood
Pantheon Books, 2011

Gorman, Amanda
Call Us What We Carry
Viking, 2021

Gyasi, Yaa
Homegoing
Random House, 2016

Harari, Yuval Noah
Sapiens: A Brief History of Humankind
HarperPerennial, 2018

Hariri, Yuval Noah
21 Lessons
for the 21st Century
Jonathan Cape, 2018

Heath, Chip and Dan Heath
Made to Stick:
Why Some Ideas Survive and Others Die
Random House, 2007

Heimans, Jeremy and Timms, Henry
New Power:
How Movements Build, Businesses
Thrive, and Ideas Catch Fire in Our
Hyperconnected World
Doubleday, 2018

Henderson, Rebecca
Reimagining Capitalism
in a World on Fire
Public Affairs, 2020

Hirshfield, Jane
Ten Windows:
How Great Poems Transform the World
Alfred A. Knopf, 2015

Hisrich, Robert and Amr Al-Dabbagh
Governpreneurship:
Establishing a Thriving Entrepreneurial
Spirit in Government
Edward Elgar, 2013

Hoffer, Eric
The True Believer: Thoughts on the
Nature of Mass Movements
HarperPerennial, 1989

Hölldobler, Bert and Wilson, Edward O.
Journey to the Ants:
A Story of Scientific Exploration
The Belknap Press of Harvard University
Press, 1995

Hopkins, Gerard Manley
As kingfishers catch fire
Penguin Classics, 2015

Ichioka, Sarah and Micahel Pawlyn
Flourish: Design Paradigms
for Our Planetary Emergency
Triarchy Press, 2021

Intrator, Sam M. and Scribner, Megan
editors
Leading from Within:
Poetry that Sustains the Courage to Lead
Jossey-Bass, 2007

Intrator, Sam M. and Scribner, Megan
editors
Teaching with Fire: Poetry that Sustains
the Courage to Teach
Jossey-Bass, 2003

Kahneman, Daniel
Thinking, Fast and Slow
Farrar, Straus and Giroux, 2011

Kauffman, L.A.
How to Read a Protest:
The Art of Organizing and Resistance
University of California Press, 2018

Kauffman, Stuart
At Home in the Universe:
The Search for the Laws of Self-
Organization and Complexity
Oxford University Press, 1995

Kimmerer, Robin Wall
Braiding Sweetgrass:
Indigenous Wisdom, Scientific
Knowledge, and the Teachings of Plants
Milkweed Editions, 2013

King, Martin Luther
Why We Can't Wait
Signet, 2000

La Piana, David
The Nonprofit Strategy Revolution
Fieldstone Alliance, 2008

Lakoff, George
Moral Politics:
How Liberals and Conservatives Think
The University of Chicago Press, 2002

Lawson, Len; Manick, Cynthia; and
Jackson, Gaby editors
The Future of Black: Afrofuturism,
Black Comics, and Superhero Poetry
Blair, 2021

Leicester, Graham and Maureen O'Hara
Ten Things to Do
in a Conceptual Emergency
Triarchy Press, 2009

Levine, Philip
What Work Is
Knopf, 1998

Levinson, Marc
The Box: How the Shipping Container
Made the World Smaller and the World
Economy Bigger
Princeton University Press, 2016

Lopez, Barry
Arctic Dreams
Vintage, 2001

MacAskill, William
Doing Good Better:
How Effective Altruism Can Help You Help
Others, Do Work that Matters, and Make
Smarter Choices About Giving Back
Avery, 2016

MacFarlane, Robert
Landmarks
Penguin Books, 2016

Maeda, John
The Laws of Simplicity
MIT Press, 2006

Mandela, Nelson
Long Walk to Freedom:
The Autobiography of Nelson Mandela
Back Bay Books, 1995

Martin, Roger
The Opposable Mind: How Successful
Leaders Win Through Integrative Thinking
Harvard Business School Press, 2007

Mazzucato, Mariana
Mission Economy: A Moonshot Guide to
Changing Capitalism
Harper Business, 2021

McGhee, Heather
The Sum of Us:
What Racism Costs Everyone
and How We Can Prosper Together
One World, 2022

McLuhan, Marshall
Essential McLuhan
Routledge, 1997

Menand, Louis
The Metaphysical Club:
A Story of Ideas in America
Farrar, Straus and Giroux, 2002

Merton, Thomas edited by Szabo, Lynn R.
In the Dark Before Dawn:
New Selected Poems of Thomas Merton
New Directions Books, 2005

Mitchell, Melanie
Complexity: A Guided Tour
Oxford University Press, 2011

Mitchell, Stephen
The Second Book of the Tao
Penguin, 1989

Mitchell, Stephen editor
The Enlightened Heart:
An Anthology of Sacred Poetry
HarperPerennial, 1993

Mitchell, Stephen editor
The Enlightened Mind:
An Anthology of Sacred Prose
HarperPerennial, 1993

Odell, Jenny
How to Do Nothing:
Resisting the Attention Economy
Melville House, 2019

Oliver, Mary
New and Selected Poems, Volume Two
Beacon Press, 2005

Olson, Mancur
The Logic of Collective Action:
Public Goods and the Theory of Groups
Harvard University Press, 1965

Ostrom, Elinor
Governing the Commons:
The Evolution of Institutions
for Collective Action
Canto Classics, 2019

Payne, Charles M.
I've Got the Light of Freedom:
The Organizing Tradition and the
Mississippi Freedom Struggle
University of California Press, 1996

Pendleton-Jullian, Ann M. and
Brown, John Seely
Design Unbound: Desiging for Emergence
in a White Water World
The MIT Press, 2018

Pfeffer, Jeffrey
Power: Why Some People Have It —
And Others Don't
Harper Business, 2010

Piketty, Thomas
Capital in the Twenty-First Century
The Belknap Press of Harvard University
Press, 2014

Pinker, Steven
The Sense of Style:
The Thinking Person's Guide to Writing
in the 21st Century
Allen Lane, 2014

Pope Francis (Jorge Mario Bergoglio)
Laudato Si:
On Care for Our Common Home
Libreria Editrice Vaticana, 2015

Pope Francis (Jorge Mario Bergoglio)
Gaudete et Exsulate
Wellspring, 2018

Poundstone, William
Prisoner's Dilemma:
John von Neumann, Game Theory,
and the Puzzle of the Bomb
Anchor, 1993

Reich, Rob
Just Giving:
Why Philanthropy Is Failing Democracy
and How It Can Do Better
Princeton University Press, 2018

Reinsborough, Patrick and
Channing, Doyle
Re: Imagining Change:
How to use story-based strategy
to win campaigns, build movements,
and change the world
PM Press, 2017

Reiser + Umemoto
Atlas of Novel Tectonics
Princeton Architectural Press, 2006

Ries, Eric
The Lean Startup:
How Today's Entrepreneurs Use
Continuous Innovation to
Create Radically Successful Businesses
Crown Business, 2011

Robinson, Kim Stanley
The Ministry for the Future
Orbit, 2021

Roy, Arundhati
The Algebra of Infinite Justice
Penguin Books India, 2002

Sapolsky, Robert M.
Behave: The Biology of Humans
at Our Best and Worst
Penguin Books, 2018

Sharp, Gene
Sharp's Dictionary of Power and Struggle:
Language of Civil Resistance in Conflicts
Oxford University Press, 2012

Shaw. Catherine
The Campaign Manager:
Running and Winning Local Elections
Routledge, 2018

Sheldrake, Merlin
Entangled Life:
How Fungi Make Our Worlds, Change
Our Minds and Shape Our Futures
Random House, 2020

Sinclair, Upton
The Cry for Justice:
An Anthology of Social Protest
Seven Stories Press, 2019

Smith, Huston
The World's Religions:
Our Great Wisdom Traditions
HarperSanFrancisco, 1991

Smucker, Jonathan Matthew
Hegemony How-To:
A Roadmap for Radicals
AK Press, 2017

Solnit, Rebecca
Hope in the Dark:
Untold Histories, Wild Possibilities
Haymarket Books, 2016

Solnit, Rebecca
A Paradise Built in Hell: The Extraordinary
Communities that Arise in Disaster
Penguin Books, 2010

Stavans, Ilan
Selected Translations: Poems 2000-2020
University of Pittsburgh Press, 2021

Stavridis, Adm. James and
Ancell, R Manning
The Leader's Bookshelf
Naval Institute Press, 2017

Steffen, Alex editor
Worldchanging: A User's Guide for
the 21st Century
Abrams, 2008

Stein Greenberg, Sarah
Creative Acts for Curious People
Ten Speed Press, 2021

Suzuki, Shunryu
Zen Mind, Beginner's Mind: Informal Talks
on Zen Meditation and Practice
John Weatherhill Inc., 1988

Taylor, Adam Russel
A More Perfect Union: A New Vision for
Building the Beloved Community
Broadleaf Books, 2021

Teilhard de Chardin, Pierre
Building the Earth
Dimension Books,1965

Tell, Gillian
Anthro-Vision:
A New Way to See in Business and Life
Avid Reader Press, 2021

Thaler, Richard H. and Sunstein, Cass R.
Nudge: Improving Decisions About
Health, Wealth, and Happiness
Yale University Press, 2008

Thanissara
Time to Stand Up: An Engaged Buddhist
Manifesto for Our Earth
North Atlantic Books, 2015

Thomas, Lewis
The Lives of a Cell:
Notes of a Biology Watcher
Penguin Books, 1978

Thoreau, Henry David
Walden and Civil Disobedience
Barnes & Noble Classics, 2005

Tolstoy, Leo, translated by Sekirin, Peter
A Calendar of Wisdom:
Daily Thoughts to Nourish the Soul
Scribner, 1997

Tsing, Anna Lowenhaupt
The Mushroom at the End of the World:
On the Possibility of Life
in Capitalist Ruins
Princeton University Press, 2017

Tufte, Edward R.
The Visual Display of
Quantitative Information
Graphics Press, 2006

Venkataraman, Bina
The Optimist's Telescope:
Thinking Ahead in a Reckless Age
Penguin, 2019

Vialet, Jill and von Moos, Amanda
Substantial Classrooms:
Redesigning the Substitute Teaching
Experience
Jossey-Bass Kindle edition, 2021

Villanueva, Edgar
Decolonizing Wealth: Indigenous Wisdom
to Heal Divides and Restore Balance
Berrett-Koehler, 2021

von Clausewitz, Carl
On War
Princeton Paperback, 1989

Waldrop, M. Mitchell
Complexity: The Emerging Science
at the Edge of Order and Chaos
Touchstone, 1993

Weil, Simone
Gravity and Grace
Bison Books, University of Nebraska
Press, 1997

West, Geoffrey
Scale: The Universal Laws of Growth,
Innovation, Sustainability,
and the Pace of Life in Organisms, Cities,
Economies, and Companies
Penguin Press, 2017

White, Micah.
The End of Protest:
A New Playbook for Revolution
Alfred A. Knopf Canada, 2016

Wiener, Norbert
Cybernetics: Control and Communication
in the Animal and the Machine
The MIT Press, 1965

Wilkerson, Isabel
Caste:
The Origins of Our Discontents
Random House, 2020

Williams, J.D.
The Compleat Strategist:
Being a Primer on the Theory
of Games of Strategy
Dover, 1986

Wright Edelman, Marian.
The Measure of Our Success:
A Letter to My Children and Yours
Beacon Press, 1992

Yunkaporta, Tyson
Sand Talk:
How Indigenous Thinking
Can Save the World
HarperOne, 2021

Endnotes

Introduction

1   "The Calling of Delight: Gangs, Service, and Kinship." Interview with Greg Boyle. *On Being*. February 26, 2013. (Fr. Boyle has offered various versions of this quote elsewhere.)

2   *As If: Idealization and Ideals*, pg. x. Harvard University Press, 2019.

3   Lorde, Audre. "The Master's Tools Will Never Dismantle the Master's House." 1984. *Sister Outsider: Essays and Speeches*, pg. 110–114. Crossing Press, 2007.

4   Beckerman, Gal. "Radical Ideas Need Quiet Spaces," *The New York Times*, February 10, 2022.

5   See Wright Edelman (1992), section 1. She may have been referencing Muhammad Ali's quote, "Service to others is the rent you pay for your room here on earth," which he wrote in a note to the staff of the Atlanta Hilton on April 19, 1978.

6   Ben Paynter, "GuideStar and the Foundation Center are merging to form the definitive nonprofit transparency organization." *Fast Company*. February 5, 2019.

Chapter 1: An Age of Flux

7   "An Intellectual Entente," *Harvard Magazine*, September 10, 2009.

8   Chang (2019), pg. 180.

9   For more good news, see: https://www.vox.com/2014/11/24/7272929/global-poverty-health-crime-literacy-good-news

10   From "Monomyth." Gorman (2021), pg. 191.

11   https://blogs.worldbank.org/opendata/17-statistics-world-statistics-day-and-why-we-need-invest-them

12   https://blogs.worldbank.org/opendata/17-statistics-world-statistics-day-and-why-we-need-invest-them

13   https://www.worldometers.info/

https://plasticoceans.org/the-facts/

https://www.worldometers.info/

https://www.sentencingproject.org/
riminal-justice-facts/

Butler, Octavia E., *The Parable of the Talents*,
g. 72. Grand Central Publishing Reprint Edition,
ugust 20, 2019.

Laudato Si, Chapter 1, Paragraph 18.

"From the Chairman: The Pace of Change."
int Forces Quarterly, January 26, 2017. Quoted
Wood, David. "We Need a Slow War Movement."
ackbencher, March 16, 2021.

Chakravorti (2003).

Quoted by Hugh Raffles in *The Book of
nconformities: Speculations on Lost Time*.
antheon Books, 2020.

Nearing, Helen and Scott. *Living the Good Life*,
g. 39. Shocken Books, 1954.

Toffler, Alvin. *Future Shock*, pg. 2. Bantam
eissue Edition, June 1, 1984.

Our fragmentation is not just a virtual phenom-
on. A spatial dynamic helped build our islands
belief. In the United States, this has come to be
nown as the "Big Sort" — the physical relocation
people to neighborhoods full of people just like
emselves. This geographic division complicates
asic human communication, not to mention the
ork of changemakers.

*Artificial Life: Proceedings of an
terdisciplinary Workshop on the Synthesis
d Simulation of Living Systems*. Pg 43. From a
orkshop in 1987 hosted by Los Alamos National
aboratory and co-sponsored by the Center for
onlinear Studies, the Santa Fe Institute, and
ple Computer Inc. Later published as a book by
utledge in 2019.

See, for example, Jared Diamond's *Collapse*.
enguin, 2011.

27 For a discussion of the link between pollution
and discriminatory housing practices see,
"Redlining means 45 million Americans are breathing dirtier air, 50 years after it ended" by Darryl
Fears in the Washington Post, March 9, 2022.

28 *Reflections on the Human Condition* (1973).
(Quoted in Stein Greenberg 2021.)

29 See https://candid.org/explore-issues/
us-social-sector/money

30 In China, you even see influential GONGOs,
"government organized
nongovernmental organizations."

31 Quoted by George Packer in "America's Plastic
Hour is Upon Us." *The Atlantic*, October 2020.

32 Recent science has demonstrated the human
brain's extraordinary capacity for change — a phenomenon known as "neuroplasticity." Old dogs can,
in fact, learn new tricks. Perhaps human society
can show a similar capability, a socioplasticity.

33 Roy, Arundhati. "The pandemic is a portal."
Financial Times, April 3, 2020. I cannot help but
to note another dimension to Roy's remarkable
metaphor. In physics, "flux" is defined as a volume
passing through a surface over a given amount of
time. As we think the "flux" of a changing world, the
equations of science match her image of passage
through a portal.

34 Serious thinkers have suggested that the
21st century may be the most important in history.
See, for example, https://www.cold-takes.com/
most-important-century/

35 Merton, Thomas. *Contemplation in a World of
Action, pg. 149*. University of California Press, 1968.
Quoted in Odell (2019), pg. 59.

36 From *Prejudices: Second Series*, pg. 155. Alfred
A. Knopf, 1920.

37 Brown, Eliot and Maureen Farrell. *The Cult of
We: WeWork, Adam Neumann, and the Great Startup
Delusion*. Crown, 2021.

Chapter 2: The Shape of Strategy

38   Interview with Alvin Toffler by James Daily, September 26, 2000. http://iranscope.ghandchi.com/Anthology/Alvin_Toffler00.htm

39   The poster was originally designed and distributed by the Canadian magazine *Adbusters*. You can find an — admittedly controversial — telling of the story in Micah White's *The End of Protest*. For a nuanced analysis of Occupy Wall Street, see Smucker (2017).

40   Taylor, Astra and Jonathan Smucker. "Occupy Wall Street Changed Everything," *New York Magazine*, September 17, 2021. https://nymag.com/intelligencer/2021/09/occupy-wall-street-changed-everything.html

41   McGhee (2021), pg 129

42   Lathrop, Yannet. "Impact of the Fight for $15: $68 Billion in Raises, 22 Million Workers". National Employment Law Project. Retrieved March 13, 2019.

43   Havel@80 — The Vaclav Havel Library Foundation (vhlf.org). https://www.vhlf.org/news/havel80/

44   From his course on social movements at Duke University in Spring of 1998.

45   Ellenberg (2021), pg. 19.

46   In particular, I'd recommend this online toolkit from the Stanford Center on Social Innovation: "Developing a Strategy for Social Impact." https://tinyurl.com/impacttoolbox. For creating a social enterprise business model, see: https://socialbusinessdesign.org/business-models-for-social-enterprises/; For a variety of strategic and operational templates, see https://diytoolkit.org/

47   Kaizen is a Japanese business philosophy — often translated as "continuous improvement" — that aims to increase quality, productivity, and morale. It is cyclical in structure, often oriented around a "plan-do-check-act" iteration. Kaizen seeks to empower individual employees to make small changes to a process while also creating space to think about the overall process or structure.

48   Agile is a methodology commonly used in software development. It offers a framework for teams to organize their activities. See the discussion in the **Design Thinking** chapter.

49   Lean Startup is a methodology for start-up companies outlined by Eric Ries in his book *The Lean Startup*. It has been used by countless start-ups — especially in technology. The Lean Startup methodology emphasizes constant learning and user engagement. In large part, it accounts for the common use of terms like "minimum viable product" and "pivot" in Silicon Valley.

50   The OODA loop was originally developed by Colonel John Boyd of the United States Air Force as a framework for fighter pilots. He suggested that pilots go through a constant cycle: observe-orient-decide-act. Quickly moving through the loop can make one more responsive and interrupt the decision-making of an opponent. Over time, this framework was expanded to military strategy in general and then to other disciplines.

51   This quote appears to be apocryphal. I could not find a definitive citation.

The International Futures Forum has proposed framework for how to approach strategic lanning worth mentioning here. They imagine our quadrants defined by two axes: agency and ncertainty. If you have high agency and face low ncertainty, you can simply make a "roadmap" of our plan. With low agency and high uncertainty, ou can go through a process of considering different "scenarios." If you have low agency but also ow uncertainty, you can create a forecast. And if ou have high agency in a situation of uncertainty, ou have to make your own "pathway." (Quoted in hioka and Pawlyn, 2021, pg 29.)

From the translation by William Butler Yeats nd Shree Purohit Swami. Quoted in Mitchell (1991).

Thinking about preservation, I'm struck by uotes from political opposites saying much the ame thing. First, environmentalist Edward Abbey rote, "At some point we must draw a line across ne ground of our home and our being, drive a spear to the land and say to the bulldozers, earthmov- s, government and corporations, 'thus far and no rther.'" Second, conservative William F. Buckley, ho, in the mission statement of the conservative ational Review explained that "it stands athwart story, yelling 'Stop,' at a time when no one is clined to do so, or to have much patience with ose who so urge it."

For more monitoring, evaluation, and learning sources, see Ebrahim (2019); Doerr (2017); d Coffman, Julia and Tanya Beer. "The Advocacy rategy Framework." Center for Evaluation novation, 2015.

The Human Condition, page 250. Second lition. University of Chicago Press, 2019 (first blished 1958).

Select resources compiling evidence out which interventions work: What Works earinghouse, https://ies.ed.gov/ncee/wwc/ ducation); Spotlight on Poverty and Opportunity, tps://spotlightonpoverty.org/ (poverty); chrane, https://www.cochrane.org/ (health).

58   Appiah (2006), pg. 145.

59   Chenoweth and Stephan (2012).

60   Pg. 52, Odell (2019).

61   Mearsheimer, John J. "Assessing the Conventional Balance: the 3:1 Rule and Its Critics." *International Security*, Volume 13, No 4 (Spring, 1989, 54–89. and Davis, Paul K. "Aggregation, Disaggregation, and the 3:1 Rule in Ground Combat." RAND Corporation. Prepared for US Air Force, US Army, Office of Secretary of Defense. 1996. (Application to non-human animals: Clifton, Elizabeth. "A Brief Review on the Application of Lanchester's Models of Combat in Nonhuman Animals." *Ecological Psychology*, 2020, Vol. 32, 181–191.)

62   From "Observations on Spanish Affairs," a letter to his brother Joseph from August 27, 1808. A related argument can be found in Clausewitz (1976), 77: "Power of resistance… can be expressed as the product of two inseparable factors, viz. the total means at his disposal and the strength of his will."

63   In this quote, Johnson was paraphrasing Collete Pinchon Battle. From Episode #5, "Black Lives Matter and the Climate," *How to Save a Planet*, September 2020.

Chapter 3: Ethics and Social Change

64   brown (2017), 134.

65   Quoted in Tolstoy (1987), pg. 199.

66   As philosopher Kwame Anthony Appiah says, "We enter every conversation — whether with neighbors or with strangers — without a promise of final agreement." Appiah (2006), pg. 44.

67   "Digital Impact 4Q4: Alison Carlman and Alix Guerrier on the Paradox of Platform Neutrality." https://digitalimpact.io/a-new-approach-to-solving-the-paradox-of-platform-neutrality/

68   Malunga, Chiku and Charles Banda. *Understanding Organizational Sustainability Through African Proverbs*. Impact Alliance Press, 2004.

69   Barber, Gregory, "Ada Palmer and the Weird Hand of Progress." *Wired*, February 10, 2022. https://www.wired.com/story/ada-palmer-sci-fi-future-weird-hand-progress/

70   Venkataraman (2019).

72   Sigal, Samuel. "What we owe to future generations." *Vox*, July 2, 2021.

73   For resources on long-term scenario planning, see the website of the Institute for the Future: http://iftf.org

73   Singer, Peter, *The Life You Can Save*. Random House, 2009.

74   *Gaudete et Exsulate*, paragraphs 88–89. Wellspring, 2018.

75   https://candid.org/explore-issues/us-social-sector/money

76   This quote is widely attributed to Hinmatóowyalahtqit but may be apocryphal. It undoubtedly describes his remarkable approach to communications.

77   "Inclusion is patriotism of the highest order." *Washington Post*, July 2, 2021.

78   *The Late Show with Stephen Colbert*. November 18, 2016. When first introducing the concept on *The Colbert Report*, season 1, episode 1, October 17, 2005, he added, "The gut. That's where the truth comes from, ladies and gentlemen, the gut." See also: Bullshit. Bullshit is talk for the sake of talk, discourse that advances the conversation to nowhere. As the philosopher Harry Frankfurter said in *On Bullshit*, "It is impossible for someone to lie unless he thinks he knows the truth. Producing bullshit requires no such conviction...neither on the side of the true nor on the side of the false."

79   "Lies and honest mistakes," AEON, July 5, 202 https://aeon.co/essays/our-epistemic-crisis-is-essentially-ethical-and-so-are-its-solutions

80   See Wilkerson (2020).

81   "The Truest Eye." *O, The Oprah Magazine*. November 2003.

82   "The Faith of a First Lady: Eleanor Roosevelt's Spirituality." Truman Library Institute https://www.trumanlibraryinstitute.org/faith-first-lady-eleanor-roosevelts-spirituality/

83   It is worth highlighting that Sambuli emphasizes that this phenomenon is especially present f fundraisers in the Global South raising money fro the Global North.

84   Packer, George, "America's Plastic Hour Is Up Us." *The Atlantic*, October 2020.

85   See *The Happy, Healthy Nonprofit: Strategies for Impact without Burnout* by Beth Kanter and Ali Sherman. Wiley, 2016.

Chapter 4: Storytelling

86   See Hariri, *Sapiens* (2018).

87   From Levar Burton's course on storytelling. https://www.masterclass.com/classes/levar-burton-teaches-the-power-of-storytelling

88   Cone, Kitty. "Short History of the 504 Sit-in," Disability Rights Education & Defense Fund. ` https://dredf.org/504-sit-in-20th-anniversary/short-history-of-the-504-sit-in/

89   See Stith Thompson's *Motif-Index of Folk-Literature: A Classification of Narrative Elements in Folk-Tales, Ballads, Myths, Fables, Mediaeval Romances, Exempla, Fabliaux, Jest-Books, and Loc Legends* (Rosenkilde and Bagger, 1955–58).

90   Campbell, Joseph. *The Hero with a Thousand Faces*. 1949, Pantheon Books.

The desire to be a hero can become fraught with moral and psychological conflict. For example, as explained by Heather McGhee, "It's just human: nature we all like to see ourselves as on the side of the heroes in a story. But for white Americans today who are awake to the reality of American racism, that's nearly impossible…It can cause contradictions and justifications, feelings of guilt, shame, projection, resentment, and denial. Ultimately, though, we are all paying for the moral conflict of white Americans." McGhee (2022), Pg. 222.

Brockington, Guilherme, Ana Paula Gomes Moreira et al. "Storytelling increases oxytocin and positive emotions and decreases cortisol and pain in hospitalized children." *PNAS*, May 24, 2021. https://www.pnas.org/content/118/22/2018409118

Quoted in Smith (1991), pg. 35.

From a 1970 interview between Cesar Chavez and John Moyer. This interview took place near the end of the Delano grape strike, the first successful organizing effort of farmworkers in the United States. https://libraries.ucsd.edu/farmworkermovement/essays/essays/MillerArchive/037%20A%20conversation%20with%20Cesar%20Chavez.pdf

"Best Story Wins." February 11, 2021 https://www.collaborativefund.com/blog/story/

As compiled in the Wikipedia entry "Once upon a time." https://en.wikipedia.org/wiki/Once_upon_a_time

See further discussion of public narrative in Battilana and Casciaro (2021) and Taylor (2021).

Solnit (2016), pg. 31.

Blackwell, Angela Glover, "The Curb-Cut Effect," *Stanford Social Innovation Review*. Winter 2017.

Chapter 5: Mathematical Modeling

100   If a customer buys once a year, average revenue for a product is the same as price.

101   See Brest, Paul, Hal Harvey, and Kelvin Low, "Calculated Impact," *Stanford Social Innovation Review*. Winter 2009.

102   Notes on these calculations. These expected value calculations are on an ongoing annual basis. They could also be calculated for a fixed time period. Strategy One assumes (a) you can buy — and plant — 20 acres of degraded land at $5,000/acre and (b) that leads to steady-state of 4 tons of CO_2 reduced per year. All of these assumptions would vary significantly by local economic and ecological factors. (See: U.S. Environmental Protection Agency, Office of Atmospheric Programs, "Greenhouse Gas Mitigation Potential in U.S. forestry and Agriculture," EPA 430-R-05-006, November 2005, Table 2-1.)

103   Mathematically, an S-curve can be called a Sigmoid or Logistic function. It is often rooted in an equation such as $dN/dt=rN(1-N/K)$. Consider an ecosystem in which N is the population of a given species; dN/dt represents the rate of change of that population; r is a rate of reproduction; and K represents the capacity of that ecosystem. Once $N=K$, the population can't grow anymore. While N is small, the population grows slowly; then there's a period of fast growth, and then it reaches the natural limitations of the ecosystem. Evolutionary biologists talk about two different strategies a species may take: r strategies (reproduce as fast as possible) and K strategies (steadily dominate your niche of an ecosystem). In general, r strategies are best in unstable contexts, K strategies in stable ones.

104   Clayton, Aubrey. "How Eugenics Shaped Statistics." *Nautilus*, October 23, 2020.

105   You would see a similar pattern with any other aggregation of consistently random events. This is known as the "Central Limit Theorem."

106   A power law relationship may be formally represented as: y is proportional to x raised to the a power.

107   Anderson, Chris. *The Long Tail: Why the Future of Business is Selling Less of More*. Hachette, 2008.

108   Taleb, Nassim Nicholas. *The Black Swan: The Impact of the Highly Improbable*. Random House, 2007.

109   "Q+A — Edward Tufte," *PRINT*, December 27, 2007.

110   See, for example, the Urban Institute's resources here: https://www.urban.org/data-viz.

111   Nirenberg, David and Ricardo L. "Numbers and Humanity," *Liberties*, Winter 2022, Volume 2, Number 2.

112   Banerjee, Abhijit and Esther Duflo. *Poor Economics: A Radical Rethinking of the Way to Fight Global Poverty*. PublicAffairs, 2012. Also see Dean Karlan and Jacob Appel. *More Than Good Intentions: How a New Economics Is Helping to Solve Global Poverty*. Dutton, 2011.

113   For a nuanced discussion of counterfactuals, see Chiara Marletto, "Our Little Life Is Rounded with Possibility," *Nautilus*, June 9, 2021.

Chapter 6: Behavioral Economics

114   Dickinson is widely credited with this quote, but I could not find a definitive citation.

115   https://www.oracle.com/a/ocom/docs/industries/utilities/utilities-opower-31twh-info.pdf

116   Translated by Donald Finkel. In *A Splintered Mirror*, North Point Press, 1991. Appears to be out of print.

117   From *The General Theory of Employment, Interest and Money*. Palgrave Macmillan, 1936.

118   Quoted in brown (2017), pg. 121.

119   "The War on Objectivity in American Journalism." *Liberties*. Volume 2, Number 3.

120   Conversation with Dana Milbank, cited in his *Washington Post* opinion column on March 28, 2022.

121   "Beyond Comprehension: We know that genocide and famine are greater tragedies than a lost dog. At least, we think we do." Shankar Vedantam, *Washington Post*. January 17, 2010.

122   "Motivated Numeracy and Enlightened Self-Government," Behavioural Public Policy, 1, 54–86. Yale Law School, Public Law Working Paper No. 307. September 2013. https://papers.ssrn.com/sol3/papers.cfm?abstract_id=2319992%20

123   From *Interpretation of Cultures*, Basic Books 2017. Quoted in Tett (2021).

124   https://web.archive.org/web/20130902053532/http://web.utk.edu/~glenn/GopacMemo.html

125   From Mitchell, Stephen. The Second Book of the Tao, Penguin, 2010: section 23, pg. 46.

126   Scarcity quickly gets tied up in dynamics of pride and fairness. Consider what researchers call the "ultimatum game." Two people are told they will split a pot of money, say $10. The first person gets to decide the split; the second gets to decide whether to take the offer or to reject it. The rational thing for the second person to do is to accept any offer. But experiments show that people will reject offers they see as unfair. If the first says the split is $9 for them and $1 for the second, often the second will reject the offer outright. So in this case, the presence of real scarcity leads people to hurt themselves because they see another's offer as unfair. (See the work of Soyoung Q Park at the Charité Universitätsmedizin Berlin.)

127   McGee (2021).

128   "The Brain-Gut Connection." Johns Hopkins Medicine. https://www.hopkinsmedicine.org/health/wellness-and-prevention/the-brain-gut-connection

29   Here she was citing work such as Scott Carney's *The Wedge: Evolution, Consciousness, Stress, and the Key to Human Resilience.* Foxtopus Ink, 2020.

30   brown (2017).

31   In *On Trails*, Robert Moor suggests three terms that can help you visualize the clues you will choose to provide. A trace is the faint line left by the passing of one person or animal. A trail is emergent, forming over time by the overlapping steps of many who have passed a certain way. A path is intentional and constructed, perhaps of gravel or concrete. (Simon & Schuster, 2017.)

32   "That Is Not How Your Brain Works," Lisa Feldman Barrett. Nautilus. December 18, 2021.

33   https://www.xprize.org/about/mission

34   For example, see this analysis: https://web.archive.org/web/20100330204202/ http://www.socialedge.org/blogs/forging-ahead/ archive/2009/12/15/the-dark-side-of-online-voting-contests

35   See, for example, "The Effects of the Kalamazoo Promise Scholarship on College Enrollment, Persistence, and Completion." Bartik, Timothy et al. *Journal of Human Resources,* Winter 2021, vol. 56, no. 1, 269–310.

36   Adam Phillips, *On Getting Better*, Penguin General. Cited in "A different view of self-improvement" by Baya Simons. *Financial Times*, November 1, 2021. https://www.ft.com/content/ dac9e05-073b-4be5-8bd9-601b5784f26f

37   See Brest and Kreiger (2010) and Galef, Julia, *The Scout Mindset: Why Some People See Things Clearly and Others Don't*. Portfolio, 2021.

38   Odell (2019), pg. 81.

39   See Schwartz, Barry, *The Paradox of Choice.* Ecco, 2004.

140   A definition of intuition from Nobel Prize–winning political scientist Herbert Simon: "The situation has provided a cue: This cue has given the expert access to information stored in memory, and the information provides the answer. Intuition is nothing more and nothing less than recognition." From "What is an explanation of behavior?" *Psychological Science*, 3(3), 150–161. Quoted by Gary Klein and Daniel Kahneman, "Conditions for Intuitive Expertise: A Failure to Disagree." *American Psychologist*, October 2009.

141   See *American Psychologist* paper cited in previous note and Strategic decisions: When can you trust your gut?" *McKinsey Quarterly*, March 1, 2010.

Chapter 7: Design Thinking

142   Source: Vialet and von Moos (2021) and interview with Jill Vialet and Amanda von Moos, September 6, 2021.

143   Listening can also be powerful even when you are the one conveying information. One of the most powerful techniques in public speaking is targeted silence: a break after you have said something important where you let an idea sit quietly. An unexpected silence can pull your audience out of unconscious reception (assuming they aren't just looking at their phones) and nudge them to conscious consideration of your last statement. In a sense, this targeted silence is an invitation to listen to an idea together.

144   The first five quotes come from Mitchell, Stephen. *The Enlightened Mind* (1991) and *The Enlightened Heart* (1989).

145   Suzuki, Shunryu. *Zen Mind, Beginner's Mind.* Weatherhill, 1970.

146   Battilana and Casciaro (2021), pg. 36.

147   Chang (2019), 48.

148   From a lecture at Presidio School of Management in San Francisco, California, c. 2010.

149 Battilana and Casciaro (2021). pg. 32.

150 Stein Greenberg, pg. 123.

151 Quoted in Pendleton-Jullian and Brown (2018).

152 Used with permission; https://dschool.stanford.edu/about.

153 Nicely described as a "a not-very-old, not-nearly-famous-enough saying" in Stein Greenberg (2021), pg. 144.

154 Chang (2019), pg. 71.

155 See, for example, Paul, Ann Murphy. *The Extended Mind: The Power of Thinking Outside the Brain*. Mariner, 2021.

156 Appiah (2006), pg. 99.

157 Geertz, Clifford. "Thick Description: Toward an Interpretive Theory of Culture," *The Interpretation of Cultures: Selected Essays,* Basic Books, 1973, 3–30.

158 Tett (2021), pg. 27.

159 For more on ethnography and social change, see Gillian Tett's book *Anthro-Vision: A New Way to See in Business and Life*. Avid Reader Press, 2021.

160 Beynus (2002), pg. 253–254.

161 See Miller, G. A. "The magical number seven, plus or minus two: Some limits on our capacity for processing information." *Psychological Review*, 63(2), 81–97, 1956.

162 From the prose piece *Worstward Ho*, Grove Press, 1984.

Chapter 8: Community Organizing

163 Letter to Gerrit Smith, March 30, 1849.

164 Personal correspondence with Mario Lugay, November 2021.

165 Gbowee (2011).

166 Battilana and Casciaro (2021).

167 See Shaw (2018).

168 Smucker (2017), pg. 160–161.

169 Friere (1970).

170 The March on Washington was far more than the "I Have Dream" speech, brilliant as it may have been. It is often forgotten that its full name was "The March on Washington for Jobs and Freedom." The event was not solely focused on civil rights, it included deep engagement on economic issues; indeed, the organizing committee was chaired by labor leader A. Phillip Randolph. And the efforts to organize the event were themselves complicated by questions of identity. Bayard Ruskin was arguably the most important single organizer of the event — despite the innumerable difficulties he faced as a gay man. Women leaders were essential in planning the March and yet had no representation on the organizing committee.

171 See Chenoweth and Stephan, (2012).

172 "Letter from Birmingham Jail," from King (2000).

173 It is worth noting here the story of Claudette Colvin. Colvin was arrested nine months earlier (March 2, 1955) for refusing to give up her seat on the bus. But Colvin did not get the same strategic support of key civil rights organizations. These organizations believed she was less likely to get sympathy from the local white population because she was pregnant, unmarried, and had darker skin (See "In the Shadow of Rosa Parks: 'Unsung Hero' Civil Rights Movement Speaks Out" in *The Cardinal Inquirer* by Vanessa de la Torre, January 20, 2005.)

174 Solnit (2010), pg. 173.

175 *The Body Keeps the Score: Brain, Mind, and Body in the Healing of Trauma*, by Bessel van der Kolk, pg. 335. Penguin 2015.

176 Lois Gibbs. *Love Canal: and the Birth of the Environmental Health Movement*. Island Press, 2011

177 See the analysis of Zeynep Tufekci, such as "#Kony2012, Understanding Networked Symbolic Action & Why Slacktivism is Conceptually Misleading" on Technosociology.com.

8   Movement Commons/Justice Funders webinar, October 2021.

9   Smucker, Jonathan Matthew. "Occupy: A Name Fixed to a Flashpoint," jonathansmucker.org, April , 2013. https://jonathansmucker.org/tag/291/

0   Bennett, Jessica. "What if instead of calling people out, we called them in?" *The New York Times*, November 19, 2020. https://www.nytimes.com/2020/11/19/style/ loretta-ross-smith-college-cancel-culture.html

1   Freeman, Jo. "Trashing: The dark side of sisterhood." JoFreeman.com. https://www.jofreeman.com/joreen/trashing.htm Written for *Ms.* magazine, April 1976.

Chapter 9: Game Theory

2   Ostrom (1990).

3   This chapter draws from an article I wrote for the *Stanford Social Innovation Review*, "The Collaboration Game: Solving the Puzzle of Nonprofit Collaboration." April 26, 2017.

4   For the goals themselves, see: https://sdgs. un.org/goals. For a tool to map any organization's work, including your own, to the SDGs, see https:// sdgfunders.org/wizard/.

5   Chen, Can, and Sukumar Ganapati. "Do transparency mechanisms reduce government corruption? A meta-analysis." *International Review of Administration Sciences*, August 31, 2021. Available in Sage Journals: https://journals.sagepub.com/ doi/abs/10.1177/00208523211033236

6   Axelrod, Robert; Hamilton, William D. (27 March 1981), "The Evolution of Cooperation," *Science*, 211 (4489): 1390–96.

7   I'll add that another successful strategy is a modified version of tit-for-tat where you show random preemptive forgiveness. We could call it a grace strategy."

188   Carse (1986). The first quote is from pg. 3; second from pg. 25.

189   Sheldrake (2020), pg. 88.

190   Sheldrake (2020), pg. 17.

191   See Suzanne Simard's *Finding the Mother Tree* (Knopf 2021) and Peter Wohlleben's *The Hidden Life of Trees* (Greystone 2016).

192   Thomas (1978), pg. 10.

193   Lecture, "Working Together for a Peaceful World," organized by Dr. APJ Abdul Kalam International Foundation. October 15, 2020. The Dalai Lama was speaking from the Thekchen Chöling complex in Dharamsala, Himachal Pradesh, India.

194   Turner, John C. "The significance of the social identity concept for social psychology with reference to individualism, interactionism and social influence." *British Journal of Social Psychology*, September 1986, 237–252.

195   Wei-Skillern, Jane, and Norah Silver. "Four Network Principles for Collaboration Success." *The Foundation Review*, Volume 5, Issue 1, 2013.: https://scholarworks.gvsu.edu/cgi/ viewcontent.cgi?article=1009&context=tfr

196   Kania, John and Mark Kramer. "Collective Impact." *Stanford Social Innovation Review*. Winter 2011.

Chapter 10: Markets

197   "The Wherewithal of Society: An Accountability Challenge to Private Enterprise." *Nonprofit Quarterly*. Fall-Winter 2011.

198   CDP, "The Collective Effort to End Deforestation: A Pathway for Companies to Raise Their Ambition." March 2021. www.cdp.net.

199   Pg. 363, Hariri, Sapiens (2019)

200 From Matisse, Henri, *Notes of a Painter* (1908). Quoted in Kramer, Hilton, "Matisse's Dream," *New York Times*, March 10, 1974.

201 See Clara Miller's seminal article, "The Looking Glass World of Nonprofit Money," *Nonprofit Quarterly*, Spring 2005.

202 Foster, William and Gail Fine. "How Nonprofits Get Really Big," *Stanford Social Innovation Review*, Spring 2007.

203 Lopez (2001), pg. 127.

204 Heron. "Introduction to Net Contribution." The F.B. Heron Foundation, 2022. https://www.heron.org/ introduction-to-net-contribution/

205 Maxim #33, quoted in Sinclair (2019)

206 See Cohen (2020); Federal Reserve of San Francisco (2017); and the Impact Investing Initiative at the Duke University Center for Advancing Social Entrepreneurship: https://sites.duke.edu/casei3/

207 Ostrom (2019), pg. 15.

208 Crawford, Krysten. "Stanford study finds medical debt is double whammy for the poor." news. stanford.edu, October 7, 2021. https://news.stanford.edu/2021/10/07/ study-finds-medical-debt-double-whammy-poor/

209 This section draws from an article I wrote for *Stanford Social Innovation Review*, "The Collaboration Game: Solving the Puzzle of Nonprofit Collaboration." April 26, 2017.

210 E.g. see "About MDC," Miami Dade College website. https://www.mdc.edu/about/community.aspx

211 Tsing (2017), pg. 38.

212 Lopez (2001), pg. 258.

213 For further discussion of social discount rates, see https://www.lse.ac.uk/granthaminstitute/ explainers/what-are-social-discount-rates/

214 Robinson (2021), pg. 411.

215 "Internalizing the externalities." *The Economist* Special report on ESG investing by Henry Tricks. July 23, 2022.

216 See Fleishman (2009); Giridharadas (2018); Reich (2018); Buchanan (2019); Villanueva (2021).

217 Drutman, Lee. *The Business of America is Lobbying: How Corporations Became Politicized and Politics Became More Corporate*. Oxford University Press, 2015.

Chapter 11: Complex Systems

218 Sheldrake (2020), pg. 7.

219 Hölldobler and Wilson (1994).

220 This chapter draws heavily from a paper I wrote while at GuideStar, "A whole greater than the sum of its parts: What philanthropy can learn from complex systems theory" (published at Candid in 2019).

221 Berlow, Eric. "Simplifying complexity." TEDGlobal 2010, July 2010. https://www.ted.com/talks/eric_berlow_ simplifying_complexity?language=en

222 Weaver, Warren. "Science and Complexity," *American Scientist* #36 (1948): 536. More precisely what I'm describing here as "complicated" Weaver referred to as "disorganized complexity " later in "Science and Complexity." Weaver highlighted two "wartime advances" he considered promising for tackling organized complexity: the new power of "electronic computing devices" and a rising trend toward academic interdisciplinarity (what he called "the 'mixed team' approach of operations analysis [pg 541]). It seems he was prescient in more ways than one.

223 Seelos, Christian and Johanna Mair. "Mastering System Change." *Stanford Social Innovation Review* Fall 2018, pg. 36.

224 Schrodinger, Erwin. *What Is Life?* Cambridge University Press, 1944; Ilya Prigogine, *Order Out of Chaos.* Bantam, 1984.

225 von Neumann, John. *Theory of Self Reproducing Automata.* University of Illinois Press, 1966; Bernard Mandelbrot. *The Fractal Geometry of Nature.* Freeman, 1983.

226 Wiener (1965); Claude Shannon and Warren Weaver. *The Mathematical Theory of Communication.* University of Illinois Press, 1971.

227 Kauffman, Stuart. *The Origins of Order: Self-Organization and Selection in Evolution.* Oxford University Press, 1993; Geoffrey West. *Scale.* Penguin Press, 2017.

228 Holland, John et al. Induction: *Processes of Inference, Learning and Discovery.* MIT Press, 1986.

229 Anderson, Philip et al., eds. *The Economy as an Evolving Complex System.* Addison-Wesley, 1988; Eric Beinhocker. *The Origin of Wealth: Evolution, Complexity, and the Radical Remaking of Economics.* Harvard Business School Press, 2006.

230 Watts, Duncan and S.H. Strogatz. "Collective Dynamics of 'Small World' Networks. '" *Nature* 393, June 4, 1998, 440–42.

231 The Santa Fe Institute has played a critical role in the emergence of complexity science as an influential discipline. See Mitchell (1993).

232 Gaddis (2019), pg 155.

233 There is evidence that many real-world networks follow a precise, fractal-like pattern where connections among nodes follow a power law distribution. See A. Barabasi and R. Albert. "Emergence of Scaling in Random Networks." *Science* 286, October 15, 1999. Others argue that this relationship has been exaggerated; see, for example: A. Clauset, C.R. Shalizi, and M.E.J. Newman. "Power Law Distributions in Empirical Data." SIAM Review 51, no. 4, Nov. 6, 2009, 661–703.

234 Again, there is no consensus on these characteristics. But see, for example, John Holland, *Hidden Order.* Addison-Wesley, 1995.

235 See, for example, pg 83 in Kauffman (1995). The structure can take other forms, too, such as the emergent tiers of trophic levels in an ecosystem.

236 These rules need not be immutable — they can change over time. But if there is not some stability, it is unlikely the system will exhibit truly complex behavior.

237 Summarized by Thomas Piketty as "r>g" — the rate of return on capital is higher than the economic growth rate. Piketty (2014). See further discussion in the Markets chapter.

238 This is known as an open system. Per the Second Law of Thermodynamics, a system needs to be open to external energy if it is to consistently retain or increase its order over time.

239 That information could take many forms, such as DNA or securities prices.

240 This is related to — although not the same as — Joseph Schumpeter's concept of creative destruction, what he called the "process of industrial mutation that incessantly revolutionizes the economic structure from within, incessantly destroying the old one, incessantly creating a new one." From *Capitalism, Socialism, and Democracy.* Routledge, 1942.

241 Leicester and O'Hara (2009), pg. 19.

242 See the "Money for Good" analyses from Hope Consulting and the Camber Collective in 2010, 2012, and 2015. The trend line is clear (3% in 2010 to 6% in 2012 to 9% in 2015) and matches an immense amount of anecdotal evidence. Still, it is worth noting that there was a slight shift in the wording/framing of this question between 2012 and 2015 and that extrapolations assume similar behavior across income groups — an assumption that matches some but not all of the data.

243 https://journals.sagepub.com/doi/full/10.1177/0148558X18814134

244 See, for example: Susan Colby, Nan Stone, and Paul Carttar, "Zeroing in on Impact." *Stanford Social Innovation Review*, Fall 2004.

245 The idea of a boundary is essential for life. "It takes a membrane to make sense out of disorder in biology. You have to be able to catch energy and hold it, storing precisely the needed it amount and releasing it in measured shares." Lewis Thomas, *Lives of a Cell*, pg 145.

246 Odell (2019), pg. 81.

247 brown (2017), pg 78.

248 Generally, the value of a network is seen as increasing as the square of the number of nodes (Metcalf's Law). But others argue that if you include the value of sub-groups within the network, its value grows as 2^n (Reed's Law). Still others say the reality is more subtle (what you could call "Briscoe's Law" — the value of a network grows as n*log(n)). See the "Network Effects Manual" from the venture capital firm NfX: https://www.nfx.com/post/network-effects-manual

249 *Ethics of Identity*. Princeton University Press, 2010.

250 Thanissara (2015), pg 107.

251 Solnit (2016), pg. 3.

Chapter 12: Institutions

252 https://en.wikipedia.org/wiki/Wikipedia

253 Neufeld, Dorothy and Joyce Ma (graphics). "The 50 Most Visited Websites in the World." visualcapitalist.com, January 27, 2021. https://www.visualcapitalist.com/the-50-most-visited-websites-in-the-world/

254 From Henry George Liddell, Robert Scott, "A Greek-English Lexicon." tufts.edu. https://www.perseus.tufts.edu/hopper/text?doc=Perseus:text:1999.04.0057:entry=o)/rganon

255 The March of Dimes was originally devoted to addressing childhood polio but broadened its purpose to addressing newborn health more broadly.

256 Thomas (1978), pg. 58–59.

257 Ibid.

258 *Approximations*. University of California Libraries, 1922.

259 This has been attributed to management thinker Peter Drucker, but there's no definitive citation.

260 The phrase "we are what we repeatedly do" first appeared in a discussion on Aristotle in Will Durant's *Story of Philosophy*. Durant used the phrase to bridge two of Aristotle's ideas: first, "these virtues are formed in man by his doing the right actions"; and second, "as it is not one swallow or a fine day that makes a spring, so it is not one day or a short time that makes a man blessed and happy." From pg 87, *Story of Philosophy*. Simon and Schuster, 1926.

261 See, for example, "Challenges in Cross-Sector Collaboration and Learning from Doing" in *The Intersector: How the Public, Nonprofit, and Private Sectors Can Address America's Challenges*. Brookings Institution Press, 2021, and Insights from Philanthropy, "Rules and Rituals: How to Drive Change" in *What Matters: Investing in Results to Build Strong, Vibrant Communities*. Federal Reserve Bank of San Francisco and Nonprofit Finance Fund (2017).

262 Quoted in brown (2009), pg 134.

263 The text from this table represents a selection from the table in Heimans and Timms (2018), pg 17.

264 Quoted by John Thornhill in "Innovation still requires smart, even barmy, innovators." *Financial Times*, September 23, 2021.

265   This phenomenon was described as "institutional isomorphism" by sociologists Paul DiMaggio and Woody Powell in their paper, "The Iron Cage Revisited: Institutional Isomorphism and Collective Rationality in Organizational Fields." *American Sociological Review*, Vol. 48, No. 2, April 1983, 147–160.

266   Candid offers a free diagnostic tool for people deciding whether to start a new nonprofit organization: https://learning.candid.org/resources/nonprofit-startup-resources/ (Citation for the figure of 1.8 million organizations: https://candid.org/explore-issues/us-social-sector/organizations)

267   See Fleischman, Joel. *Putting Wealth to Work: Philanthropy for Today or Investing for Tomorrow?* Public Affairs, 2017.

268   My choice of "space, time, and scale" here is no accident. In it, I'm referencing the work of historian John Lewis Gaddis. He defined "grand strategy" as the alignment of capabilities and ambitions over space, time, and scale. See Gaddis (2018). I believe that frame is particularly relevant when thinking about organizational development.

269   Falkvinge, Rick. *Swarmwise: The Tactical Manual to Changing the World.* Self-published, 2013.

270   Kaal, Wulf. "Decentralized Autonomous Organizations — Internal Governance and External Legal Design." *Annals of Corporate Governance.* U of St. Thomas (Minnesota) Legal Studies Research Paper No. 20–14 (2021).

271   Lalley, Steven; Weyl, E. Glen. "Quadratic Voting: How Mechanism Design Can Radicalize Democracy." *American Economic Association Papers and Proceedings*, Vol. 1, No. 1, 2018.

272   See Clara Miller's seminal article, "The Looking-Glass World of Nonprofit Money: Managing in For-Profits' Shadow Universe" in *Nonprofit Quarterly.* Reprinted June 12, 2017.

273   Kerr, Steven. "On the Folly of Rewarding A, while Hoping for B." *The Academy of Management Journal*; Vol. 9, No. 1 (February 1995), 7–14.

274   Chang (2019), pg. 235.

275   Which itself a version of Goodhart's law: attention on a metric will distort that metric.

276   Kerr, Steven. "On the Folly of Rewarding A, while Hoping for B." *The Academy of Management Journal*; Vol. 9, No. 1 (February 1995), 7–14.

277   https://www.census.gov/newsroom/releases/archives/governments/cb12-161.html

278   Henderson (2020), pg 19.

279   See "The Hashtag That Changed the Oscars: An Oral History." *The New York Times,* September 9, 2020.

280   Internet: U.S. Defense Advanced Research Projects Agency; World Wide Web: CERN, the European Organization for Nuclear Research; portable computing: NASA, National Aeronautics and Space Administration; GPS: U.S. Navy. See Mazzucato (2021).

281   Mazzucato (2021), pg 55.

282   See William MacAskill's *What We Owe the Future*, Basic Books, 2022.

Sources
and Permissions

"Poems mark a trail of identities;
poems laid end to end
are a map of the human voice."

Elizabeth Alexander
(pg xvii, Chagnot and Ikkanda, 2017)

Introduction

Ieshia Evans photo: Photo by Jonathan Bachman. Used with permission from Reuters.

Kuzmickas poem: From "Logic Problem." Used with permission from the author.

Issa poem: Issa, Kobayashi, translated by Robert Hass, 1989. "The man pulling radishes" in *The Essential Haiku: Versions of Basho, Buson, & Issa* edited and with an Introduction by Robert Hass. Introduction and selection copyright ©1994 by Robert Hass. Used by permission of HarperCollins Publishers.

Chapter 1: An Age of Flux

Seaside Heights photo: Photo by Julie Dermansky. Used with permission from the photographer.

Pablo Neruda poem: "Ode to the Moon" from *Selected Translations, 2000–2020* by Ilan Stavans, 2021. Reprinted by permission of the University of Pittsburgh Press.

Elizabeth Alexander poem: Elizabeth Alexander, excerpt from "Praise Song for the Day" from *Crave Radiance: New and Selected Poems 1990-2010.* Copyright © 2008 by Elizabeth Alexander. Reprinted with the permission of The Permissions Company, LLC on behalf of Graywolf Press, graywolfpress.org

Amanda Gorman quote ("These are the things..."): From "Monomyth," *Call Us What We Carry.* Copyright © 2021 by Amanda Gorman. Used by permission of the author.

Ángel González poem: From *Astonishing World: The Selected Poems of Ángel González.* Milkweed Editions, 1993. Out of print, used with permission from Pedro Gutierrez Ruvuelta (co-translator with Steven Ford Brown).

Chapter 2: The Shape of Strategy

Ray Charles photo: Photo by Bill Ray. Used by permission from Time Inc., via Shutterstock Editorial.

Occupy Wall Street poster: Used by permission of the Adbusters Media Foundation.

William Stafford poem: William Stafford, "The Way It Is" from *Ask Me: 100 Essential Poems.* Copyright © 1977, 2004 by William Stafford and the Estate of William Stafford. Reprinted with the permission of The Permissions Company, LLC on behalf of Graywolf Press, graywolfpress.org.

Cynthia White poem: From "Quail Hollow," in Crewes (2012).

Amanda Gorman quote ("To be accountable..."): From "Ship's Manifest." *Call Us What We Carry.* Copyright © 2021 by Amanda Gorman. Used by permission of the author.

Emily Dickinson poem: "I dwell in Possibility" (466) *The Poems of Emily Dickinson: Reading Edition,* edited by Ralph W. Franklin, Cambridge, Mass.: The Belknap Press of Harvard University Press, Copyright © 1998, 1999 by the President and Fellows of Harvard College. Copyright © 1951, 1955, by the President and Fellows of Harvard College. Copyright © 1979, 1983 by the President and Fellows of Harvard College. Copyright © 1914, 1918, 1924, 1929, 1930, 1932, 1935, 1937, 1942 by Martha Dickinson Bianchi. Copyright © 1952, 1957, 1958, 1963, 1965 by Mary L. Hampson.

A. Van Jordan Poem: From Lawson et al. (2021). Used with permission from the poet.

Chapter 3: Ethics and Social Change

"Senseless Kindness" photo: By Dylan Martinez. Used with permission from Alamy.

Wisława Szymborska poem: From "The Century's Decline," from *Map* by Wisława Szymborska. All works by Wisława Szymborska copyright © The Wisława Szymborska Foundation. English translation © 2015 by Houghton Mifflin Harcourt Publishing Company. Used by permission of HarperCollins Publishers.

Dulce María Loynáz poem: "I Dream of Classifying..." from *Selected Translations, 2000-2020 by Ilan Stavans*, © 2021. Reprinted by permission of the University of Pittsburgh Press

Gerard Manley Hopkins poem: "As kingfishers catch fire" from *As kingfishers catch fire*, Penguin Classics 2005.

Chapter 4: Storytelling

Plastic art installation: "Giant Plastic Tap" at the UNEA 5.2 in Nairobi 2022 © Benjamin Von Wong www.TurnOffThePlasticTap.com. Used with permission from the artist.

Emily Dickinson poem: "Tell all the truth but tell it slant –" (1263) *The Poems of Emily Dickinson: Reading Edition*, edited by Ralph W. Franklin, Cambridge, Mass.: The Belknap Press of Harvard University Press, Copyright © 1998, 1999 by the President and Fellows of Harvard College. Copyright © 1951, 1955, by the President and Fellows of Harvard College. Copyright © 1979, 1983 by the President and Fellows of Harvard College. Copyright © 1914, 1918, 1924, 1929, 1930, 1932, 1935, 1937, 1942 by Martha Dickinson Bianchi. Copyright © 1952, 1957, 1958, 1963, 1965 by Mary L. Hampson.

Chapter 5: Mathematical Modeling

Wisława Szymborska poem: Excerpt from "Starvation Camp Near Jaslo" from *Map* by Wisława Szymborska. All works by Wisława Szymborska copyright © The Wisława Szymborska Foundation. English translation © 2015 by Houghton Mifflin Harcourt Publishing Company. Used by permission of HarperCollins Publishers.

Ferreira Gullar poem: "Two Plus Two Is Four" from *Selected Translations, 2000–2020* by Ilan Stavans, © 2021. Reprinted by permission of the University of Pittsburgh Press

Old Faithful image: Public Domain http://en.wikipedia.org/wiki/File:Oldfaithful3.png.

Anscombe's Quartet image: Data: Anscombe, Francis J. (1973) Graphs in Statistical Analysis. *American Statistician*, 27, 17–21. Image: CC By 3.0 by Wikipedia user Shutz. https://en.wikipedia.org/wiki/Anscombe%27s_quartet#/media/File:Anscombe's_quartet_3.svg.

Normal Distribution image: CC By 3.0, created by Wikipedia user Ainali. https://en.wikipedia.org/wiki/Normal_distribution#/media/File:Standard_deviation_diagram_micro.svg.

Power law distribution: Image based on Public Domain picture by Hay Kranen (www.haykranen.nl).

John Snow map: Map adapted by author based on public domain image. Original map by John Snow showing the clusters of cholera cases in the London epidemic of 1854, drawn and lithographed by Charles Cheffins. https://en.wikipedia.org/wiki/John_Snow#/media/File:Snow-cholera-map-1.jpg

Chapter 6: Behavioral Economics

Elephant photo: Public domain image.

Yeats poem: Excerpt from "The Second Coming," 1920.

Leonard Cohen lyrics: excerpt from "Anthem," 1992.

Chapter 7: Design Thinking

Landscape photo: "Landscape of the Four Seasons in the Styles of Old Masters," Wei Zhike, 1625. Public domain image from Metropolitan Museum of Art.

Chapter 8: Community Organizing

Climate march photo: Photo by Julie Dermansky. jdsart.com Used with permission from the photographer.

Student Nonviolent Coordinating Committee photo. By Jim Karales. Photo is from SNCC Passive Resistance Training Program in 1960. Copyright, Estate of James Karales. Courtesy of Howard Greenberg Gallery, New York.

"We the People" poster: By Shepherd Fairey, commissioned by art and activism group Amplifier. Made available for free download at https://amplifier.org/campaigns/we-the-people/.

Chapter 9: Game Theory

Isaac Cordal photo: "Follow the Leaders." Montreal, Canada. 2015 ©Isaac Cordal. Used with permission from the artist.

Jeff Daniels lyric: Jeff Daniels and the Ben Daniels Band, "Good on the Bad Side of Town." Used with permission.

Chapter 10: Markets

Man Controlling Trade photo: By Tom Shearer. Used by permission from the photographer.

Fearless Girl photo: By Richard Zinken. naturweinwelt.de. Used with permission from the photographer.

Shipping container photo: Photo by shaunl. Used with permission from Getty Images/iStock.

Chapter 11: Complex Systems

Vine photo: By author.

Amanda Gorman poem: From "Displacement," *Call Us What We Carry*. Copyright © 2021 by Amanda Gorman. Used by permission of the author.

Malena Mörling poem: excerpt from "An Entrance" from *Astoria: Poems by Malena Mörling*. © 2006. Reprinted by permission of the University of Pittsburgh Press.

Starling murmuration photo: By Doug Scarr. www.drbsphotography.weebly.com. Used with permission from the photographer.

Chapter 12: Institutions

Keiunkan photo: Photo by Takato Marui; Creative Commons Attribution-Share Alike 2.0.

Building photos: Tempodrom, Berlin, Germany. Creative Commons CC0 license. https://pxhere.com/en/photo/644194; Budapest Central Market: Used with permission from Alamy.

Concluding Materials

Iceberg photo: By Ulrik Pedersen/NurPhoto. Used with permission from the Associated Press.

Oblique Strategies: From the "Oblique Strategies" cards by Brian Eno and Peter Schmidt. Fifth Edition. 2001. Used with permission from Shakedown Records.

Wordsmything: From the Twitter feed of Andrew McLuhan (@amicusadastra), 2021–2022. Used with permission from the author.

"Ways and Methods of Doing Good" from *An address to persons of quality and estate* by Robert Nelson, Esq. 1752. Public domain image from Wellcome Collection.

Rabindranath Tagore poem: Excerpt from "New Birth." Public domain under UK law.

Index

I am stubborn
I build ten theories out of stone
In a stone wall Eden
An unknown flower loves me more
I do not know it
The fire in the center
However is still there
And smoulders

Thomas Merton

Finance:

of institutions, 263–264, 278

and long-term planning, 66

and markets, 225–226, 236

Fleming, Heather, 150, 162

Flow, in systems, 253, 256

Fog of war, 56

"Follow the Leaders" (Cordal), 192*f*

Ford Motor Company, 210–211

Foundation Center, 17, 74, 200–201, 249

Founder's syndrome, 74

Fourth Industrial Revolution, 24–25

Fractals, 242, 245

Fragmentation, 26, 295n24

Framing, 93, 96

Francis, Pope, 22

Frankfurter, Harry, 298n78

Friedman, Milton, 218–219

Frola, Francesco Gabriele, 60*f*

Fundamental attribution error, 127

G

Gaddis, John Lewis, 307n268

Game theory, 58*f*, 192–215

defining, 13

enabling collaboration, 209–213

and equilibrium, 197–198

models in, 194–195

in natural world, 206–207

and social change organizations, 208

tools to improve outcomes, 198–205

Gandhi, Mohandas, 90, 176

Ganz, Marshall, 94

Gawande, Atul, 135–136

Gbowee, Leymah, 166–167

Geertz, Clifford, 157

Generosity, as strategy, 214

Germany, 276

Gibbs, Lois, 181, 182

Goal orientation, 247

Goals, 224

Golden Rule, 70

Goodwyn, Lawrence, 41

Google, 221

GOPAC, 131

Gorman, Amanda, 44

GOTV (get out the vote) canvassing, 182

Governance, 276

Governing the Commons (Ostrom), 202

Government:

changes in role of, 29

regulation and role of, 274–275

Grasstops organizing, 180–181

Greenberg, Sarah Stein, 151

Green Corps, 173

Greenpeace, 17, 177–178

GuideStar, 17, 63, 74, 101–102, 200, 201, 205, 228, 231, 247, 249, 251, 271, 274

Guilt freeze, 72

Gyasi, Yaa, 88

H

The Handmaid's Tale (Atwood), 180

Harry Potter series, 84

Hassan, Shira, 61

Hasso Plattner Institute of Design, 152

Hawes, Emma, 60*f*

Hedonic treadmill, 130

Henerson, Rebecca, 274

Hernandez, Isaac, 60*f*

The Hero's Journey, 84–86, 96, 299n91

Heuristics, 142

Hewlett Foundation, 17, 126, 228

Hippocratic Oath, 64

The Hobbit (Tolkien), 87

Home Energy Report, 123

Homegoing (Gyasi), 88

Horizontal gene transfer, 207

Housing, 253

Hume, David, 195

Humility, 75, 117

Humor, 91–92

I

Identity, 62, 70–71, 77, 128–129, 248

Illusions, 126–133, 142

Ilulissat, Greenland, 280*f*

Improv, 155

Oblique Strategies

In 1975, Brian Eno and Peter Schmidt released a deck of cards they called "Oblique Strategies." Each card in the deck included a few words suggesting an approach, a question, or a challenge. An artist or entrepreneur or other human could draw a card whenever they got stuck or simply wanted the jolt of a new perspective. You'll find a few of these oblique strategies below.

Simply a matter of work

Not building a wall but making a brick

Use an old idea

Retrace your steps

Question the heroic approach

Don't be frightened of clichés

Work at a different speed

When is it for?

State the problem in words

Remove specifics and covert to ambiguities

Remove ambiguities and convert to specifics

Do something boring

Question the heroic approach

Don't be afraid of things because they're easy to do

Voice nagging suspicions

Discard an axiom

Accept advice

About the Design

The Toolbox was designed by Open (http://www.notclosed.com) in New York City.

Its design was inspired by the "access to tools" of the *Whole Earth Catalog*, W.E.B. Du Bois' data visualizations, Quentin Fiore's design of Marshall McLuhan's books, Ladislav Sutnar's "principles of visual flow," instruction manuals for electronics and machinery — and Franz Joseph's 1975 *Star Trek Star Fleet Technical Manual*.

Open sought to distill these precedents (and more) into an engaging but utilitarian system designed to help you find your way through the information while enjoying yourself along the way. Besides a few phrases in Chinese, Greek, and Hebrew, *The Toolbox* is entirely set in the Public Sans type family.

Public Sans (https://public-sans.digital.gov) is a typeface designed by Dan Williams and released by the U.S. Digital Service (https://www.usds.gov) as part of the U.S. Web Design System (https://designsystem.digital.gov). It's an open-source tool, built to further the goals of universal accessibility and readability, that anybody can use — for free.

The Toolbox is mostly black-and-white, except for anything related to the nine tools, which have their own colors — and their own icons. Reminiscent of those used by mass-transit systems around the world, the icons were designed at Open by Yasmin Ali. ■

About the Author

Jacob Harold is a social change strategist, author, and executive. His story parallels the intellectual arc of *The Toolbox*: he's traveled from farm to monastery to jail to laboratory to boardroom, all in search of the best ways to do good.

From 2012 to 2021, Harold served as President & CEO of GuideStar and co-founder of Candid. *Fast Company* called Candid "the definitive nonprofit transparency organization." Each year, more than 20 million people use its data on nonprofits, grants, and social sector practice.

Candid was formed in 2019 by the merger of GuideStar and Foundation Center. Harold co-led the $45 million capital campaign to launch Candid, wrote Candid's guiding strategy document, Candid 2030, and served as EVP during post-merger integration.

During his tenure leading GuideStar, Harold oversaw a financial turnaround, a tripling of GuideStar's reach, and major partnerships with organizations ranging from Google to the Gates Foundation. In 2013, Harold launched the Overhead Myth campaign to shift attention from nonprofits' financial ratios to their programmatic results. Since then,

GuideStar's Profile Program has been used by more than 200,000 nonprofits to tell their full story to the world.

Harold joined GuideStar from the William and Flora Hewlett Foundation, where he led a $30 million grantmaking initiative to build a 21st-century infrastructure for smart giving. Before that, he worked as a consultant to nonprofits and foundations at Bridgespan and as a climate change campaigner and strategist with the Packard Foundation, Rainforest Action Network, and Greenpeace USA. He began his career as a grassroots organizer with Green Corps.

Harold earned his AB *summa cum laude* in ethics and intellectual history from Duke University and an MBA from the Stanford Graduate School of Business. He was a term member at the Council on Foreign Relations and has further training from MIT, Bain, the Chinese Academy of Sciences/Santa Fe Institute, and the SIT Tibetan Studies Program, where he did the first translations of newly discovered poems by the Sixth Dalai Lama.

The NonProfit Times named Harold to its *Power and Influence Top 50* list seven years in a row. He has written extensively on climate change and philanthropic strategy and his essays have been used as course materials at Stanford, Duke, Wharton, Oxford, and Tsinghua. Harold has been quoted in media outlets including the *New York Times*, *Washington Post*, *Financial Times*, and *Wall Street Journal*. Harold serves on the boards of the U.S. Climate Action Network, Rewiring America, and the Duke University Center for the Advancement of Social Entrepreneurship and as an advisor to investors, startups, foundations, and government agencies.

Harold spent his early childhood on a corn farm in rural North Carolina. When he was 10 years old, his family moved into Winston-Salem, where his parents led small, community-based nonprofit organizations. He lives in Washington, DC, with his wife Carolyn Sufrin — a physician-anthropologist at Johns Hopkins — and their two sons.

Now, let's put the tools to work.

Find additional resources and support at:
www.jacobharold.org

This is not the first attempt to offer tools people can use to build a better world.

And nor will it be the last.

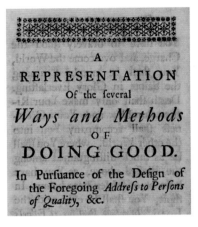

A

REPRESENTATION

Of the several

Ways and Methods

OF

DOING GOOD.

In Pursuance of the Design of the Foregoing *Address to Persons of Quality,* &c.

Robert Nelson
An Address to Persons of Quality and Estate
1752